LABYRINTH

My Journey to Belonging

GW00645315

MORIAH AMA HOPE

ISBN:

978-1-913590-67-3 (Paperback)
978-1-913590-68-0 (ebook)

Cover design by Lynda Mangoro.

The Unbound Press
www.theunboundpress.com

Hey unbound one!

Welcome to this magical book brought to you by The Unbound Press.

At The Unbound Press, we believe that when women write freely from the fullest expression of who they are, it can't help but activate a feeling of deep connection and transformation in others. When we come together, we become more and we're changing the world, one book at a time!

This book has been carefully crafted by both the author and publisher with the intention of inspiring you to move ever more deeply into who you truly are.

We hope that this book helps you to connect with your Unbound Self and that you feel called to pass it on to others who want to live a more fully expressed life.

With much love,

Nicola Humber

Founder of The Unbound Press
www.theunboundpress.com

Contents

Labyrinth: My Journey to Belonging Reviews   5

The Labyrinth Speaks of the Seed of Our Belonging   13

Foreword   15

The Labyrinth   21

Full Size Labyrinth Symbol   27

The Labyrinth Speaks of the Secret of Our Belonging   28

Pre-Incarnation – The Swing Between Worlds   29

What if I Fail?   34

Once Upon a Time   35

My Early Years   36

'I Always Knew You Were a Witch!'   41

Good Girls   43

It Was Good Enough for Me, It's Good Enough for You   44

Letter from my Soul on Gathering Moss   45

The Labyrinth Speaks of Trust   47

I'll Bring You Down a Peg or Two!   48

Change your Name, Change your Life   63

I Want That Job!   64

The Labyrinth Speaks of Letting Life Unfold   69

I Said YES! - Part One   70

Musical Chairs   75

I Can't Find a Heartbeat   82

Love Yourself   90

You Can Have It All!   91

I Don't Want to Be the Soil!   96

The Soul Speaks of Feeling the Call   104

The Labyrinth Speaks of the Mystery Within 105

Awakening '99 106

Flow is the New Balance 113

I Need a Break! 114

To Mum 127

The Soul Speaks - Passenger or Pilot? 131

Dive In 133

A Thirsty Fish 134

Three Male Catalysts 140

You're Not Here to Fit In 141

The Soul Speaks of Boundlessness 144

I Said YES! - Part Two 146

'I Don't Like Who You've Become.' 147

The Labyrinth Speaks - All of You is Welcome 150

The Tale of The Labyrinth, The Void & Rennes
Le Chateau - Parts One to Four 151

I Changed My Name 162

The Labyrinth Speaks of Taking Your Time 170

Can You See the Vole, Mum? 171

The Labyrinth Speaks of Being Free to Fly 173

I Changed Beyond Measure 174

I Said YES! - Part Three 176

It Was Time 177

'Smile, Why Don't You? It Might Never Happen!' 179

An Angel in the Supermarket 181

The Labyrinth Speaks of Navigating Blindfolded 183

A Financial Resolution 184

'I'd Rather Walk on Hot Coals Than Do That!' 190

Three Wise Women   192

Dear Home   197

I Said YES! - Part Four   200

Perfectly Imperfect   201

The Soul Speaks on Being Deeply Rooted   202

The Day the Sun Broke Through the Clouds   203

Come to the Beach   207

The Soul Speaks of the Presence of Love   210

Three Months' Grace   211

Love Hearts Everywhere   218

I Wrote a List   221

'Are You Blonde?'   222

Bring Me Sunshine   225

The Labyrinth Speaks - Here I Sit   231

Funk Rocks!   232

I Had a Rant!   233

The Soul Speaks of the Power of Looking Within   239

The Soul Speaks of the Ten Guiding Principles for Life   241

White Flag   244

Come and Stay for Three Months   246

Head in the Sand   251

I Let My Belongings Go   255

Glastonbury Tor Labyrinth   264

The Labyrinth Speaks of Being True to Self   268

I Walked Out of Counselling   269

The Labyrinth Speaks of Life as a Spiral   275

The Soul Speaks of Being ENOUGH   276

I'm Worth It   280

Be the Savvy Frog 287

RAGE 289

The Soul Speaks of Grace 300

I Didn't Recognise Myself 301

The Soul Speaks of Being Naked 302

This Thing Called Life 303

The Soul Speaks of Perfection 306

Goddess Rising 308

I AM Woman 309

The Labyrinth Speaks of Love Leading to Truth 312

The Tale of the Labyrinth, The Void & Rennes le Chateau - Parts 5 & 6 316

Soul Belonging 317

The Labyrinth Speaks of Love Leading to Source 321

What Price Freedom? 322

The Labyrinth Speaks of Life as a Spiral Dance 327

Inside Out 330

Prayer – Show Me 332

Letter – The Next Decade 333

The Labyrinth Speaks of Being You-nique 336

The Red Thread 337

Afterword 343

My Prayer for You 348

Contemplation Prompts 349

Acknowledgements 350

Let's Stay Connected 352

About the Author 353

Labyrinth: My Journey to Belonging
Reviews

"Thought provoking. Brave. Inspiring. There's so much deep wisdom throughout the book. Moriah challenges the emphasis that society places on us to strive and achieve in order to be valuable. The world is shifting and there is no pushing anymore, instead we're aligning with our truths and heart's desires through being and creating. This is such a special book and a precious voice, weaving the human and soul experience as one throughout."
Debra Kilby, author of "Rosa's Choice: Healing the Wounds of the Mother."

"In reading *Labyrinth*, I found the sense of not knowing and trusting the process of Life to unfold, rather than pushing or second guessing, to be very releasing. A relief almost. Reading Moriah's stories has encouraged me to reflect on events in my own life and what I have learned from them. I have a feeling I'm going to read it over and over and gain more each time. Thank you."
Victoria Tiller, Executive Coach

'Labyrinth is a beautiful weaving together of wisdom, gentle but powerful guidance and Moriah's journey which she so generously and vulnerably shares. There is so much in here that is relatable and a reminder that we share such similar struggles and triumphs in this human existence, even though our stories are each unique. It reminds us that it's an inner journey to finding home and that to belong we must come back to ourselves.'
Tara Jackson, Intuitive Business Guide, Empathpreneurs®

"This book has something very special. It is a handbook to awaken to the wisdom of living a life of freedom. Surrender, wisdom, and love are at its core. Such a wonderful book to accompany anyone in these changing times."
Marcia O'Regan, Spiritual Business Coach

"A wonderfully inspiring book for all women who are looking to move on in their lives, whether practically or spiritually. A handbook for our modern times."
Arya Ingvorsen, Shamanic Healer

"I can hear Moriah's voice in my ear, giving me permission to rest and just be. Perfect. Thank you."
Catrina Bennett-Jane, Primary School Teacher

"The women who walk ahead are guiding the steps, offering wisdom, and sharing truths. Moriah is one such being. The sense of knowing weaves its way through the pages and catches you off guard. It nudges your thoughts back into life and presses your body into forward motion.

You are not merely a reader of Moriah's words. You are a co-author as you gain permission to write your own. Story by story, narrative by narrative, letter by letter, that permission grows and strengthens. Throughout all her words, Moriah clearly shows that hope IS eternal if you are ready and willing to allow it into your life. This book is my permission to hope and offers a clear window on the possibilities still ahead for me.

It is a gift and one I will treasure for a long time to come."
Stacey Macdonald, Story Coach

"This is a handbook for all the female keepers of the wisdom for this time. We are birthing the new spirit of our age, and it must have the earthy power and wisdom that only women or at least the feminine in all beings brings. This book is a gift and will truly help so many people, especially women who have to make sense of how life is to be lived into the crazy future we are facing."
Melissie Jolly, Founder of Colour Mirrors

"Weaving together one woman's powerful and engaging personal story with deep insights in the "voice of the Labyrinth" about authenticity, courage and true freedom, this book will stay with you long after the last page has been turned. Moriah's work of empowering people to find their soul purpose is vitally important, and needed now more than ever, at this time of global transformation."
Dr Ash Brockwell, Associate Professor, London Interdisciplinary School

"In a field of many women sharing their stories of the long and looping road that is the Labyrinth of life, we can safely, surely follow the taillights of Moriah Ama Hope. She offers a companionship to those of us who do not fit the mould of the corporate world and spend years, too many years, trying to fit in. Her gift to us is in belonging to a precious lot of women who, leaving the comfort of the old paradigm, find a home for our hearts and belonging within. This woman, her story and this book are a treasure. May all belong!"
Kerry Anne Parsons, The Women of the Well

What can I say? Reading Labyrinth: My Journey to Belonging feels like an alchemical journey. Moriah has managed to create a book that's so very personal, sharing her own stories and experiences, whilst also capturing the essence of the spiral path we're all on. So often in life, we can feel in the midst of chaos, like we have no direction and it's one step forward then three back! In Labyrinth, Moriah reminds us (and herself) that even in the most challenging times, there is a divine intelligence at play. I feel like I could read this book over and over again, each time experiencing it in a different way - just like the labyrinth! Highly recommended for any woman wanting to make sense of her own unique and magical journey."
Nicola Humber, Founder of The Unbound Press

"So powerful. Moriah has created something very beautiful that people are really going to resonate with."
Jesse Lynn Smart, Writer & Editor

"It's beautiful, poetic, authentic and true. I know that I'll be able to dip into it again and again to unearth riches and wisdom to savour. Thank you."
Jackie Henry, Astrologer

The pathway from the head to the heart is a journey that calls forth our deepest inner resources, a soul-guided North star, and a determination for Truth that fortifies and supports all aspects of our lives. In Labyrinth - *My Journey to Belonging*, Moriah reveals for us the myriad ways she has travelled to find her unique pathway of belonging… so that we may find it, too.

From the world of fashion to the world of heart is a giant leap of many steps. As Moriah walked that journey, she opened inner doors of awareness, wisdom, and trust. In so doing, the doors of her inner and outer worlds unified, bringing a firm and resolute sense of the balance and clarity possible when one creates through the compassionate and kind intention of the heart.

Moriah's nurturing spirit is felt through her stories, tools, poems, and the voices of her soul and the Labyrinth. She greatly cares that our paths be easy and our psyches sound. As we read the words from Moriah's soul, we also feel the power of the soul's connection, which offers guidance and direction to weave its presence into our lives as it has Moriah's. Her journey to belonging becomes a guidepost for us on the path of our own spiritual awakening and evokes the longing within each of us for the peace that comes when we choose to live from the inner world of our heart and soul.

Flo Aeveia Magdalena, author of *I Remember Union: The Story of Mary Magdalena* and *The Voice of the Mothers*

The Labyrinth Speaks
of *the Seed of Our Belonging*

The seed of our belonging lies within us.

To discover it and to truly *feel* it is the nectar of Life itself,

for when we find it, we can call off the search.

Until that point, we are all lost in the wilderness,

finding our way Home.

Foreword

Hello and a very warm welcome to *Labyrinth: My Journey to Belonging*.

I know that your time and energy are precious, and I appreciate you creating time to read and experience the stories, journal entries, poems, musings, and stream-of-consciousness writings contained within.

This book is the story of the journey I undertook to find my place in the world and to ultimately answer the calling of my Soul. I was, both consciously and unconsciously, seeking to belong, to fit in, to be validated and loved by the worlds I occupied – familial, corporate, and spiritual – until eventually, step by step and over time, I found my way home to the seat of my belonging. It had been there all along, but like so many, I had been looking in all the wrong places.

Although this is my very personal account, it echoes the universal experience of many women and what it feels like to be human in a world that wants us to conform. How being true to ourselves initially feels like an act of rebellion and then evolves into an act of radical self-love. I share my stories with you. Some are raw, some sweet, some poignant. All are real.

Although it is not designed to be a self-help book, I trust that the stories and the messages throughout will support, encourage, soothe, inspire, and perhaps catalyse you.

Each of the chapters are standalone pieces. Imagine, if you will, a series of photographs taken at different times of my life. Each one a story, a memory, a glimpse into my life as it happened in real time. Once strung together, they appear as if markers on a single thread, charting my journey to belonging. They appear largely in chronological order.

There are three voices who speak throughout the book: me, the voice of my soul, and that of the Labyrinth.

My voice speaks through my stories, musings, reflections, and journal entries.

There are letters, postcards, and passages written as the Voice of my Soul. It could equally be experienced as a universal message to all of us from the level of the soul, a loving voice, whispering to us of its guidance.

And finally, the voice of the Labyrinth speaks at certain points throughout the book too.

The poems, postcards, letters, and stream-of-consciousness pieces were all written as they came to me in one continuous flow of words. The postcards and letters came to me fully formed during a time of my life when I felt particularly alone and challenged. They soothed and inspired me through those times. The poems arrived almost two decades prior to the writing of this book, and it was clear that they belonged here. I've kept journals and notebooks through the years, so all the material was ready at hand.

I didn't set out to write this book. I had, in fact, felt a calling to write a different book altogether. It was called *Love Your Karma – Making Peace with Life and Coming Home to Love*. It was close to completion, having been through its first edit, when I felt a distinct change in my relationship with it. My interest and energy for it completely dropped away, and over the course of a few weeks, it was clear to me that it wasn't coming back. Another version of it began to form in my mind, and this version had the name *A Life of Spaghetti: How to Survive and Thrive through Messy Times*. This version felt lighter, more fun, and I could see that it would be a collage of all the self-help tips, self-enquiry questions, and experiences that my clients and I had lived through. I collected ideas lightly, on post-it notes and, in my notebook, taking care not to cling too tightly and race off ahead. This book idea lasted but one week before the third and final idea dropped in.

And this book was conceived. At first, all I could see, and feel was that I was to write about my own life experience. I had a string of stories come to mind during the first few days, and it would be a full three weeks before I heard its name drop into my head whilst washing dishes one morning. I never imagined that I would set off on a book-writing expedition to share some of my most personal stories. In fact, it felt more likely that I would resist, squirm, and wriggle my way out of it. And yet, the calling to write this book was so clear, pure, and strong that I surrendered into the process and let the essence of the book mingle with my consciousness.

One day, I asked for a message about how to approach writing the stories. Later that morning, whilst walking on the beach, my eyes were drawn to a beautiful, wispy, pure white feather. As I walked further, I began to see identical white feathers along the beach ahead of me.

In my head, I heard the message, 'Follow the feathers.'

As I continued further along the beach, sure enough, the feathers kept appearing. Each feather was as pure white and fluffy as the first and all at an equal distance from each other. And then I suddenly understood. I was being guided to write my book one story at a time, to let the stories lead the way. I was to trust in the unfolding of the book. I was to trust the wisdom at work behind the scenes. As soon as I understood and acknowledged the message, the trail of white feathers came to an end.

When I first began to write this book, it was simply a collection of my personal stories. After a few weeks of writing, the name of the book dropped into my awareness, and I became curious as to how the Labyrinth would show up here in my writing, for me as the author and for you as the reader. Although I had an inkling about how this might work, it was only towards the very end of the book-writing journey that I began to glimpse the intelligence at work behind the scenes. And it wasn't until I had printed all the individual stories and pieces that I understood how they would come together in the order in which you see them now. If you would like to hear more about how this book was written, there is a bonus chapter for you to discover on my website. Please turn to the back of the book for more details.

I am certain that I haven't grasped all of it even now. It will reveal and illuminate whatever you need to know, feel, or experience in the moment, just as you would if you were walking a physical Labyrinth. You can gaze at the symbol or simply hold this book within your hands and receive a transmission of energy from the consciousness of the Labyrinth.

The stories that I am about to share with you are deeply personal. In the interests of privacy, I have largely chosen not to refer to the people in my stories by name. Any resemblance to any person or persons with similar circumstances is purely coincidental and unintentional. I am deeply grateful to everyone who has been part of my story, regardless of circumstances.

This book works on many levels and can be experienced in various ways. I know and trust that you will find your own ways of connecting with its messages. If, however, you would like some inspiration, here are some ideas you might like to consider.

Read the whole book from cover to cover.

Read the everyday stories exclusively.

Read the mystical passages of the Soul Speaks and the Labyrinth Speaks exclusively.

Consider a challenge or an opportunity you are facing. Open the book and see where your eyes land. Does it give you an answer or the next step?

Cast your eyes over chapter names, notice which one catches your attention and read that one.

Trace the Labyrinth symbol on page 27 with your finger, with or without a question in mind. Try alternating between left and right hands and experiment with different fingers to see how different it feels.

Hold the book in your hands or against your body and invite a transmission of energy to fill you.

Try reading the mystical pieces out loud. It provides a different experience from simply reading them. It becomes a more felt, embodied experience when read aloud.

It may be that you read little and often, giving yourself time to digest it before returning.

Return to re-read it wholly, or read individual pieces as and when you feel called to. Each time you read or engage with it, you will receive something new.

If you have the paperback version, please do feel free to write in it, turn its corners, allow it to be a living, breathing part of your life. I believe books are to be fully experienced and their wisdom embodied.

Share it with others, pass it on if you feel called, gift it to loved ones. It is designed to be shared. The everyday stories of miscarriage, workplace bullying, living with chronic pain, divorce, and loss are shared with so many. If even just one chapter in the book helps another, then it has done its work.

Try engaging with the symbol over a twenty-one-day period to support you in your personal growth. You could focus on a single question or challenge. Perhaps engage with it as part of a contemplative or meditation practice. I find that twenty-one days is the time it takes for a change in attitude, habit, or belief system to integrate and fully land in our daily awareness.

As with life, there is no right or wrong way – there is only your way.

There are some journal prompts and a list of resources that you might like to make use of at the end of the book.

May this book bring you whatever you most need and desire at this time, even though you may not know what that is.

May the mystery scoop you up in her arms and return you Home to your own belonging, time and time again.

From my heart to yours,

The Labyrinth

A Labyrinth is an archetypal symbol based on the circle, a universal symbol of wholeness and unity.

It differs from a maze in that it has only one pathway in and out, with a resting place at the centre. A maze, on the other hand, has multiple entrances and is a puzzle that challenges the mind to locate the way out. In a Labyrinth, the mind can rest and take a back seat as one follows the singular pathway.

You turn 180 degrees each time you enter a different circuit. This shifts your awareness from right brain to left, helping to induce a receptive state of consciousness and bring you into a greater state of presence.

The Labyrinth I work with is the classical seven-turn Labyrinth. There is one pathway in, a space in the centre to pause and reflect, and then there is one pathway out. We cannot get lost. It represents our journey or path to our own centre and back out again into the world. For me, this links with the rhythms of the moon and the tides, our own in and out breath, the seasons of winter retreat and summer expansion, and so much more.

Each of the seven turns in and out represents one of the chakras or energy centres of our energetic system. The Labyrinth is a universal symbol, and yet my sense is that it relates uniquely to each of us, and its consciousness works with ours to meet us exactly where we are on our own journey.

I have a confession: I love Labyrinths. Labyrinths, mazes, and spirals have always fascinated me. I remember drawing and painting spirals as a child and enjoyed doing this with my own children long before I began working with the symbol. On rainy days, I would often get coloured pens and paints out. My sons and I would then create whole pictures made of spirals. We all got involved. Giant rolls of unused wallpaper would be turned over and we would each begin with a section. These sections would then merge into one long piece of art. Our kitchen walls were often adorned by our spiral creations.

My relationship with the ancient symbol of the Labyrinth goes back decades to when I first began exploring the mysteries and stories of Labyrinths and mazes. I became fascinated by them and wanted to experience them for myself. I sought out mazes near me in the UK and tried navigating them in different ways – first by logic and research, then by intuition, and more recently by following the pathways using my hand or a finger in one continuous motion. It never did work when I tried to think my way through. It always worked best when I used my intuition and felt my way around.

Looking back on my life, I would say that this experience mirrors my evolution from head to heart and then to feeling my way through life in a more embodied way. And herein lies the magic of the Labyrinth. It mirrors so much of what we experience of life, as well as the capacity to support our transformation and our unfolding evolution.

I have run Labyrinth walks in England, Ireland, and France. My personal experience of walking Labyrinths – as well as facilitating Labyrinth walks for others – is that we always receive what we need from the experience. We may not always know what we need, yet we can trust that the consciousness of the Labyrinth knows exactly what we need. It also knows how we need to experience it to grow, evolve, and mature in accordance with our own life's path. It holds an intelligence way beyond logic.

Our ancestors knew the power of this symbol. It is found all over the world and especially so in caves and at sacred sites such as Newgrange in Ireland. Labyrinthine symbols date back to the Neolithic Age, also appearing in places like India, Ireland, Greece, and Turkey. They are found in Minoan palaces as symbols of royal power and appear on old Cretan coins. There is a giant multi-course Labyrinth built from limestone, measuring approximately 13 metres in diameter, on the floor of the central knave in Chartres Cathedral. For 2,500 years, Chartres has been one of the most sacred sites in France. Druids revered the location. Christians built a cathedral over the site. Celtic priests believed that energy emanated from the ground and that the underground waters were sacred and held healing properties. From the Labyrinth, you can look up and see the rose window. The rose symbol is often associated with the

Labyrinth. It is thought that pilgrims would pause at Chartres to walk the Labyrinth as part of their journey to the Holy Land.

They knew how to be in touch with nature's rhythms, rising with the sun and withdrawing at sunset. They worshipped and lived in accordance (accord-dance) with the seasons and the turning points of the year, the Equinoxes and Solstices in particular.

The Labyrinthine symbol also links with the da Vinci Fibonacci series, which is found everywhere in nature and within certain geometries of our own bodies. The symbol itself pre-dates 1,000 B.C. and is believed to have manifested through a prayer or intent of 'please show me the way home'. I personally believe that the Labyrinth is a gateway into other worlds, including our inner world and that of mystery.

I think that this ancient symbol is ever more relevant and powerful for our contemporary lives. In a time when we look outside of ourselves for answers, solutions, and quick fixes, the noise of the world serves to disconnect and distract us even more. We are increasingly out of balance with ourselves, our own personal rhythms, and our capacity to simply rest, go at our own pace, and be fully present.

As a woman myself and having worked primarily with women over the past two decades, I believe it is essential to our holistic health and well-being to balance activity with rest and renewal. Our Feminine nature is often exhausted by over-activity, over-stimulation, over-socialising, and holding space for everyone other than ourselves. Many of us in the western world have become out of balance with our innate yin energy, having grown up in an overly masculinised world regulated by structure, expansion, activity, logic, timetables, quantitative results, and speed. This is inherently detrimental to us and to society. Men, too, need to experience the benefits that true, deep rest can bring. So often, we can find ourselves experiencing enforced rest when our bodies say, 'Enough', and give us little choice but to stop and take stock.

In walking the Labyrinth, our logical mind is balanced with our intuitive, creative mind. It helps that it is a non-linear construct because it serves to scramble our logical brain and bring it into balance with the non-linear. As life is not experienced in a straight line, the Labyrinth supports us in remembering how to walk a non-linear path.

The Labyrinth will meet each of us where we are at right now. Its consciousness weaves its way within, through, and around our energy field and resolves the core issue of anything getting in the way of us being Home and true to self. Its core mission is to facilitate our homecoming. Connecting with it daily can help us to stay on track, manifest our hopes and dreams, and relax into our own unique, true nature. It is simple yet profound. It is a mystery that, by its very nature, is deeply Feminine. It's not a linear path, and neither is life. We can have a grasp of some of its power and potential, and yet so much of it remains a mystery. So much is known, and much remains a mystery, much like our lives and the world and cosmos that we live in.

When I run Labyrinth days, I create a sense of sacred ceremony and celebration to enhance the transformational potential of the Labyrinth walk experience. I allow time to reflect, time in meditation, and time to walk it slowly. Women often remark just how surprised they are that it takes so long to walk what looks like such a simple path. Once they begin walking, they slow down, they naturally want to stop at certain points, and in some cases, they feel lost or a sense that they are doubling back on themselves. These are all natural responses. The experience of walking a Labyrinth is like our experience of life itself. I have seen women laugh, cry, fall to their knees and feel panic on their inward pathway whilst many walk more swiftly and even skip with delight on the outward one.

In the process of writing this book, I am even more convinced that the Labyrinth symbol, walk, and consciousness, all mirror life. As we trace or walk the Labyrinth pathway, we are led to the centre without having to engage our logical minds. We simply follow the path. Indeed, our logical mind can become confused or disoriented as the pathway doubles back on itself. It is easier to simply follow the path ahead, one step at a time. This is a skill that serves us well in navigating our life.

The Labyrinth is whole and complete in and of itself. We walk in. We rest at the centre. We walk out.

It flows. We can get stuck within ourselves with too much introspection. We can get lost in the outside world of convention, tradition, rules, distraction, other people's expectations of us, and the media projections. In this way, it serves to balance our yin or Feminine energy with that of our yang or masculine energy.

It shines a light on where we get stuck. As we navigate each twist and turn, we move through the seven main energy centres or chakras of our energetic system. We can get stuck at certain points, and the location within the Labyrinth where we get stuck or confused can shine a light on which chakra and corresponding life theme require our attention. Our blind spots can be illuminated, which helps us to work more consciously to contemplate and transform those parts of us that we have disowned and shut off from, all of which helps us integrate our mind-body system and come into greater wholeness. It can show us which characteristics, attitudes, beliefs, or behaviours of the corresponding chakra to look more closely into. The process of walking or tracing the Labyrinth supports us in getting unstuck – it helps to transform the underlying issue at the root cause. In this way, it can shine a light on our blind spots and heal them.

Working at an unconscious level, each time we walk the Labyrinth or trace its shape, we make more of our unconscious beliefs, drivers, and behaviours conscious. This gives us a wonderful opportunity to engage with them, determine what is relevant and resonant with us and discard the rest.

Each time we do this, we shed layers upon layers of old programming from childhood, society, peers and learned experience. It gives us the opportunity to get closer to who we are without any of the should, musts, coulds, needs, and expectations. We become more fully whole. We come Home to ourselves and our innate essence and gifts.

We unlock power, portals, and energetic pathways – imagine the motion of turning the key of a safe or spinning the numbers of a combination lock, unlocking the pathway to our own individual buried treasure within.

The Labyrinth holds the space for us so that we don't have to. The ancients knew that it was a symbol of renewal and balance, and the centre of the Labyrinth was often called 'The Womb of Hope'.

Tracing and walking the Labyrinth can be a meditative experience. It unconsciously helps us to slow down, to re-balance and be present. It creates an energetic resonance to set the balance of in/out into our energy fields. It also facilitates an opening, a relaxing of our mind-body system, which creates space for our energy field to soften and for us to feel the presence of our Soul more acutely.

I believe that the Labyrinth works at the subconscious, conscious, and superconscious levels. Whilst we engage with the everyday-ness of life, it facilitates our evolution. Its consciousness interacts with ours to facilitate potent transformation. I have witnessed this for myself and for others.

As well as organising in-person Labyrinth walks, I also offer online meditations globally to connect with and attune to the energy of the Labyrinth to enable more people to benefit from the experience of connecting with its consciousness.

This book holds within it the consciousness of the Labyrinth. May its ancient wisdom and mystery guide you Home to the seat of your own belonging.

The Labyrinth Speaks
of *the Secret of Our Belonging*

In the soft underbelly of each of us lies the secret of our belonging.

We are not alone.

The trick is to remember that we are not alone.

It is an illusion that feels so real.

We are made of stardust and connected to the cosmos.

How could we possibly be alone?

Pre-Incarnation – The Swing Between Worlds

A conversation between The Ones with No Names and my Soul, pre-incarnation, in the space and time immediately prior to incarnation into physical form. It speaks to the themes and flavours of the life to come, the contract that I agreed to at a Soul level and how the challenges I would face would help me to grow and ultimately how they would help me serve more widely in the world.

The life you have planned will stretch you beyond measure. It will take you out of your comfort zone and challenge you in ways that may, at times, bring you to your knees.

You will lose your way on many occasions.

You will feel lost and alone – although, in truth, you will be neither lost nor alone.

You will feel powerless, confused, even angry.

You will descend into your human-ness, and it will feel like a thick, dense fog has enveloped you.

It will feel suffocating at first.

You will quickly come to forget what it was like to feel expansive, limitless, and free.

You will forget what it was to be connected, to know yourself as a free spirit, bound by none.

You will forget what it was like to be able to breathe deeply.

You will feel empty, flat, and will seek to fill the void with all manner of drama, distraction, and distortion.

Your Design will be simple yet profound.

You will be born into a genetic ancestry and spiritual lineage, which ensures you experience and feel acutely the disempowerment of the

Feminine nature of your being.

You will know what it is to be disconnected from all that is inherently true of the Feminine, and you will sink deeply into the patriarchal world of humankind.

Your Design requires you to disconnect from your psychic and sensory gifts, your body, your ancient wisdom, the many gifts that you have honed through hundreds of incarnations and aeons of existence, and to become disconnected from your personal power.

You will slip into survival mode.

You will forget that your Divine human birth right is abundance and love.

You will experience helplessness and hopelessness.

You will tumble into victimhood, and at times you will feel shame, guilt, and despair.

You will experience all of this and more so that you learn how to unbury, unravel, and unbind yourself from the emotional, mental, psychic, and societal debris that has bound you. This will give you an embodied experience of how it is to feel lost, alone, confused, and restricted.

You will do this for yourself and for your ancestors first and foremost.

You will transform, transmute, and resolve ancestral karma.

As you learn to reclaim your sovereignty, so too will you help others to do the same.

Your experiences will serve to remind others that they too can experience peace, love, and abundance.

You will help them navigate their own unique pathway through the pain and back home to a life of connection, harmony, and joy.

You will transform the corrupted disk that you were born with into a blueprint for how to live lightly upon the Earth, living in right ways and in synch with the rhythms of life and the cosmos.

You will need to lose yourself to find yourself, and you will give your power away so that you can learn the value of discernment and personal boundaries.

You will look outside of yourself for answers and for a place to belong in the world. You will place your faith in others and be let down, disillusioned, and feel betrayed. You will continue to do this until you learn to trust yourself and to value your own innate wisdom and the truth that lies within.

And you will know the trauma of not valuing your deeply Feminine gifts because society has shunned them. And so, you too will shun them.

You will learn all of this and more as an initiation into belonging.

The themes of belonging, Home, lost, found, and sovereignty are all bound together as one.

One song, one dance; now this, now that.

There will be key players along the way to support you in your endeavours.

There will be heroes and villains, although in truth, sometimes the villains will be the heroes, and the heroes will appear as villains. You will play these roles for others too.

Everyday actions at certain times in your life will signal significant moments and points of change.

Some you will recognise, and others you will not.

The number three will be significant for you.

You will learn how to be in synch with your personal rhythms, the rhythms of the Earth and those of the cosmos.

You will learn to heed the call of Spirit and know what it is to follow your spiritual signature without hesitation, even when it makes no sense or seemingly puts you at a disadvantage.

You will learn to let go and surrender over and over again.

You will experience much loss in your life, and you will come to understand its value in your awakening.

Your ego will be broken down until it is fully integrated, at which point your Soul will pick up the reins. In the first forty years, your masculine energy will predominantly lead the way. The final forty years will see your Feminine call the shots.

You will be many things to many people.

You will fulfil many roles, arguably the most important one being that of Mother.

You will love and guide your sons so that they know how to stay true to themselves and to their own Design. In this way, they will not lose themselves and will retain connection. They will inherently know their sacred 'Yes' from their sacred 'No' and will be more equipped to fulfil their destinies with greater ease and grace than many. You will learn many things from your sons, and they will be catalysts for your growth and unfolding, including the realisation that you are not here to suffer or sacrifice in your role as Mother. You will learn to value your role and appreciate how you model what it means to be in right relationship with oneself and others.

You will come to appreciate your Design and its contribution to your unfolding and evolution.

You will, eventually, come to love your karma.

Through all of this, you will be amassing and embodying wisdom from your lived experience, which you will feel guided to share in very specific ways. The more you engage and immerse yourself in acts of empowerment, the more aligned you will be to your Design, and the more you surrender to your spiritual signature, the easier and more joyful life will be. Immerse yourself in creativity, and you will be deeply fulfilled.

And you will know and experience great love.

Knowing all of this, do you accept your Soul's Plan and soul contracts for this lifetime ahead?

Are you willing to accept and live your Design in accordance with the sacred laws of the cosmos?

'Yes. I am willing.'

Then let us proceed to the journey into form.

Remember that you are loved beyond measure.

Remember that you will find and live your Design and help others to do so too.

Remember that the power lies within.

Remember that there is a pathway through the pain.

Remember that Union is to be experienced first within before it manifests without.

And that all is well and that all will be well.

And now it is time to descend into form.

Are you ready?

'I am ready.'

What if I Fail?

'But what if I fail?
What if I don't do you justice?'
You could never fail me.

'What if I don't complete the contract?'
It is in the Design that you will complete the contract.
You cannot fail.
It is already written in the Design.
You will succeed.
And that will be your greatest fear.
That you will succeed.

Once Upon a Time

Once upon a time, a baby girl was born.

She was bright, bubbly, and popular.

She grew into a woman, had a successful career, and offered her innate qualities of intuition, love, and creativity to the world and was much loved by all.

She married, had babies, and lived happily ever after.

Er, nope, plot twist.

Are you kidding?

Where's the soul learning and growth in that?

Do you want to know the real story?

Are you sitting comfortably?

Then let's begin.

My Early Years

I was born into early 1960s suburbia in a town northwest of London, England. In breech position until hours before making my journey through the birth canal, I emerged into the world many hours later. Strawberry blonde hair and big blue eyes. My mum was still sedated when I was born, and so I was taken, like all the babies were at that time, into a nursery full of newly born infants. Born on my great grandfather's birthday and into a family where I was much wanted and loved.

For the first few years of my life, we lived on the first floor of the semi-detached house that we shared with my father's parents. Looking back, it can't have been an easy start to married life, especially with then having a new-born. Listening to my mum's account of life then, she had to take me out on frequent, long walks to give my grandparents peace from my early, noisy explorations. I cried a lot, apparently, for the first twelve weeks. She lost a lot of weight. She regrets now not listening to her own intuition, which was telling her that I was hungry and not getting enough milk from her. She listened to the midwives who told her not to bottle feed until I was at least twelve weeks old. This would be repeated in my own mothering journey three decades later when my firstborn was admitted to hospital at six days old because he was losing weight and becoming dehydrated. It was my mum who spotted it and intervened. At first, I trusted what the midwives were telling me, although after five days or so, I was challenging them because I knew something felt off. My mum is more intuitive and much wiser than she gives herself credit for, and she has been one of my guiding forces throughout life. She has always let me learn from my own mistakes and as a parent myself, I know how difficult that can feel. She also taught me to "follow my nose," in other words, to follow my intuition.

My earliest memory is of lying in my pram in the garden, looking up at the sky, and listening to bird song. I have a distinct recollection of feeling connected to nature and to life, and I would babble, my way of chatting and communicating with what I could sense, see, feel, and hear.

I grew into a happy, curious toddler who had invisible friends, chatted with fairies, and apparently predicted the future. I would spend hours in the garden, hopping from one stepping-stone to the next, up and down the full length of the grass. I would walk across the rockery surrounding the edge of the pond, much to my father's horror. He was always worried that something bad was going to happen to me. The rocks provided me with a seat closer to the pond life, and I was equally fascinated and startled by the frogs that used to jump out from the water or from underneath a plant. The water lilies fascinated me too. From my vantage point, I created stories of water fairies and boats and floating islands.

Another memory is that of lying on my bed, around the age of five, asking my mum what the shapes were that I could see floating around in front of my eyes. I could see circular shapes, sometimes clear, sometimes coloured, floating in the space above me. I saw colours around people too and questioned why. Mum advised me that it would be best not to talk about such things to others for fear of being misunderstood. And so, I stopped. Slowly but surely, I began to shut down some of my innate senses until intuition and imagination were all that remained.

I turned instead to the world of books. My mum fostered in me a love of reading and books from birth. She would read to me as a baby and speak to me as she would an adult. Music was always playing in the house, and I remember listening to the radio and dancing in the kitchen to the tunes of the 60s. By the time I was three, I could tell a good story from illustrations and from memory. My maternal grandad made a two-tiered doll house which I adored. It kept me occupied for hours, with tiny pieces of handmade furniture, carpets and even curtains at the windows. I would make up stories with my dolls and act them out.

On Fridays, we would take a walk to our local library. I was always excited to choose new books. There was a little wall to the front of the library building, and I would hop up and walk along it, arms held out to my sides for balance. I was fascinated with the librarian and the process of returning books and having them allocated. The sifting through endless small, brown oblong tickets and the click of the inky date stamp as it hit the first page of the book. I remember that I would often cast my eye over the list of dates on the paper sticker on the inside sleeve showing previous loan dates. I thought that I'd like to be a librarian when I grew up. Books were a big part of my early life – that, and visits to parks. Books fed my imagination. Parks and our garden fed my communion with nature and my sense of adventure and freedom. When I was around two years old, I had my first experience with the sea. We went to the south coast for a holiday. Legend has it that I ran directly into the sea, fully clothed, beaming and laughing. My mum was distracted momentarily, and I broke loose. I was safely retrieved, and they bought me my first bikini later that day.

When I was old enough to go to a local playgroup, I didn't enjoy the experience. It took me months to adapt. I was sensitive and very shy, unaccustomed to being with lots of other children. I remember feeling lost and overwhelmed at the volume of noise and the amount of running around and snatching of toys. It felt like angry chaos. I felt like the proverbial 'fish out of water'. I spent a lot of my time with water play and in the sandpit. I made friends with several of my young playmates, many of whom were boys. This was a theme right the way through to senior school. I found boys easier to relate to and less complicated than girls, who were frequently falling in and out of friendships, with endless squabbles.

My dad worked shifts and often worked nights. He was a good provider for the family and, on reflection, was probably always highly introverted. He needed a lot of space and silence. Working in a factory and shift work probably left him out of kilter. I don't remember him reading to me or playing with us as children.

My brother was born a few months before I started school. I remember the point at which my mum told me that she was expecting him. I was watching her place bed linen into the airing cupboard in our bathroom. I also remember that being the first moment when I questioned whether I was enough.

By the time I started school, I could write, and I could read some basic words and sentences. I loved school and learned that if I got through the work quickly that I was allowed to go out to play. I worked hard. I loved learning and had a ferocious appetite for books. I worked my way through all the children's book section of our local library by the age of eight. I was ahead of my classmates academically for the whole of my school life, and this gave me a sense of pride and accomplishment as well as the origins of not fitting in'. There were several times that I remember trying to rebel and not do the homework. Times when I stopped putting my hand up to answer the teachers' questions so that I didn't get teased or just so that I could attempt to 'blend in'. It didn't feel good, though.

I immersed myself in my imagination, numbing my pain and confusion about not fitting in, not being popular, not looking the part, not being the first to be picked for sports teams, not being fast enough, pretty enough, confident enough or good enough. I lost my happy demeanour and became withdrawn and pale. I became a picky eater.

I had flashbacks and fragments of memory of something that I was supposed to be doing. I have a vivid memory of standing in my infant school playground, around age six or seven, watching the other children playing. Some played with a skipping rope, others were running around, and some played hopscotch. I remember feeling crystal clear that I was supposed to be getting on with something, that we were all here for a reason. I couldn't remember the detail. I just knew it to be true. The memory would come and go, but I couldn't make sense of it. And then the flashbacks stopped altogether.

When I was seven, my maternal grandmother introduced me to ballroom and Latin American dance lessons. I won medals, progressed through the levels and competitions. Here I was welcome, popular, and more than enough. I felt like I had a home here. It was something that I could excel in. It helped me to develop more confidence in myself. I made friends and had a regular dance partner. I continued with dancing until I was fourteen, when the pressure of public exams and the lure of boyfriends began to take hold.

I came back to my love of stories and immersed myself in the English language. I wrote stories for the Radio for the Blind and narrated my own stories from time to time. Something new began to change too. I was now much taller than most of my classmates, and I was being picked for sports teams for defence positions. I discovered that I was good at most sports that involved throwing or batting a ball and enjoyed them. I went on to represent my school at county level in tennis, hockey, and netball. At about the same time, I was being asked out by boys, most of whom I had little interest in. At the age of sixteen, however, I met and fell in love with a boy who became my first love and first partner in life. We stayed together for eight years, through public exams, university, and first jobs. Memories of Dean evoke long, sweet summers, togetherness, ease, loving connection and road trips to Cornwall in the southwest of England, in his Mini.

University was, in many ways, the making of me. I was independent, I had chosen topics that I loved and had a natural affinity with and talent for, and I met wonderful friends. I spent a year in France deepening my fluency in the language, went on numerous geomorphology field trips, and cycled for miles around southwest London. Summers were spent at my parent's home, working to earn money for the following year, or on some occasions, I worked at the Wimbledon Tennis Club, washing up and gaining access to the tennis matches whenever I could. It was a happy time. I have fond memories of my undergraduate years. I had matured into a woman who was preparing to find her place in the big, wide world beyond education.

Halcyon days, memories stored, friendships made, an excellent honours degree in the bag and three graduate job offers secured, I left Uni feeling excited, full of hope and with a great sense of anticipation.

'I Always Knew You Were a Witch!'

These were my mum's words to me the day before I set out on my first Reiki attunement. I was 37. She had never told me this before. I asked her what she meant, as I was curious to know what she had seen in me as a child to lead her to believe this. I share them here at this point of the book because it gives an insight into how I was as a child before I lost my connection with my innate abilities.

She thought for some time and then reeled off a list.

I avoided people who were critical, unkind, or loud.

As soon as I could talk, I asked questions about why people were sad even though they said they were fine.

I voiced long-held family secrets, including pointing out that my great-uncle wore a toupee.

I talked about things that hadn't yet happened, but which often took place within a day of me mentioning them.

I made choices based on how my body felt.

I would put my hand over my heart for things that I wanted and were a 'Yes'.

I would put my hand over my stomach for a 'No'.

I made up stories of fairies and invisible friends and had conversations with them.

I was happiest in nature and on my own.

I didn't need people around me like other children of my age did.

My eyes followed the birds when I was lying in my pram in the garden, and I would make noises as if I were having a conversation with them.

I used to *see* energy.

When my brother had his tonsils removed in hospital, I had my one and only incident of tonsillitis.

I read people's body language from a very young age.

I could *make things happen*.

And I knew the time and way my grandad had died before being told.

Some of this I do remember, and some of this I have no memory of. I was surprised and happy to know that I had had these abilities from birth – an ability to see and *feel* things, empathy, sensitivity, and intuition – and it gave me hope that I could re-connect and plug back in.

I had no idea what lay ahead of me when I drove off from home that day to have my Reiki attunement, but what I did know was that this felt like a plan I had made a very long time ago.

Good Girls

Programming:
England. Early 1960s. Female. Caucasian.

De facto programming as follows. Good Girls:

```
Are seen and not heard.
Don't talk back
Don't swear.
Know their place.
Please others.
Put others first.
Don't rock the boat.
Don't raise their voice.
Don't rebel.
Respect authority figures.
Don't cause trouble.
Don't ask for what they want.
Wait to be invited.
Are sugar and spice and all things nice.
Are grateful for their lot.
Settle for what they are given.
Don't have sex before marriage.
Play by the rules.
Play nicely.
Conform.
Don't complain.
Don't have ideas above their station.
Don't push back.
Blend in.
Look pretty.
Grin and bear it.
Play by the rules.
Colour inside the lines.
Follow.
Put up.
Shut up.
```
Programming degree of difficulty = 100%
Activation: At birth.
Acceleration: Three years of age.
Full Absorption: Seven years of age.

It Was Good Enough for Me, It's Good Enough for You

When I was eleven, it was time to choose my next school. I had always had great school reports, and my teacher and headteacher both recommended me for the local grammar school. I remember feeling so excited. In my mind, I imagined it to be a place where everyone wanted to learn and where I could excel and take my love of learning to a whole new level.

My parents and I went to the open evening, and it didn't disappoint. It had an awesome library and a very grown-up kind of feel to it. I wanted to go to this school. It felt like a big jump, and I felt ready. In my mind, this was the one for me, and I was going to apply.

One evening, my dad called me over to his armchair and had a chat with me. He suggested that it would be too expensive to send me to grammar school. The uniform, the school bus fees, the extra books, and the school visits would all be very costly.

He closed by saying, 'The comprehensive was good enough for me, so it's good enough for you.'

The eleven-year-old me sensed a subtext. Firstly, 'You're not going to grammar school,' and secondly, 'People like us don't go to grammar school.'

It seemed that the decision had been made for me. I was not going to grammar school. I was going to the comprehensive school. My dad had made himself clear, and I knew better than to challenge his word.

Letter from my Soul
On *Gathering Moss*

Dear Moriah,

You will go through many transformations in life.

It will be a little like gathering moss. The first half of your life will be taking on other people's expectations and conditioning. The more conditioning you take on, the more you will be wrapped in moss and the thicker it will become until it's so thick, you will barely be able to see, breathe, or move.

The second half of your life will be about loosening, unbinding, detangling, releasing, breaking free, dissolving, transmuting and finally liberating yourself fully from all conditioning. It will be like rolling down a hill, and as you roll, the layers of moss unroll with you.

Except that it won't always be quite as simple or as fun as it sounds. There will be humps and bumps, stones, inclement weather, twists, turns, ledges, sharp corners, as well as times when you seem to go nowhere at all.

I will be cheering you on, sending you signs, clues and people to help you.

I will send you love bombs from afar when things feel tough and you feel my absence.

Trust in the mystery of it all.

There is rhyme and reason in everything that happens as well as in that which does not happen.

And you will look back and smile.

You will know that it was a good life, well lived.

You will know peace.

You will know love.

And in living all of this, you will also help others to do the same.

Embodied.

Enriched.

Enlivened.

I love you, always and all-ways.

Your big, beautiful, moss-loving Soul X

The Labyrinth Speaks
of *Trust*

I trust and I am led.

I trust, and I am shown.

I trust, and I understand.

I trust, and I love.

I trust, and I act.

I trust, and I know.

I trust, and I am in flow.

I trust, I AM.

I'll Bring You Down a Peg or Two!

September 1984

I was just starting out in my second placement of my post-graduate career. I had thrived in my first six-month placement in Oxford Street, at the epicentre of London's West End. I had loved working there. It was a vibrant, fast-moving culture and environment to be learning about fashion retail management. I had chosen this company to work for because I was already familiar with their working practices and culture. I had previously worked for them on Saturdays whilst I was studying for my A Levels and then later during the long university holidays. I also knew that they had an excellent three-year management training programme, and I instinctively knew that this was what I both wanted and needed as a good grounding into my working career.

I lived with my parents for the duration of my induction period. It was a relatively brief commute into London from my childhood home, and it meant that I could save a sizable amount of money. It was good to spend more time there too – it provided a psychological safety net of sorts whilst I began this new phase of my adult life out in the big wide world. It also gave me an opportunity to spend some quality time with my parents, which was lovely. I discovered that I enjoyed the commuting time. I walked a forty-minute sprint either to or from the railway station each day and spent the twenty-minute train journey either dozing or reading. It was a good transition time for me to prepare for or reflect on the day's events.

I already knew the manager of my first placement. He had interviewed me for my Saturday job, and then he appeared again five years later when I had my first interview for the management training scheme. He knew that I was a hard worker and got things done, that I was reliable and good with colleagues, so I guess you could say that I had less to prove than others might have. That said, however, he was no pushover. He demanded one hundred per cent, but he was fair, had a good sense of humour and believed in the importance of a good work-life balance.

After successfully completing my first six months' placement, I was posted to a large store in the far north-eastern suburbs of London, in Essex. It was going to be a new area for me to explore and hopefully make new friends. I was looking forward to a new challenge and an opportunity to extend my learning and deepen into my career. The company offered a generous relocation package, and my long term boyfriend and I decided to buy a flat as part of this move.

When I arrived for my first day, I was invited into a meeting by my new manager, together with my seven new colleagues, including one of whom, like me, was also new to the store. I felt both apprehensive and excited all at the same time. I tried hard not to show any of this or the tiredness from not sleeping well the night before. I put on a brave face and pretended that I was confident and competent.

I quickly sensed that there was a distinctly different tone to this team. The manager spoke, they listened. They seemed downbeat, looking mostly at the floor. It was a weekly briefing that felt more like a dictate of orders and expectations with a generous sprinkling of sarcasm and caustic wit. There was little interaction, and I sensed a lot of anxiety.

He had not yet made any reference to myself and the other new member, which I thought was odd if not downright rude, but I gave him the benefit of the doubt and waited to see how we might be welcomed. At the end of his monologue, the manager introduced the other new member by name and said that he was here as the new deputy manager.

And then the manager turned to face me directly, and with a big smirk across his face, announced to all my new colleagues:

'This one is fresh from the West End, and I will take great pleasure in bringing her down a peg or two. Let's see how she fairs against our own home-grown management trainee.' He looked at the woman standing beside him as a father might to his own daughter.

Even though I was stunned at his rudeness, I managed to voice my own name and to say that I was looking forward to getting to know everyone.

And that was the end of the briefing. A few people came over to welcome me and wish me well. Some nodded their acknowledgement of me and then left me to get on with their day's work. Some just walked out of the room in keen anticipation of getting the manager's attention.

I was in shock. My heart sank. I was confused. I had worked for this company on and off for five years and had just experienced six months of management induction courses and in store training, none of which looked or felt like the experience I had just had. It seemed a parody of how not to do things. Could a manager with regional responsibility really behave like this? Was this the same company? Had I just landed in a parallel universe?

It seemed that this was his regular style and that he could and frequently did get away with it. Everyone knew that he had some questionable methods and favourites; however, it appeared that the store was financially successful, and so he was left to his own devices as far as I could tell.

I was swiftly allocated a department of my own to merchandise. Sportswear and Accessories was to be my domain. It was the smallest square meterage of any department and the category that most managers liked the least because it had such a wide range of merchandise from swimwear to jewellery, from shoes to scarves. It was highly seasonal too, which meant if merchandise hadn't been sold by the end of each season, it would potentially show up as a loss, which no one wanted on their watch. It was also very messy. Think tangled necklaces, odd shoes, and string bikinis!

There and then, I decided that the only choice I had in this store was to make the best of things and look for the silver linings along the way. I went immediately down to the ground floor showroom to find the member of staff who was allocated to my new department. She was a few years younger than me and was bright and feisty. She had a depth of knowledge about the department that I lacked, an experience of a year's worth of hard work with little input from her previous merchandiser. She wanted to know how hands-on I was going to be. I could feel her energy dip when I explained it was my first real placement, and I wanted to dive right in and would like to learn from her as much as from other merchandisers about how they did things.

I wanted to find a way to make it work well for both of us, and I invited her to have a think about how we might do this together. I could see her weighing me up. I wasn't surprised, given the ice-cold welcome I had received from the others earlier. I imagined it would take a while for her to trust me. We spent the first week working together full-time on the showroom and behind the scenes so that she could show me how things worked and where everything was kept. I spent a lot of time listening which gave me the advantage of getting to know her and understanding her frustrations.

I could see that little time or attention had been given to her over the past year. She had a lot of potential, and I wanted to bring that out so that she could shine and get the recognition she deserved. I quickly grew to like and respect her, and she softened with me.

Within the first three weeks, we had been out and about in town looking at our competitors and what they were offering and the shopping experience they offered. We had completed a review of how stock was being stored and had come up with a more efficient and reliable way of storing it. I had cleared a backlog of admin and had also applied for some freely available equipment which would enable us to sell more of the reduced and out-of-season merchandise quickly and out of sight of the main showroom.

As we got to know each other more, we began to enjoy each other's humour which brightened our days considerably. She was an influencer in the wider staff team, which meant that her peers began to trust me, which was helpful given the general mistrust bred from fear that prevailed like a low-lying, dense fog. This young woman was my silver lining in a cloudy, stormy, unpredictable world. Our small part of the showroom was a happy place, at least.

The manager, however, seemed to be displeased with the impact I had made. Despite sales figures being up since my arrival, he began to undermine me by making snide remarks, criticising, and even interfering with how we were displaying merchandise. I once caught him taking an orderly line of garments and throwing them onto the floor, remarking to a passing team member how shocking I was. I called him out on that occasion. He told me that I was mistaken and that my department was a shambles.

He also tried to pit me against the woman who was his home-grown trainee. She was the only clear favourite in the whole team, and she took full advantage of her elevated status. She could frequently be seen following him around and updating him on every detail of her activity. I, on the other hand, avoided him and updated him once a week or as and when he demanded it. I did not want to play the brown-nosing game. That wasn't my style. I wanted the results to speak for themselves.

Things were about to sink to a whole new level of misery.

Nothing was good enough for this man. No amount of effort or results brought a kind or encouraging word. He seemed to seek me out as if it were a sport to him. He appeared to take a great deal of pleasure in 'bringing me down a peg or two'. At first, I shrugged it off and wholeheartedly imagined that he would change his behaviour once he saw that I was making a positive impact and contribution. Instead, he seemed to get worse the more successful the department became. Sadly, I couldn't sustain my optimism in the face of his regular, daily barrage of spite and venom.

He was a small, blonde, skinny man, around 1.6 metres in height, Scottish. He often had a frown, a smirk, or a look of disbelief on his face and wore a moustache that comically moved as he spoke. His small stature meant that he was able to hide behind merchandise and pillars of the showroom. He sometimes spied on me and would often jump out in front of me and bark criticism. He didn't appear to do this with anyone else.

He would follow me from behind the scenes as I took the newly delivered merchandise onto the showroom to display and would tell me to hurry up, go faster, do better. He could be almost pleasant one minute and fly into a vile, angry tirade the next. I once encountered him at the lift, banging on the closing doors and swearing. It seemed that the member of staff hadn't kept the doors open long enough for him to get in. That was a brave woman, whoever she was. I had never encountered someone quite so angry before, and I didn't know how to handle it. In truth, I felt frightened of it. It felt personal when he flew into a vile, verbal attack. And, of course, it was personal. It was designed to cut me down and erode my self-esteem. It was a power game that he played. The combination of attack and intensity was powerfully damaging. The fact that he was my manager and had an influence on how my performance would be rated was a difficult path for me to navigate. I was poorly equipped to know how to deal with him or my feelings. Most of the time, I dared not feel anything for fear of overwhelm and not being able to get on with the day-to-day tasks.

He was an outright bully. Nothing was ever good enough. He was never satisfied. I went from being an inexperienced but confident management trainee to a nervous wreck. I slipped into wanting to please him, first to win his approval and then to simply get him off my case. I knew that I was doing well, the sales figures were improving year on year, and our department was outperforming not just the others in the region but also across the country.

Logic told me that I was doing well. My heart, face, and body told a very different story. I felt anxious and scared for most of my working day. His day off would be the highlight of the week – and not just for me but for everyone. The whole store was a happier place when he wasn't around. It was palpable, the difference his miserable presence made. I felt my whole body relax on those days. I remember noticing that even my breathing changed. I had gotten used to short breaths and sometimes even holding my breath. On the days that he wasn't in the store and on my days off, I felt my breathing come back to its original rhythm of long and deep.

I was just twenty-three and in only my second placement with a manager who could potentially make or break my career. I was in a job and a company I loved but with a tyrant for a boss. I had a mortgage to pay now. I had little disposable income and couldn't afford to buy a car. Public transport was poor. I got one Saturday off each month, and I would go and spend it with my family or with friends. The quicker I was out of the area, the better. I could almost forget for a day just how miserable I felt. My midweek days off would be spent in the local parks or in just sleeping and catching up with life admin. I didn't feel much anymore. I was numb. It was as much as I could do to get through each day and survive it.

I had a good-sized two-bedroom flat, which didn't feel like my home. This was my first home, and I'd been lucky enough to buy it fresh out of uni, and yet I felt no excitement and no connection to it. It was a crash pad. It was functional. It was transactional. And this is how my life had become. Transactional. It was how I had become too. I knew I would most likely be moving on within two years, and so I furnished it with second-hand furniture or left it bare. Nothing wrong with that, except it was shabby and nothing quite fitted together. My desire for harmony and coherence was not met here, and somehow, I was oblivious. I was desperately, hopelessly disconnected from my core self, my creativity, and my ability to fully nurture myself. This was not a nourishing space to come home to, but it was a safe space, and I needed *that* for sure. Evenings found me curled up in front of the television, and I was generally in bed by nine. The one thing that I looked forward to seeing at the end of each working day was my cat, Sophie. A beautiful, sensitive, jet-black rescue cat who relished being indoors and who brought me such comfort during that first difficult year. She was a good listener and a total delight. Looking back, I think we were each other's therapists. I helped her recover from her trauma, and she helped soothe me after a long, hard day at work.

My long-term boyfriend had moved in with me; however, he spent most of his time back at his parents, and so we barely saw each other. I understood that the journey from this new flat to his place of work on the other side of London was just too far for a daily commute. I tried to explain what was going on at work, but he didn't really understand and didn't seem to care too much either. Home life was joyless and lonely. Work life was fraught with stress, anxiety, and a dreaded sense that something terrible could happen at any minute. He and I were growing in different directions. He was working to earn money to pay for his football and other sporting interests. I was working to invest in a future and develop my career. I stopped talking to him about work; it seemed a fruitless exercise, really. There was no one to talk to about it because my colleagues were watching their own backs and kept close counsel on how they really felt. I could tell that they were either in the camp that says, 'I don't care, I'll play the game, keep my head down and stay out of trouble,' or they would be in a never-ending and thankless game of 'catch-up and please me, try harder, be perfect'. The men tended to be in the former camp with the women in the latter.

I wondered who I could talk to about what was going on. Who could I trust? Could I ask for a move to another store? Was this going to be the norm? Who would believe me anyway? I was just a management trainee. I concluded that I would just have to stick this one out and hope for a miracle.

Within six short months, I had changed beyond recognition. I didn't recognise myself or my life. This was not how I envisaged my career and working life to be. My usual positive outlook had gone, and in its place was an anxious and sad woman who felt utterly incompetent and a total failure. This was not how I wanted to live my life. I felt so isolated and unhappy. I used to see and expect the best in everyone and everything, and now I was looking over my shoulder and trying to gauge whether it was safe to let my guard down. I became hyper-vigilant. I began a perilous game of trying to anticipate attacks from others. I stopped trusting and giving colleagues the benefit of the doubt. Instead of naturally trusting them until they transgressed my trust, I now waited for signs that they were trustworthy. I shut off and I shut down. I developed what I would call tunnel vision. As I went into work each day, my task became the thing I focused on most. I blanked everything and everyone out except for the job in hand and the people I was directly managing. I kept myself to myself.

Oddly, I don't remember ever crying during this period, even though I was very unhappy. After the initial shock of landing in this cold, hostile, alien landscape, I don't remember feeling very much at all. I didn't want to feel. I couldn't function if I allowed myself to feel everything, so I had to learn how not to feel. It wasn't safe to feel fully. I didn't feel safe with the volume and intensity, and so I had to turn it all off and dial it right down. My manager was constantly barking insults, criticism, and orders at me daily. I had to find a way of protecting myself. I had to find a way of blocking him and the environment OUT. I grew a thick skin and put up barricades all around me so that I could be in what felt like a safe bubble all of my own making.

After a while, the barricades took hold and created a thick wall of protection all around me. This affected my capacity to feel anything deeply. I began to *flat line*. I couldn't feel anything above or below a certain octave. Everything was OK. 'I'm fine. I'm OK,' was my mantra. And it was fine. I couldn't feel anything that was anything other than fine. I was now numb to life and to myself. I didn't feel anger or fear or sadness as such, but neither could I feel joy or happiness. I could pick up on other people's emotions but not my own. I still needed to feel other people's emotional waves so that I could discern whether I was safe. Feeling my own emotional waves did not feel safe.

On days off, I would catch myself staring out of the window, wondering, 'There must be more to life than this? Is this what my life has become? How did I get here?' My life had drained of all colour. I was now living life in black and white or, at best, sepia. Life had lost its joy and sparkle. I was suffering from low mood and anxiety, and maybe even depression; however, there was very little emphasis on mental health back in the late 1980s, and the work culture was very bullish and masculine. I would have been considered weak if I had taken leave for how I was feeling. I would have to push on and be strong and hope that this nightmare would resolve itself soon. I didn't know how else to take care of myself at that age. My self-esteem and confidence plummeted, and I lost all belief that I could make any change here. I felt that I had no control over the situation, and this was a crushing experience for me. I felt alone and very disempowered.

I researched other careers and began to look for other jobs. I was now, however, buying a flat in a part of the country I didn't particularly like and needed a certain level of income to maintain it. My options were limited, given I had only worked for a year. The cost of selling now would eat up the profit gained so far on the price of the property. It might also look to future employers that I couldn't hack working and was giving up. Giving up was not in my nature, though, and so this wasn't going to be an option. There had to be another way.

It was at the twelve-month mark, after months of trying to please this man and to make a good impression, that things began to change. I recognised that I had to find the validation I wanted from him, from within myself. My self esteem had taken a nosedive and I didn't want to feel so anxious and miserable.

I could see by now that nothing I did was ever going to be enough for him, and so it was a fruitless pursuit. It made me unhappy, and I felt anxious most of the time. This was not how I wanted my life to feel, and so I would have to change something. But what and how?

In the past, achieving results had always reaped praise and rewards, but this was not the case in this instance. I decided that I would measure success purely on the results that we were able to achieve, the consistency of the results and how I felt inside. I would measure success by the quality of my relationships. This way, it wouldn't matter what my manager decided to throw at me – I would know I was doing a great job, and I would be fully focused on enjoying it instead of trying to gain his approval. No one could argue with great results. If he wanted to shout and stamp, then that was up to him. I would no longer allow him to intimidate me. This was a game changer for me.

It sounds so simple now as I'm writing this; however, my 23-year-old self was highly approval-oriented and was hard-wired to do all that she could to please. She was also programmed to avoid conflict at any cost. This was a big inner shift that she would have to make. Thankfully, things were about to change. My younger self wouldn't have to wait long to put her new perspective to the test.

The ski season was approaching, and this was my first-time merchandising skiwear. It was still a relatively new line of clothing and accessories for the company, and there was an opportunity to sell to a market who were new to the skiing scene. There was a wave of nouveau riche with whom skiing was becoming more popular. The time was ripe.

I set a high weekly sales target, one that I thought was out of reach for a provincial town. I decided to merchandise in a slightly different way. Instead of following the layout guidelines that were issued from our head office, I decided that we would do it intuitively. It was something that both of us were good at. We could see or feel that something wasn't quite right, and we would change things around until we knew they looked just right. There were only the two of us, however, we knew the sales trends and the stock so well that we could re-merchandise the showroom every other day, which meant that customers had a dynamic shopping environment to visit. We engaged in conversations with our customers to find out what they liked about the range and what they felt we were missing. I fed this information back through the regional merchandise representatives and to the buyers. I began to build up relationships beyond the store.

We decided that we would host a ski evening. It was an event that very few stores had offered, and we knew that we could make a real success of it. I pitched the idea to my manager, and he agreed to go ahead, making it perfectly clear that if it failed, it was down to me. I had no intention of failing. This would be a fun challenge that we would both rise to. And we did.

The event ran between 5 and 9 p.m. one Thursday evening. We had organised for additional stock to be delivered and had taken over the whole front half of the showroom. I had persuaded all my management colleagues to help. Other members of staff offered their services too. I had some colleagues dress in ski outfits which they thought was great fun. We played Tyrolean music through the sound system. We had a licence to serve mulled wine, and we had cheese and biscuits. Adverts and articles had been in the local press and on the local radio for the four weeks leading up to the event. I loved the planning and the execution of it. I thrived on the adrenaline and the excitement I felt. I didn't care what my manager was up to or how he would respond. I was in my element, and I loved it. I was beginning to feel more like *me* again. The regional operations director and many other regional representatives made an appearance. My manager was a transformed man for the evening. He became the perfect host – bouncing and smiling, and of course, it was all his idea! Even hearing him voice this to others still didn't get to me. Nothing and no one were going to get in the way of me enjoying this moment.

We received a lot of kudos for that evening having made thousands of pounds more in one evening than in an average 3 full days of trading. We shifted hundreds of pieces of merchandise and had clients ordering garments. We appeared in the local newspaper. It was so successful that I was invited to present to the skiwear buyers and to create a template for other stores to run future skiwear events. Our store became a flagship for skiwear sales. My manager was visibly delighted, but he neither acknowledged nor thanked me.

It was about this time that my boyfriend's mother was putting pressure on us to get married and *settle down*. I had instigated a few conversations with him about how I wanted things to change in our relationship, and this added pressure from her felt intrusive and unwelcome. When it reached a peak, however, it served me well because it made me realise that I didn't want to marry him. I could no longer see a future for us together. It didn't feel right. We no longer shared the same outlook, values, or experiences. He had begun to resent that I was earning more than him and that I worked most Saturdays. He didn't want me to be the main earner. He didn't want to live with me in Essex and wanted me to leave my job and return to Hertfordshire, where our families lived. He wanted me to get a regular job, with regular hours and one that wasn't a career. This clearly was not going to work for me, and although I felt a great deal of sadness, I knew it was time to bring things to a close.

Our relationship had been failing for quite a while. I think I had clung to it and to him for the familiarity and the sense of safety and comfort it gave me whilst the rest of my life was imploding. My recent successes and shift in perspective had given me the clarity and confidence I needed to bring things to a close. It took several months for him to finally accept that I meant what I said, and he moved his things out. It wasn't his fault. He didn't like who I had become and didn't feel he could relate to me. I had changed entirely. I had just been through the toughest year of my life so far. I can't have been an easy person to be around. The glue that had held us together during our late teens and early twenties had gone. Our love for each other had dissolved. He had been 'The One' for me. We had shared everything together. We'd had so much love for each other, had such happy formative experiences and grown into adults together. And yet, despite our very best efforts, it seemed that our path was not a 'forever' one. And it was sad.

Several months later, the next training module of the company's management training course became available to me, and I jumped at the opportunity to be out of the store environment for a whole week. It was a course teaching us how to display merchandise on mannequins and other equipment. It was something that I had a natural flair for, so it wasn't particularly taxing. Something did happen, though, that I hadn't expected. I had my one, and so far only, one-night stand. He was a guy who was on the same course. It was frowned upon within the company to have personal or sexual relationships with colleagues, but there was an instant and very strong chemistry between us, and for me, it felt like I was getting in touch with a wild, carefree aspect of myself that I hadn't felt for a very long time. In fact, I'd go as far as to say I was rebelling and perhaps exorcising all the frustration and demons of the past 12 months. It was wonderful. It was liberating and it was great fun. And it was so very needed. I felt like a new woman.

When I got back from the course, a new colleague had arrived. He was a breath of fresh air. An East Ender from birth, he was funny, honest, and very good at his job. He taught me a lot and was also great company. We would confide in each other about the crazy-man shenanigans of our manager, and it felt good to let off steam with someone I could trust. He had great integrity and was devoted to his wife and children. He had worked for the company for thirty years and knew the trade inside and out, but he wasn't the type to play the game of getting ahead. He didn't score cheap points like some of the others. We got on well, and he was most certainly a silver lining.

At around the same time, a new graduate management trainee began at our store. We immediately hit it off, and now I had a friend I could socialise with out of work too. Life was beginning to feel very different – colour was returning, slowly but surely.

Shortly afterwards, we arrived at work one Monday to discover we had a new manager. It seemed the madman had been moved into an admin role in head office, and we had a new manager who seemed the opposite of our Scottish tyrant. It was a highly unusual experience not to know that a manager of his seniority was being relocated. It caught us all by surprise.

This new man was a very talented people manager who had been in the company for twenty-plus years and was greatly respected by his peers. He had a good reputation. He was intrinsically a good man. He had decent values, listened more than he spoke, had a firm but gentle manner about him, and was interested in team working. He called me into his office and asked me about the previous manager, reassuring me that the company was aware of his inappropriate behaviour and the impact that it had on staff and management alike. He wanted my opinion. I carefully began to share some of my experiences and views, mindful that I wasn't entirely sure to what extent I could trust him at the beginning. He encouraged me to continue, and I spent several hours with him. He apologised for the treatment I had received, and he noted that regional colleagues spoke very highly of me. He wanted to give me some new opportunities to shine and invited me to take on the responsibility of being the store's training coordinator, plus a few other roles.

I thrived in this new environment. I was moved to the biggest department in the store and had a team of five people to manage. I loved the training aspect and was seen as one of the training specialists in the district of nine stores.

After six short months under this new manager's careful wing, I was promoted to a deputy manager role in a different store. I was delighted. I got a further relocation package and bought another flat closer to my new store and near a beautiful nature reserve. This time I took great delight in decorating. I painted the walls, bought new furniture and blinds, and experimented with patterns and textures. I was beginning to know my style with colours and accessories. In the summer evenings, I would come home from work and open wide the skylight windows, lie on the sofa, and listen to music. It was a very happy period in my life.

I joined a local yoga group and a jazz dance studio and began to make new local friends.

I would walk by the river estuary, over the sand dunes and through the fields of wildflowers. I arrived in late May when the poppies were out in full bloom. I still remember that time whenever I see poppies, even now, several decades on. It was an experience of Home and of being able to be more fully myself again. To feel safe once more. And perhaps to begin to thrive.

And although my external set of circumstances had changed for the better, the effects of the previous eighteen months had settled from emotional scabs to scars and would colour my experience of the workplace and life on and off for years to come. He hadn't 'brought me down a peg or two' as he had threatened, but he had triggered various drivers that were hard-wired into my system. 'Please me',' try harder', 'hurry up', and 'be strong' got deeply activated. I succeeded and my career thrived. My confidence had taken a battering, though, and I would repeat the habit of looking outside of myself for approval and validation for several decades until I remembered to look within and trust myself.

Always remembering and forgetting, forgetting, and remembering, until finally, when I was older and wiser, it was finally resolved.

Change your Name,
Change your Life

Dear Moriah,

You will change your name. This will seem ludicrous to the 20-year-old you, even to the 40-year-old you, but by the age of 44, it will make total sense and feel inevitable.

Fear not. It will be your Salvation, ultimately. It will help you to relate to yourself, others, and the world you live in, in a completely different and quite unique way. Do it. Change your name. It will work wonders. For you see, dear Moriah, it will help awaken your unconscious, and you will awaken from the Dream — slowly at first, but gradually you will achieve full wakefulness, and at that time, you will see all worlds as One. No separation. No illusion. Just One.

'Til then, adios, my friend X

I Want That Job!

I had been in my deputy manager role for eighteen months and had been thoroughly enjoying it. I had a lot of responsibility and autonomy as I was just twenty-five. The store manager was often in regional meetings or away and out of contact, so I had free rein for much of the time. I had built a good reputation for my management style and for being a good stand-in for other managers when they were ill or off on holiday. I enjoyed the variety of the job, the operational challenges, staff scheduling, and the leadership skills that I was developing along the way. I was now respected and well-liked by staff and management teams alike as well as gaining the respect of the regional specialists who pretty much let me go off-piste with my merchandising as I was now doing it all intuitively and getting great results. I was now entrusted with the welfare of more than one hundred members of staff, plus the development of several trainee managers and the merchandising roles I still held.

From this happy, successful position, I now looked back on the previous role and manager, and I was glad that I stuck it out. In the end, I did well and made a good name for myself even though my confidence and self-esteem nose-dived. Instead of being brought down a peg or two, which had been his intention, I had risen, succeeded, and shone. There was something fundamental that changed about my essential nature too. Up until that unhappy experience, I had always approached people trusting them until and unless they showed me that they were untrustworthy. As a result of the year with the mad Scottish man, I was now very guarded, and my initial stance was now, 'I'll trust you when I know I can be open and vulnerable with you. I'll believe it when I see it.' Some might say this was a good thing, especially in the world of business; however, it was a sea change in approach for me. Was I naïve? Probably. Was I wrong to blindly trust? Maybe. I have always seen the best in people and their potential. When their Shadows came out to play, it was a bit of a shock, especially when I was new to a career and still quite an *Innocent* in the world.

Life was good. I had settled quickly into my new flat and area. And something rather wonderful had happened too. I had been enjoying a new romance which had blossomed very quickly into love. It was surprising, it was sweet, it was fast-moving, and it felt so natural. Within several months, I was engaged to be married. I share more of our story in the next chapter.

It was true to say that I felt settled, happy, and for the first time in my career, I felt like I belonged. I had found my niche. I loved the work and the people. I was buying my second flat, and I was looking forward to married life too.

And so, it came as a surprise to me that just two months before my wedding, I made an instantaneous declaration that would change the direction of my career and influence my work and life for decades into the future.

I was walking past the manager's office one day when I stopped in my tracks. There was a new poster up on the notice board. It was an advert for a secondment. I scanned it quickly, and my immediate response was, 'I want that job!' Within seconds, my manager came out of his office, grinned at me, and told me to go for it. He told me that he thought I'd be great at the job and would happily recommend me. Before I knew it, he had set up an interview at the company's head office at Marble Arch, at the heart of London's West End. Within the space of thirty minutes, I had applied for and been given an interview.

And the job? It was a two-year secondment specialising in the role of training graduate management trainees during their first eighteen months with the company. Essentially, I was to run the courses that I had completed just four years earlier.

It was such an instinctive response. It astounded me at the time. I was so clear that I wanted that job. I had really enjoyed taking part as a trainee in the courses themselves. One of the reasons that I had chosen that company was that I knew just how good their management training scheme was first-hand. And now I was going to be interviewed for the role of leading these courses. I was so excited.

There was another reason for applying for the secondment. Within nanoseconds of thinking, 'I want that job,' I also knew that this would stretch me and make me face my fears and discomfort with training and leading. It would get to my visibility issues and help me resolve them. It would force me out into the limelight, and I knew that this was something I had to face and embrace.

The interview took very little preparation because I had so much natural interest and passion for training and development. In the previous two years, I had also gained a reputation for being a training specialist for the eight stores in our district. I was also heading up a major training programme for a new cash and merchandise handling financial system.

It went well. I enjoyed the conversation very much and was able to contribute through the wider reading that I had done over the previous three years. I had read some of the earliest of Wayne Dyer's books and others on the topic of transactional analysis.

What I didn't know until after I was offered the secondment was that my manager was a drinking and golf buddy of the Head of Function who had interviewed me. The synchronicity wasn't lost on me, even though I might have called it a coincidence. I recognised it as my path being eased. And I smiled.

My fiancé was away at sea whilst all of this was going on, and the only way to keep him in the loop was by snail mail – a letter in the post. In the three weeks between applying and landing the secondment, I didn't once consider the impact that my new role would have. I would be away from home most weeks. My fiancé would be leaving the Royal Navy in nine months' time, and I didn't yet know what job he might get and how this might play out for us. As it turned out, he was delighted with my impending move. His new role meant that he, too, would be away from home during the week, so it suited us both. My cat found a happy home with his grandmother out in the Norfolk countryside. She was one very happy cat.

There was something else that I didn't know until several months later when I arrived for my first day. The advert had been for one secondment opportunity. I discovered that during the interview process, there were, in fact, two of us who stood out as natural candidates. It seems that they wanted us both, and so created an additional secondment. His name was Ian.

He and I began our new roles and spent the first six weeks away from home in Birmingham, where the company had its management training centre. This was tough for me. I was suddenly in a whole new division of the company with work that was only vaguely familiar and colleagues who were new to me. Added to this, I was away from home and expected to socialise every evening after the courses with my colleague and the participants. It took me a while to find my rhythm and to learn how best to pace myself. By the time I began leading the courses myself, I had introduced a weeknight when participants and I could do our own thing. Ian and I were running courses together as well as individually. Each week we stayed in a different hotel, were running a different course, and had a new group of up to nine trainees or managers. It was rigorous, fun, and hugely rewarding. We were mostly running courses on listening, questioning, training, motivation, and leadership skills, with some modules focused more on personal development. It was a lot of responsibility to not only ensure they got the best possible learning experience but also to model the company's ethos and values.

We learned together, having joined the role at the same time. I was wary at first, given some of my previous experiences; however, within a few months, it was clear that here was a man who had integrity and who was a team player, both things I valued too. We got on well, shared a similar sense of humour, and always had each other's back. There was a connection between us and a natural chemistry; however, there was an unspoken boundary that was very clear.

Towards the end of the secondment, I began to consider what I wanted to experience next in my career. I knew that the company would send me back out into a store; this time, I would most likely be promoted to store manager. Whilst I knew that I would enjoy the role, I had little control over where in the country that would be, and by then, my husband and I had just settled into a beautiful little house in a village we both loved. Neither of us wanted to move.

I also knew that my heart was no longer in retail management. I could do it, and I could do it well, but my passion was now firmly rooted in personal development and supporting others to grow. I initiated conversations with my manager to let him know where my thinking was at. As I had thought, there was no capacity to have me stay beyond the two-year mark of the secondment; however, they did put me forward to an elite fast-track group. I decided to go for the panel interview to see what options might be available for me if I got accepted. My performance had been rated as outstanding during the two years I had been away from the stores, and I was welcomed into the elite group. I had, however, been applying for jobs in other companies too, and within a few weeks, I was reluctantly resigning. I knew that the only way forward was to continue along the management development route, which fascinated me.

And so, after six years, I left the company that I had loved and professionally 'grown up' in. Many seeds for my future had been sown and embedded during this last phase. It set me up beautifully for the career that was to come and unexpectedly introduced me to Ian, who would be a long-time friend and would also play a significant role in my life several decades later. I share more further into the book as my story unfolds.

The Labyrinth Speaks
on *Letting Life Unfold*

Let life unfold.

Let life be.

Allow it to move through you into expression and form.

Let Life be your Guide.

Let Life show you the next step and the next.

It will show you the way.

It will light the path,

Illuminate the shadows,

And bring you the main characters and the sub-plots too.

It will present the lessons.

It will surprise and delight you.

It will leave you b-r-e-a-t-h-l-e-s-s.

I Said YES!

Part One

Where to begin? Let's start at the very beginning. A very good place to start.

We met on 8th August in 1981, in north Wales, when we were both on holiday with our parents. He was 21 and just about to begin his naval officer training in Devon. I was 18 and just about to go to university in London. It was totally unexpected. It was one of those moments when you catch each other's eye across a room, and you know that you know each other even though you've never met before. Or, at least, not in this lifetime. There was an instant connection. He said much later in our relationship that he knew that he would marry me. I was already in a steady relationship and not looking for complications; however, I felt that he was significant, and I could feel a strong connection and attraction to him. I wanted to get to know him. We climbed Mount Snowdon that week, walked on the beach, and chatted for hours. At the end of his holiday, we exchanged addresses and went our separate ways. We met up a handful of times in the years that passed and exchanged a few letters. We developed a friendship, and there was always a great fondness and a good deal of feelings unspoken yet felt.

In 1987, not long after I had been promoted and had ended my long term relationship, his naval ship was in for a re-fit and he was home with his parents. Their home happened to be half an hour from my flat, and we began to meet up now and then. Sometimes a lunch together, sometimes a walk in the park, and on one occasion, he fixed my clapped-out car and helped me to find a new second-hand one. We got on well and enjoyed each other's company. It was easy to be with him. I didn't have to try too hard. I could be myself, and I liked that.

When it was time for me to move into my new flat, he was called back to his ship, and there was a period where we were apart for a few months. I sensed a deeper connection possible with him but was focused on my career and on moving home, and so I just let it be, thinking that if it was meant to evolve, it would, no need to push it.

Later that summer, he invited me away for a weekend in Somerset to stay with two of his friends, one of whom he had served with in the Royal Navy. On the first evening there, he and I went out for a short walk to explore the village whilst our hosts were preparing dinner. We took the route that they had suggested and began to walk towards the woods at the edge of the village. We had been laughing and larking around, and I remember beginning to run through the trees. When we emerged from the wood, I had a very strong sense that something had changed between us. I remember thinking, 'Wow, I'm falling in love with this man.'

It was only looking back on this time that I realised that our weekend away was on or around the sixth anniversary of our first meeting.

And just two months later, when he asked me to marry him on my twenty-fifth birthday, my whole body said 'Yes!' It was an easy, natural, happy 'Yes'. We were married nine months later.

We had barely spent any time together, hadn't lived together and yet we both knew that it was so right. It just felt right. This union was right. I had a full-bodied 'Yes' and a heart full of love.

No matter what the world might throw at me, I knew that he had my back. I felt safe. I felt loved. And I could let go. I could let go of worry, of carrying everything alone. I could let go of the longing. I had found a home here with this man, and in finding a home with him, I felt more at home within myself. We shared a vision of what we wanted our life to be like. Here was a man of action. We would work hard towards our goals. We felt equals in so many ways. Here was someone I could share my hopes, dreams, and worries with. I could trust him. I knew that he would stretch me and encourage me to grow and achieve, and I him.

I could call off the search.

The lead-up to our wedding was unusual in as far as he was away at sea for much of that time, and our only means of communication was by letter. It could take up to ten days to receive each other's letters, so whilst it was a romantic way of deepening our relationship, it wasn't very practical. He would send three red roses periodically as a surprise. My engagement ring had three diamonds, and the three also represented the three words, 'I love you'. It was a symbol of his love – even though he couldn't be with me in person, he was with me in thought and gesture.

The practical preparations were largely down to me to organise. I knew exactly what I wanted to wear on my wedding day. I knew the colour, the style, the accessories, the whole look. I knew how I wanted to feel. I wanted to feel beautiful, relaxed, feminine, radiant, and empowered. I wanted to get the balance just right between beauty, simplicity, and sophistication, and I think I achieved that.

So many people had said to me that I was cutting it fine to find a wedding dress that I liked in such a short space of time, given that we had set our wedding date just nine months ahead. That hadn't even entered my head. I had worked on lead times so much shorter than that for work lately that nine months seemed a long time to me and eminently doable.

Given that it was to be a naval wedding, I wanted my dress to be full length, ivory, romantic and stylish. I wanted it to be feminine to counter the naval officer uniform that my husband and his naval friends would be wearing. I wanted it to be romantic. I wanted the whole experience to be perfect. Everything had to be perfect. I rarely settled for less. You could say that I set myself a high bar in those days. You could say also that I put myself under a lot of pressure – and those around me – and I was careful about detail. It had to be just so.

A shopping trip was planned. I invited my mum to come with me to look at potential dresses. We began with the local department store. I walked into the wedding section and went straight to a dress – the dress! There it was. It was the first dress that I picked up and the only one I tried on. It fitted well, it felt exactly how I anticipated it would. I could barely feel it. It was light despite its layers of fabric. It felt like a dream. It had a good fluid movement when I walked and danced in it. It was perfect and I bought it there and then.

My mum was amazed, and she admitted to feeling a little cheated

– she had expected a full day or days of shopping to find the right dress – only to leave the shop just one hour after we had walked into it. Even the shop assistant was astonished. What can I say? I know when I know. No point searching further when I knew I had got the right one.

Frilled sleeves, a tight waist, low-cut back with a large bow above a tiered section. A petticoat and several layers gave it volume and movement. Very 80s and very *Lady Diana*. I wanted the fabric to be raw silk. I loved the feel of raw silk and I loved that it was a rare fabric for a wedding dress back then. On the day, I wore a veil with a circular headdress made from roses, daisies, and lily of the valley. A simple posy of fresh roses, carnations, lily of the valley and freesias. It smelled heavenly. A pearl necklace that my parents gifted me and a simple gold bracelet on loan from my best friend.

We married at the church in my hometown where I was christened. The vicar was delighted. He had two military weddings that day, one after the other. I had been so excited for the week leading up to the big day that I had barely slept and had lost half a stone in weight from the nervous energy. Once at the church it felt like I had shifted into a completely different gear. As I walked up the aisle, I felt like I was walking on air. It was the most joyous experience. I could see all our loved ones, smiling and happy. All there to witness our union. He looked so handsome in his uniform, my eyes locked onto him, and we stood in front of each other. I remember sending him strength, holding his hands, willing him to be OK as I could see the happy tears in his eyes. I had enough strength for the both of us.

I was full. Complete. Happy. Whole. Full of joy. I felt so very loved and so in love. I felt very lucky.

I had a sense that we were going to craft a good and happy life together. Together, we were a force to be reckoned with. Our love and respect for each other was so strong that I had no doubt that we would weather whatever Life brought our way. We left the church through a military archway of swords and travelled the short distance to our reception party by horse and carriage. So traditional.

It was a beautiful, love-fuelled reception. There were so many personal touches and special moments. Many of our family and friends had contributed something and one of the things that I most treasured was the fact that my grandad had made our three-tiered wedding cake. Love, champagne, the heady scent of fresh flowers, music and dancing made it all a day to savour. Even the pouring rain couldn't dampen our spirits.

It was a simple, romantic, beauty full day.

There was one further surprise. He had been organising our honeymoon whilst he was away at sea and together with his mother had booked the whole two weeks as a surprise. Our first week was to be in Bled and second week in Porto Roz, both in Croatia, Yugoslavia as it was then. Magical. Perfect choices.

At the end of our wedding reception, I changed into a different outfit and my mum took care of my wedding dress. The plan was to dry clean it and give it back to me in its box when I returned home from honeymoon. When the time came, though, I had a strange response. I wanted her to keep it at her house. I didn't want it to come home with me. I couldn't explain why, other than it didn't feel right or even good to be bringing it home. I felt this so clearly in my gut.

And so there it stayed, in its original box, on the top of her wardrobe for nineteen years.

Musical Chairs

Every year pretty much for the final six years of my corporate career, I had to go through an application process to keep my own job. It sounds crazy, doesn't it? In those times, it was relatively unusual and fed the hunger for an incessant drive for simplification, re-organisation, and re-invention. I was in a head office role and such roles were constantly under review, especially the service-oriented ones like mine, because there wasn't such a direct and quantitative way of measuring the value to the company's 'bottom line'. We often had to justify our existence because it was not always easy to evaluate the value add that we facilitated.

I totally understood why work simplification was a necessary and valuable exercise to do generally. It meant that as a company we would not become complacent or stagnate. Instead, we could re-invent and re-imagine our brand and offer and maintain and grow our number one status in the marketplace. I still value re-imagination and reinvention in my own life and business. I am a bit of a shapeshifter at heart too, a chameleon, changing my style, my colours to blend in.

It is only as I look back, however, that I acknowledge just how unsettling it was at the individual, human level. Imagine the underlying threat of losing your job or it being so re-engineered that you don't feel competent let alone passionate enough to deliver it. Imagine not knowing when or how this might happen. Whether it is just you or your whole team or division who might lose their jobs. Imagine the degree of responsibility on each individual and the potential collective stress that it creates. It's like anticipating that at any minute, the rug could and almost certainly would be pulled from underneath your feet. It was an invisible, unspoken, and unacknowledged stress and one I suspect that contributed to a decline in employee engagement and loyalty. Trust is tricky when a bombshell can be dropped at any minute.

And this is ironic for it was at the individual and human level that I did my best work for the organisation and had the most impact. It was a vicious cycle. We worked to improve management behaviour through self-awareness and personal change. This, in turn, had an impact on how the managers and directors felt about themselves and how they dealt with their workload and behaved with their teams. Ultimately, this manifested in a transformation from a climate of fear and mistrust to one of cooperation, mutual respect, flexibility, and innovation.

When the company added this new insidious level of insecurity and uncertainty into the mix, it not only undermined the valuable work we were doing and the progress already made, but it also added to the unconscious load that these leaders were carrying and thus making things even more difficult to improve. We were all expected to comply, conform, and shut up. Any sign of non-compliance or resistance was met with suspicion. It was seen as a sign of weakness. There was no place for emotion within the corporate juggernaut. Straight ahead, don't stop. You kept going, no matter the cost.

Managers were re-positioned in jobs they never wanted with skills they didn't have and with specialists or generalists that they had difficulty relating to and all in the name of cross-functionality and flexibility. Several excellent leaders whom I knew well had breakdowns and left. Some resigned. Most stayed on and found a way through it all.

One director once shared with me just how much he was looking forward to retiring so that he could spend all day on the golf course. He was thirty-five. He was the same age as me and yet he looked ten years older. A part of me wondered if he could wait that long. I was happy to hear that within five years of that conversation, he was managing a golf course and its club, although I don't know the full story of how it came about.

Towards the end of my time in the organisation, I longed to be made redundant and to be awarded a lump sum. This would have afforded me a happy escape route into a life that I could shape myself and a career that would work for me and my family. It was never to be. I was always retained and offered a new or different position. I got to keep my job. And whilst I was grateful and I did count my blessings, I also couldn't help wondering what it might have been like to be leaving and re-inventing my life and career in a shape that felt good to me.

Sometimes the new roles I was allocated came with an upgrade in pay, sometimes a whole new team, a different location, and a different role entirely. There was no real choice in the matter. It was always this way in my career. You go where the company sends you and do what the company tells you to do – or as they would say, 'invite' you to do. The only real choice was how I responded to the situation.

In my first company, I decided to leave because I loved the focus on learning, development and training and they wanted me instead to go back out into the field and manage retail outlets. I also wanted to be rooted in one area geographically. So, I chose to leave a company I loved but who wanted me to return to a role I no longer wanted to pursue something that was drawing me into my future. An opportunity to grow as a management development specialist and to add real value at both the individual and at the corporate level was where my interest now lay. And a home where I could confidently buy furniture and curtains and plant a garden knowing that I would not be uprooted within two years. I wanted to spend time with my husband. I wanted a life that was stable and rooted. A place to call Home. A place of safety. I wanted to feel that I worked for an organisation and had a job within it that felt like a perfect fit. I wanted to be valued for my skills and contribution. I guess what I was truly wanting – but probably couldn't fully articulate at that point – was a sense of belonging.

A sense of belonging. Yes, that was it. A round peg in a round hole. Amen to that.

I got some of what I'd hoped for. We had a home which we had lovingly created together. However, I now worked for a company where my career felt unpredictable and unstable. Team members came and went with alarming speed. Most of whom I either couldn't relate to, or I instinctively didn't trust and for good reason. Sadly, this culture of frequent re-organisations left many employees consciously or unconsciously in what appeared to be a modern-day version of 'fighting for survival' which translated in many people to behaviours of 'minding their own back' or worse, 'backstabbing'.

For me, I don't remember being overly concerned about losing my job as such. That often felt like it might have been a blessing in disguise. No, it was different. It was a dread of what the new job might look and feel like. I often felt like a 'square peg in a round hole'. I never quite fitted in. I was always trying hard to make myself fit. I got on with the work that I was told to do even though, intuitively, I felt we should be tackling root causes rather than firefighting.

Deep within me there was a deeply unsettling vortex of worry and anxiety which would rise periodically disguised as heart palpitations or migraines. I didn't dare give it space or voice because I was terrified that I would have to act upon it and that scared me. Being made redundant was one thing but beginning another job search and resigning was something else. I tried to ignore it, keep a lid on it and distract myself from it for as long as I possibly could. And for long periods of time, I did a pretty good job of it too. One astute manager once said that she got the impression that I was like a swan: beautiful, graceful, and calm, and paddling like crazy beneath the surface. I'd say she got me down to a tee.

Looking back at that time, I can see how it served a purpose for me. I learned the art of listening to my intuition and then making a strong logical case based on what I was intuitively picking up. My intuition was always spot on. I learned how to read my colleagues' behaviour and, more importantly, I suspect that I was beginning to read their energy signature – what they *weren't* saying as much as what they were saying. I was learning to read how safe I felt in sharing my true thoughts and feelings. I was learning how safe I felt about staying true to my needs and my values.

I was also learning to tune into their Shadow Self so that I could gauge what was really going on in their blind spot. I could sense what their true feelings were, the thoughts lurking beneath the words, the real version of themselves behind the layers upon layers of masks that they wore to protect themselves from detection. I could tell when someone was lying or telling a version of a truth. I got to see and feel beyond the illusion they were creating, and it fascinated me as much as it could unsettle me.

It was helpful in so far as I could dodge or avert an unwanted curveball that they might hurl in my direction. Adapt and survive was very much the name of the game. It was unsettling because I could detect and decipher the parts of them that they either weren't aware of or were desperate to hide from their colleagues. Sometimes this would show up as me hearing their spoken voice turn into that of a little boy, and I could get a sense of how they were treated as a child. It was different with each person, and it seemed to happen randomly, although I suspect it was my early warning alarm going off to keep me safe.

In hindsight, I learned some seriously helpful skills that I still use in my work today – only now, thank goodness, I don't have the highly stressful environment in which they were first honed! Now I help clients to unravel and reveal their Shadow selves so that they can understand their motivations and integrate the disconnected and disparate parts of themselves into wholeness.

I wonder at what cost to my wellbeing these newly found skills were honed. My response was to stuff down my feelings and focus on what was positive about each situation. I looked to what I could learn, gain, and achieve. I often gained financially. I got to continue moving up the corporate ladder even though it was sometimes a sideways shuffle. I got to keep some remnants of what felt familiar. And I also built a tough exterior around me to maintain my sense of balance and to be able to survive in that world.

It felt like I left my heart and Soul at home. My body and my mind came into the office, and both were exhausted by the end of the working day. I would go home and work in the garden until it grew dark. This way of being was hard at first, but I quickly got used to it. It was an automatic response. I remember looking out at the car park one day and wondering just how much valuable resource the company was wasting. Each of those cars represented a fully resourced human, except that a good half of the human was missing. And you could argue that their best parts were left in the car or at home.

At work, I was focused on the job at hand, rarely socialised with my colleagues and was very goal oriented. There was no time in the day to stop and think for any *length* of time. The day was very much activity-based and meetings-led. I barely did any training, which is what I had signed up for. My heart was not in this endless paper shuffle exercise. I loved the creative design aspect of my work, but not without the delivery piece. I loved the contact with HUMANS rather than paper.

At home, I was a different woman entirely. I had no schedules, no firm plans. I liked to be spontaneous and creative, and my focus was on relationships and crafting, shaping a home. As soon as I got in from work, I would shower and change into something more feminine and then the evening was focused on preparing a meal together and enjoying each other's company. Some nights I would go to an exercise class, do some gardening, or be out with local friends. Looking back, it was all to do with quality rather than quantity at home and vice versa at work.

As I reflect on that time, I can see the soulful aspect of me at play. I craved depth, connection, a sense of purpose and contribution. I was thrilled when I helped someone have a breakthrough in how they saw or felt about themselves. I loved helping teams work through their difficulties to reach understanding and harmony. And I loved to be creative. There was little outlet for it at work, so I guess I instinctively channelled it into my home life by way of decoration, sewing, gardening, painting, dance, and how I could put an outfit together. I naturally created beauty around me without really trying. My mind was a fertile hub that needed an outlet.

Each time it came to the game of musical chairs, I would dig deeper into my Feminine nature at home because that felt anchoring for me. My home, my marriage and my creative skills were anchors that gave me a sense of safety and certainty, a purpose, and ultimately, an experience of belonging. There was no friction or dissonance.

The coherence, resonance, and harmony in my life outside of work gave me the strength and resiliency I needed to cope with the musical chairs.

I would say that I became an expert plate spinner.

You could argue that having so many plates spinning so fast all at once might be a hazard.

And what would happen if they were to stop and crash?

I Can't Find a Heartbeat

'I can't find the baby's heartbeat.'

So that was it. My instinct was confirmed. I was no longer pregnant. It was hard to describe to my husband or to the hospital staff, but I *knew*. When I had my pregnancy confirmed, I could feel a different kind of presence inside of me, and now it was gone. I knew what I knew, and I couldn't easily explain it. When the blood came, then I was taken seriously. Even at that point, there was an outside chance that it would all be OK. But that was not to be.

It was February 1993, and I had recently turned 30.

I remember staring at the ultrasound image on the screen, desperately looking for signs, any sign that this teeny, tiny life inside me was still pulsing. Surely this must be a mistake, this can't be happening.

'I'm very sorry. Your pregnancy is no longer viable. It will abort in the next few days. You will need to wait until this happens naturally and then return to the hospital so that we can perform a procedure to fully remove it from your womb. You will need to catch it when it aborts and bring it into the hospital with you so that we can run tests.' The doctor rubbed my tummy clean of the ultrasound gel and gestured for me to get dressed. And that was that. I was no longer pregnant. I had lost my baby, our baby.

I walked into the waiting room to find my mum. She only had to look at my face to know what had happened. She hugged me gently. My dad drove us back from the hospital. I remember sitting in the back of their car feeling nothing but numb. Totally numb. Even though my instinct had been right, I still could not get my head around what had happened. My thirty years of life had not prepared me for this moment. For as long as I could remember, I had been great at 'putting a brave face' on things, concealing my feelings, using my brain to get ahead and perpetually 'looking on the bright side of life'. Once back at their house, I waited quietly in their lounge until my husband arrived back from work to pick me up, and we drove the ten minutes home in silence. There were no words.

And we waited. We waited two days. Two very long, tortuous days. I put a plastic protector onto the mattress, and I slept on newspaper and towels. We had no idea when the heavy, serious bleeding would begin and so we prepared as best we could, not really knowing what to expect and still feeling a little shell-shocked.

For the first time in my life, I let myself cry and be sad. I had lost a pregnancy and with it, the hope of being a mum. I remember us both lying together on the bed, both of us crying together. Our delight at the pregnancy now turned to sorrow. This was something that I hadn't been able to control. It was out of our hands. There was nothing that either of us could do to make this better, to make this OK.

One evening I felt a very sharp pain and went straight to the bathroom. Instinct told me that this was probably the moment that we had been told would come. And it was. I had a large plastic container that the hospital had given me. I had to crouch over it and let the remnants of my womb drop into it. It was an ungainly, uncomfortable, and miserable experience. Once it seemed complete, we closed the lid and went off to the hospital.

It was late evening when we arrived, and we were shown to a small room off the main corridor. This was to be my room for the duration of my stay. It was close to the nurses' station and, as such, was a busy junction. We stepped into the room and closed the doors behind us. My bag dropped to the floor, and we hugged, in silence, until I was ready to be alone. My husband left to go home, saying that he would return the following afternoon to pick me up. He gave me one last glance and was gone.

It was late by this point, and so I ventured outside into the corridor to locate the bathroom. Immediately and literally, I bumped into a heavily pregnant woman and, without even looking at her, mumbled my apology, wanting the ground to swallow me up. And it was then that I felt another deluge of blood leave my womb, through my already soaked sanitary towel and out onto my light blue jeans. Luckily a nurse had seen me and came over to me, putting her arm around me and whispering gently, 'I've got you. Let's go to the bathroom and we will help you get bathed and comfortable.

I'll bring your bag. Here, it's over here.' It was all such a blur. Her care and her whole presence opened a floodgate of tears. Blood was pouring from my womb. Tears were pouring from my eyes, and I didn't know which way was up. I was a mess, physically and emotionally. I felt broken. I felt hideously unprepared for all of this. I felt out of control. I felt lost, completely, and utterly lost.

The hot bath helped and being in my own pyjamas helped. So too, the hot tea and toast that the nurse made for me. She got me settled into bed and lightly touched my arm as she wished me a good night's sleep and then closed the door behind her.

I lay awake in that bed for some time. I didn't want to think, but I couldn't stop the thoughts rampaging through my mind.

How did this happen? Why did it happen? Why me and why now? How could I feel so very lost and bereft after just four short weeks of knowing I was pregnant? How could this mothering instinct have kicked in so very quickly? I remembered back to new years' eve just six weeks ago and the alcohol that we had consumed. I remembered the lack of sleep, the stress of the first few weeks back at work after the Christmas break, the long hours, poor diet, and I blamed myself. It must have been my fault. How could it not have been my fault? And I cried and said sorry a hundred times to the baby who was no longer present, no longer in my womb. Sorry, over and over. 'I'm sorry, sweet one. I'm so very sorry.'

Above me, there were the sounds of women screaming and babies crying. It seemed that I was in a room just below the delivery suite. Death and birth all in the same space. Because that's what this was. No one mentioned the D word, but I was very clear that this is what I was dealing with. Our baby had died. Regardless of whether it was an unviable foetus, a spontaneous abortion, or a miscarriage, all words the medics had used in relation to my pregnancy and the teeny, tiny baby that I had carried within me for the shortest of times. This was Death. And here I was lying in bed, still bleeding heavily, with the newness and miracle of life being born just a few feet above me. Couples becoming parents. Parents becoming grandparents. Babies arriving in this big, wide world, screaming and wide-eyed. Life. And I was angry. Why, oh why, did they put me in this room? Why? Of all the appropriate places to put me, why here?

I was losing a lot of blood. My tummy was very sore – it was cramping like a very heavy period, plus it was contracting, squeezing the remainder of the tissue out of my womb, expelling what was left of what had been my baby. I rolled over onto my side, away from the door, pulled the covers up over my head, hugged my knees close to my chest and went to sleep.

I woke up early the following morning and was wheeled down in the hospital bed to the operating theatre, where I was anaesthetised whilst my womb was *evacuated* – their word, not mine. It was scraped to ensure that every remnant of the pregnancy was gone, to avoid infection. I appreciated the attention to my physical health whilst I nursed my emotional health. It was all complete within twenty minutes. All traces of the pregnancy gone.

My husband arrived not long after the general anaesthetic had begun to wear off and I was waking up. We left the hospital together several hours later. I don't remember much of the remainder of that day, only that my husband had brought in a pack of a new variety of biscuits which we managed to consume together.

Coming home was a strange experience. I lay on the sofa whilst my husband cooked; we ate in silence and went to bed early. Neither of us really knowing how to respond to what we had just experienced. We didn't know what to say to each other or what to do. He went back to work the following day, which was probably a blessing for me, however, I'm not sure whether it helped him or not.

It was a blessing because I could feel so much emotion welling up, fit to burst, but I didn't feel I could express all of that with him or in front of him. I didn't want him to worry about me, and I didn't want him to see me like that. I didn't want him to see me bereft and empty. God knows why. If he had witnessed me sobbing, it may have given him permission to cry too. And there you have it: big boys don't cry. It was easier for me to cry alone. I guess big girls don't cry either.

I remember sitting on the lounge floor with my knees curled up to my chest, arms wrapped around my legs, sobbing. Sometimes I was still, and other times I found myself rocking backwards and forwards. Sometimes I would stare straight ahead of me, and other times, I would rest my head sideways on my knees, eyes tightly closed, barely breathing. Some days I would not get out of bed until lunchtime, curled up on my side, not wanting to think too much.

I cried for hours, for several days in a row. I was all cried out. I sobbed, gulped, and wept myself to sleep. I had never cried like this before; I didn't even know I had it in me to cry. It was a rare occurrence indeed, and yet I could not help myself. I could do nothing other than cry. I was terrified that I might never stop crying, that I might never feel OK again. I remember at one point feeling as if I were floating above my body, looking down on myself, witnessing my heart breaking wide open.

I felt so much in those first few days: shame, guilt, anger, hopelessness, lost, broken, numb. I was very withdrawn and didn't feel like talking to anyone. Sometimes I would put music on loud and cry and rant until it was out of my system. I would then feel drained, exhausted in a way I'd never felt before.

It was the first time that I had failed. It was the first time that I had felt utterly, totally out of control and had no way of fixing things. I couldn't even control my response to what was happening or how I was feeling. My raw grief scared me. I had never felt such a depth of despair before. It was like a great chasm inside of me, a bottomless well. The more I allowed myself to feel, the deeper into the well I fell. I was scared that this was never going to get any better and that I would lose myself to this insatiable misery. It freaked me out, and at the same time, there was also a knowing that somehow it would stop at some point. Intuitively I knew I had to keep feeling it until it stopped. And so, for the first time in my life, I gave myself permission to cry, for as often as I needed and for as long as I needed.

Many people didn't know how to be with me, didn't know what to say. Many just wanted me to get back to 'normal'. Some avoided me. My mum worried about me. My mother-in-law suggested I go back to work to take my mind off things. She meant well, but it wasn't my mind that was the issue. My body was still healing, I was still bleeding heavily, and I couldn't stop crying.

I lost my closest friend. She was stunned when I told her a few weeks later. She'd had an idea in her head that she and I had made a pact that we would never have children, and this was a betrayal in her mind. I don't ever remember discussing or agreeing to such a thing; it's not my style, and I had never even considered having children until six months previously. I was baffled and confused, but I had no emotional energy left to be upset. I never heard from her again after that conversation.

Others didn't know what to say or how to be with me, and so they let the silence do the talking instead. It might sound a strange thing to say, but it wasn't a lonely time for me. The grief was my company. My husband was there with me in the evenings. I never felt alone.

I discovered that it was only time that made it better. This was a new experience for me. I had become so accustomed to always being able to DO something to make things better. But nothing made this feel better for a long time. There were constant reminders of what I had lost; when I went food shopping, all I noticed were pregnant women and babies. I would put the tv or radio on and there would be talk of pregnancy or children or an aligned topic. I would see our neighbour's growing baby bump and know how many weeks pregnant she was because it was the same that I would have been, had I not miscarried.

There was no visit from a midwife or my local doctor. No follow-up. No counselling offered or helpline given. No advice other than don't try for a baby for at least three months. That was it. It was in the early 1990s and way before the internet. I was left to get on and to get over it.

My tears began to dry up around three weeks later. The well had been emptied. I was tired but was also coming to terms with the reality of what had happened and beginning to wonder when I might be ready to go back to work. It was around that time that I received a letter from my divisional director. It was a handwritten, very personal letter accompanied by a bouquet of flowers. He expressed his condolences and began to share that he and his wife had had two stillborn babies and so he knew the grief of loss. He told me to take as long as I needed and that if I needed someone to talk to when I returned, he would be happy to listen. This felt like a watershed moment for me. I felt seen and understood. I began to feel lighter.

I returned to work six weeks after the miscarriage and took things gently. My colleagues were great.

I threw myself into a new creative project. I found a trainee garden designer, and together we came up with a plan for our back garden. It took two months of hard labour, including one weekend when we invited our families and friends over to help dig in exchange for a barbecue dinner. I bought the plants in the garden centre locally to where I worked, and each evening would be out planting until the light faded. It was just coming into summertime. I loved that garden. I put so much of myself into it. It was great therapy to be outside, with my hands in the dirt and the soil. It also brought me closer to my dad, who had always been a keen gardener. Now I was learning from him and sharing one of his great passions.

The whole experience of miscarriage had softened me. I wasn't the same woman I had been. How could I be? The grief had broken through the crusty exterior that I had built up, it broke down some of the barriers, defrosted the ice. In its own way, I think it prepared me emotionally for what was to come. It opened my eyes and heart to the joys and pains of motherhood.

Five months after we lost our baby, I was pregnant again and this time I gave birth to our first son, with our second following just over two years later. A happy ending.

Grief still catches me from time to time, even after thirty years. Sometimes on the anniversary of the miscarriage, I remember, and the sadness rises. Sometimes it's when I hear another woman's story of a similar experience, sometimes it appears on television or in a film. There is still so very little written about it even though it is such a common experience amongst women. When it happened to me, I knew no one who had experienced it, and that made me feel even more alone.

Grief is not something that works to a schedule. It cannot be rushed. It has its own timing and its own unique pattern for healing. Grief is not an event. It is an acceptance, a surrender. It is a portal through which we are invited to passage. We cannot push our way through it. We can't think or talk our way through it either.

Ultimately, we must surrender to the unfathomable depth of it and allow it to permeate us. And this can be the scariest thing of all because we have no idea how long we will be in the pit of despair.

Grief has the power to transform us if we allow it to. It can bring us even more deeply into the very bones of our humanity. It can be an awakener.

Whilst writing this book, I met a wonderful healer who connects women with their babies in spirit, both those babies who have passed on and those yet to be conceived. As we talked and I shared a little of my story, I could feel so much joy bubbling up inside of me, and I began to smile. She felt it too. It was my own spirit baby who had arrived with a message for me.

He told me that he only had three months maximum to be with me and that he did a lot in that time. He couldn't stay in the density of the Earth's energy. He explained that it takes a lot to come in from a high vibrational level. I heard the words, 'I only had three months, and it was a great time!' It felt like a lifetime to him. It seemed that he could only hold the vibration in the body for that length of time.

Knowing this brought confirmation and peace and helped me to accept at a deeper level that losing my baby wasn't my fault. It was by design.

Love Yourself

Dear Moriah,

Care for yourself as if you are the most precious thing on Earth. Take time out to be alone in silence and stillness. Listen. Really listen. Tune into your deepest needs and desires. Seek as best you can to supply them for yourself.

When you can love yourself with such extreme care, you will be able to love another without expectation or need.

And the world needs more LOVE.

You've got this! And I've got you!

Your big, loving Soul X

You Can Have It All!

Summer 1995

It was the mid-1980s when I was leaving university and starting out on my career. It was the time of Margaret Thatcher and the rise of padded shoulders and bow-tied fashion for career women. New magazines were spawned at this time, packed full of images and articles about female assertiveness. Women were no longer expected to give up their careers to have a family – however, it took a long time for this expectation to filter through. The reality was that we were judged whether we stayed at home to bring up our children, became full-time working mums, or decided not to have children. The message that I received loud and clear was that I should feel lucky because I was born into a generation of women who could have it all.

Whilst on maternity leave with our firstborn, I'd had a promotion, and we had moved into a new build, a bigger house, closer to my company's headquarters. I went back to work when he was seven months old. I found the first year stressful. I had no support network. My husband was a great dad, but his job meant that he was often abroad. The childcare I had put in place crumbled within weeks of my return, and it took nine months to resolve fully. I was in a new role. No training or support was offered. My manager had little tolerance for the unexpected hiccoughs of childcare and a sick child. The team members I had been working with prior to maternity leave had all gone, and new ones were now in place. My new colleagues were ambitious, back-biting, insecure women, all looking out for themselves. I lost weight through sheer exhaustion and anxiety.

I felt disoriented, unhappy, and lost for most of my time at work in those days. I missed being with my son and felt like I was not doing a good enough job at work, being a wife or a mum. I didn't recognise myself. I didn't know how to change things. The mantra of the times for women was that we could have it all. It was a lie. I felt like my whole life was a compromise and that I was stuck in the middle with no way out.

I could have it all, but at what price?

My health deteriorated, and I had various 'mystery viruses' which knocked me out for a week at a time. I was disappearing. My faith in life was fading. I felt like I was playing a role, going through the motions, looking forward to the evening bedtime routine and time alone with my husband. I was exhausted. I wasn't sleeping well.

It broke my heart to leave my son each morning even though I knew that he loved his time in nursery. He was happy, had many friends and was learning rapidly. He was, in fact, thriving. It got to the point early on when we agreed that my husband would drop him off in the morning and that I would do the evening pick-up. He was less emotionally affected, and it suited us both well. Still, I could not reconcile the feelings of guilt and the sadness at missing time with our son.

I remember leaving the office one evening and hearing one of my colleagues say out loud and in a sarcastic tone to the rest of the team:

'Perhaps I should have a baby! Then I could leave work early too.'

I was leaving the office at 5.30 p.m. to pick my son up from nursery. The nursery closed at 6 p.m. and so there was no room for lateness. I remember feeling shocked and being flooded with a cocktail of emotions. Embarrassment that she had just voiced this aloud and to my new team. Shame that I was failing at work and as a mum. Guilt that I couldn't seem to get anything right. I was giving everything as a mum, and yet it was still not enough. Others were seen to be working longer and harder than me. I felt like I wasn't perceived to be 'pulling my weight'. My contribution wasn't enough, and the conclusion I came to was that I wasn't enough either.

Anger and indignance. How dare she! She could have chosen to leave at 5.30 p.m. I was angry that she would use me as a scapegoat for not taking responsibility for her own time management or wellbeing.

Disbelief that she had no concept of what the next four hours entailed – any working parent knows that the evenings with your children are both precious and packed with activity, usually with little or no 'me time' or 'us time' with my husband and falling into bed exhausted.

Fear. Of not fitting in and of being alienated because I was the only working mum in the team, of being lazy, of not being committed enough. I felt anxious each time I was expected to work late into the evenings to host course participants, and I had to make sure that appropriate care was available for our son.

Looking back on these times, I often felt afraid and unappreciated. Lonely and alone. I felt compromised being a full-time working mother. I had little or no energy for me or my marriage, and I felt sad about that. I was not talking to anyone about how I felt. I bottled it all up. I put on a brave face and focused on the job at hand to the best of my ability.

I didn't talk to my husband because he had enough on his plate with his own career and was often abroad on work trips. I didn't want to worry him. And in a peculiar way, I didn't want to seem weak to him. I wanted to maintain the strong, capable, 'Super Woman' persona that I had adopted.

I didn't share how I was feeling with my family either. My mum could see the strain on me but couldn't completely understand the pressure because she had been a stay-at-home mum, and so her pressures were different to mine. And I didn't want to worry her.

My mother-in-law applauded my career. Her view was that I would be bored if I had stayed at home to nurture and that I should not take any notice of what other people think. In many ways, she was right. I did not feel cut out to be a stay-at-home mum. I feared losing my foothold in the career market and the loss of income too. And I was also very aware of the potential to lose my identity too. Who would I be if I didn't work?

Through all of this, I don't ever remember crying. I don't remember getting truly angry and feeling it fully. I didn't even respond to the woman and her comments. I remember walking out of the office with my head held high and ignoring her. This was a behaviour I had learned from school days and the bullies who would follow me home and pick on anything from my intelligence to my blue eyes or my knock knees, as they called them. I remember actively trying to walk with my legs bowed as a result.

I was a contortionist, I now realise. I would shapeshift to fit in with what other people expected or wanted of me. I would squeeze my values and integrity at times to get the job done and to pay the mortgage. I would hold in and down immense, loud, painful feelings and emotions so that I did not have to feel them because, my goodness, if I felt them, there would be no coming back, and I would not be able to continue and function the next day and the next. Deep down, I suspect that I was terrified. Terrified that I would disappear from the world, lose my place in it, make a total hash of motherhood, and fail my son. I felt ashamed. I feel so much compassion for the woman I was then. I wasn't as resourceful as I am now. I was scared of the strong emotions I was experiencing, and I didn't like being out of control. I relied on my roles and external identities to feel safe, to belong.

I judged myself too. I had bought into the contemporary belief that you could be a great mum and have a thriving, successful career. Perfection. Perfect mum. Perfect wife. Perfect employee. Perfect house. The inner conflict that I felt was immense. I wanted to be good at everything. After a full day's work, I was mentally exhausted. I put my whole self into evenings and weekends with our son, and I would be physically exhausted. I was compartmentalising. At work, I would shut off from my feelings and go into my head as a coping mechanism. Once work was complete, I would drop back into my heart. It was something that I developed; I didn't think about it. What I now understand of how energy works, it would have taken a vast amount of energy to keep that level of separation and disconnection running. One woman at work and another at home. And I wasn't being honest with myself either. I was changing, rapidly. Love for my son was transforming me. My earlier miscarriage had broken me wide open emotionally. The love that I felt for our son and that he showed me was immense. I missed him. I loved him fully, unconditionally. I had fun with him. He fascinated me. He made me smile and laugh. I was a better human around him. He reminded me how to play, and he showed me just how far away I was from being present.

Something would have to change because I knew that this was not sustainable.

I began to make some changes to my diet, took care of my hydration, and hired a kinesiologist and an aromatherapy massage therapist. I went back to yoga classes once a week. I discovered that one of the nannies who looked after my son at nursery also offered herself out at weekends for babysitting, and so I booked her for two evenings a month. I began to feel as though I had some influence and control over my life again. The other major change that made a difference was in designing, planning, and creating our back garden. It had been rubble for our first year of living there, and it was time to create a fun, nurturing outdoor space.

It took three months to complete, and the week that the turf was laid, I discovered that I was pregnant with our second son.

I Don't Want to Be the Soil!

September 1996

I was on a team-building day, and for once, I was a member of the team rather than the facilitator.

It made a nice change to be on the receiving end. It felt good to be together for two whole days as a team. We were so often out running events elsewhere that we rarely got to see each other for a good stretch of quality time. I was looking forward to our time ahead and catching up with everyone.

We were a team of six women plus our manager. She wasn't the type to want to spend extended time together, so we were all curious to know what had prompted this event. The explanation we were given was that there was money in the budget and that the facilitators had a cancellation elsewhere in the company and so we would be making good use of them. Hardly the best reason to have a team event, and we still weren't clear about the intention. We were, however, happy to spend time together.

Our manager usually kept herself to herself. She wasn't what some might call a 'people person'. She was a highly introverted, critical, logic-driven woman who found it difficult to connect with people. Her humour was most often 'off' and rarely landed well with us, her team members. She valued facts, evidence, detachment, and objectivity, and these were also her strengths. I valued the fact that I could take a piece of work to her, and she would spot the flaw, the blind spot and ask the right questions to help me make it more robust. I didn't go to her for inspiration, encouragement, or creative input. She and I engaged on an as-needed basis. Nothing more, nothing less.

She had a sweet smile when it was genuine, and she could also turn mighty quickly and deliver caustic, sharp, critical comments designed to wound. And they sure did. They went right to the core of another's pain. And she knew it too. I'd watched her mouth curl at the corners in a quiet, sneery kind of smile when she knew she had hit her target. She was a cold fish, no doubt about it. Bizarre, given that our department was all about developing and encouraging talent within the organisation. I often wondered whether she had been allocated this role to help her develop her 'soft' skills.

I could sometimes see her trying hard to make a connection, but somehow, she always managed to miss the opportunity, the tone or the right words. I could sense the loneliness within her, the sense of isolation she felt even when she was with us all. She kept herself apart from us for most of the time and then tried to engage periodically. So, I was surprised and curious when she told us that we were going to take two days out of our work programme for a team event. I wondered if she had an ulterior motive. And why now?

As I was getting ready that morning, there was a familiar unease settling into the pit of my stomach. I recognised it from some time in my past, yet I couldn't quite put my finger on what it was that I felt uneasy about. A general low-level sense of anxiety that something unpleasant was about to happen. I was about to discover the source of this unease later that morning.

I drove down the long, winding gravel drive to the management training centre where I worked. I deliberately went even more slowly than usual that morning so that I could take in the beauty of this place. I pulled over and got out of the car. I consciously and deliberately gazed up at the blue summer sky and listened to the birds, breathing in the beauty as I did so. Horses were galloping across the fields in the distance, and there were sheep grazing beneath the trees nearby. I had worked in some very grotty parts of England, but this had to be the most beautiful venue so far.

The grounds were designed by Capability Brown and swept out for around two hundred acres from the main manor house, where much of the training took place, to the outlying fields beyond. A beautiful lake formed the focal point. We were blessed for sure to be able to work in such extraordinary surroundings. I breathed it all in before getting back into the car and drove the remaining short distance to the car park. One of my teammates arrived just as I did, and we made our way in together to grab a coffee before meeting up with everyone in our main room.

Our facilitator was a genuinely nice guy. He was ahead of his time in the wisdom he brought to these events and was one of the first to bring creativity, music, and visualisation into organisations. He was quietly powerful, and I appreciated his sensitivity.

We all gathered in the main room, chose a seat within the circle of chairs, and settled into the day. After doing some breathing exercises, we moved into the first session, which was all about appreciation. We were invited to consider two questions.

'What do we appreciate about each of our fellow team members?' and based on our answers,
'If they were each an aspect of a garden, what would they be and why?'

The facilitator stuck a page of flip chart paper to the walls whilst we were jotting down our answers in our own notebooks. Some looked pensive. Some were busy writing, and others were gazing out of the window. Our manager seemed to be mostly looking at her watch and nervously shuffling on her chair. The Verve's 'Bittersweet Symphony' was playing in the background. An ironic choice, as it turned out.

We were invited to answer the first question one at a time, and the facilitator wrote the feedback on the flip chart with our names on it.

Feedback from my fellow team members for me consisted of familiar tones and adjectives: warm, kind, intuitive, creative, sensitive, empathic, deep, inspiring, gently powerful, a good listener, humorous, encouraging, approachable, engaging, intelligent, visionary, wise, trustworthy.

And then my manager answered by saying:
'I honestly can't think of anything that I value about you.'

She shook her head and shrugged her shoulders. You could feel the shock waves running through the whole team. Everyone went quiet. The facilitator looked visibly shaken. He was highly experienced but looked as though he had never expected or come across this response before. He took what seemed like ages to respond.

Personally, I had several responses going on at once. I was shocked that she truly could not find anything she valued in me, especially given that I'd had good performance reviews and was generally respected throughout our division and with the directors I worked with. I could feel a kind of freeze response too. The situation felt vaguely familiar, but it was like it was there somewhere buried deep within me under layers of thick ice, so I couldn't feel it or access it. It must have been a faint reminder from another time. I did what often came naturally to me at that time and brushed it off, pretended to myself that I didn't care, that it didn't matter, and yet somewhere deep inside of me, there was an echo of this. I felt disoriented.

Looking back, I can see that my head was spinning and that I was in shock. I felt like I could be sick at any minute. My jaw was tightening, and my eyes locked onto the patterns of the floor carpet. My hands were clammy, stomach tightening. All signs that really should have been red flags, however, I wasn't yet equipped, courageous, or connected to my body enough to acknowledge my full response. It would have been sensory overload at that point. So, I said nothing.

I smiled to myself and rationalised the situation to make myself feel better about the words spoken and the deafening silence that was still hanging in the air.

I was six months pregnant, and I knew that I only had to sit this role out for seven weeks before I was away from work for eight months. That was a long time in this company, and the chances were that she would be gone by the time I got back, or I would have been re-assigned. So, it would be easy to grow an even thicker skin than I already had and just ride the waves for now. My family was my priority at that time, as was my health. I knew that I had banked enough performance credit for this episode not to matter too much to my career.

My team members were still quiet. The facilitator clearly did not know how to handle this situation. He suggested we have a tea break. There was no apology from my manager. My teammates rallied around me, all as clueless as to what was going on as I was. I reassured them that I was OK. But I clearly wasn't as OK as I thought

I was, and my thick skin had just developed a whole new crust to it.

The tea break was a weird experience. The facilitator checked in with me. He knew what my manager could be like but hadn't anticipated that she could be quite so caustic with her own team. I replied along the lines that I was used to it. The other women checked in too, clearly all still stunned. They were also wondering who was going to be on the receiving end of her sharp tongue next. My manager was in the foyer catching up with phone calls, so at least we didn't have additional awkwardness to deal with.

When we arrived back after our break, the facilitator launched straight into the second question without making any reference to the comment. The older, wiser, and more empowered me would have tackled all of this very differently; however, I was younger, less equipped to deal with what I perceived to be conflict and more likely to yield to authority figures.

And so, the team event continued.

'If we were each an aspect of a garden, what would we be and why?'

We all shared our answers, and the facilitator summarised our responses by assigning us each a word associated with the summary decision.

Mine was SOIL.

It was unanimous that I was most likely to be – the SOIL.

My fellow teammates described me as the rich, fertile soil which nourishes and nurtures life into being. They loved it. They loved and appreciated me. I wasn't jumping up and down with delight. Who wants to be the soil? Not terribly glamorous or sexy. That makes me the one who everyone walks on, digs, flattens, puts manure and artificial fertiliser on. I'm the one that gets dumped on. I clearly didn't see how being the soil was desirable. I couldn't access the appreciation that my teammates had for me and the contribution that I made.

I was in my early thirties, and I wasn't ready to be the soil. I wanted to be experienced as the sun, a sunflower or perhaps even the dew.

Someone who was appreciated for getting things done, achieving things, adding a clear, tangible contribution. But not the soil. I did not relish being thought of as the soil for the team. I had had a belly full of feedback over the recent years to say that I was too gentle, too kind, too reserved and that I needed to be bolder, louder, and more forceful. In other words, I needed to match the men in the organisation and the women who had learned to be like the men. He who shouts loudest and longest got noticed and won the 'game', It seemed. The Enablers often went unseen, undervalued, and overlooked from what I could tell, with their contribution being too intangible to measure and quantify. Qualitative contribution was a secondary bonus in this organisation but not a necessity. And I had learned to undervalue it too. Which meant that I had automatically rejected myself and my value add.

I had repeatedly been advised to be more assertive, forceful, louder and to stand out from the crowd. In other words, I was being asked to be something other than Me. It wasn't my essential nature. It felt impossible to go against the grain.

And yet, my teammates were very sincere in their allocation of soil. I was valuable to them. I was not so valuable to the senior leaders. I was valuable to the directors I worked one on one with, and I was valuable to the teams I facilitated. None of this was enough for my manager, though. She clearly didn't value me. My contribution wasn't enough. And if I were the soil, I was probably not enough for the organisation either. It was just more evidence that I didn't fit in and couldn't deliver in the way I was being asked to. And yet, how could I be anything other than the soil?

My heart sank.

I couldn't be anything other than myself.

Truth be told, I was indeed the soil.

In the right circumstances, I could also be the sun and the sunflower.

And I was always the soil. Always had been and always will be.

I was the one who spotted and nurtured the talent in others and their confidence to actualise it.

I was the one who people came to for support.

I was the one who held the team together when our manager went AWOL.

I coached them in numerous ways.

Listened to their woes.

Celebrated and cheered their wins.

I was the rich, fertile soil, encouraging their growth and feeding them nutrients.

I was the intuitive, creative one, the mother figure, the emotional glue that held everything together.

Yet, the soil often went unseen, overlooked, and undervalued.

It was the glorious, magnificent sunflower that got noticed and the sun whose warmth and sunny disposition felt good to be around.

If I couldn't appreciate my contribution, how could I expect the organisation to value the soil?

The colourful ones, the loud ones, the ones who made themselves known, got themselves noticed, were valued more highly. The ones who quietly and efficiently got on with their work and delivered consistently highly without the additional noise, drama, and fanfare did not. I was the latter. I used to get so frustrated when people were promoted because of who they knew and the effort they had put into brown-nosing those in authority and then got promoted way beyond their level of skill.

The team build ended with seemingly very little achieved, and I, for one, was mighty glad to be going home to see my husband and son.

A few weeks later, my manager called me into her office. Almost before I had even sat down, she began to confide in me about her desire to have children and that she and her husband had gone through two failed attempts at IVF. She began to cry. And then she really began to pour her heart out. Her feelings, her husband's indifferent responses, the difficulties they were going through, and the pressure of the IVF process. His long absences, reliance on alcohol to survive the stress of his job and her lack of female companionship, how sad she felt when she saw women who were pregnant or who had small babies. She didn't ask anything of me, and I had the sense that I needed to listen, without response, and simply to witness her.

Bearing in mind that I was six months pregnant with our second son, I recognised that this was a courageous conversation for her to be having with me and that she was likely to be feeling vulnerable.

She talked of her jealousy of me. She acknowledged that she could never have what I had. She was talking about my gentle, loving nature and how everyone loved me. And, of course, that I was able to have children.

I listened and witnessed her tears. She thanked me and then suggested it was time to draw things to a close, wiped her eyes with her sleeve and then signalled for me to leave her office. I smiled gently and said that I was sorry that she was going through such a tough time. I let her know that she could talk again if she needed or wanted and affirmed that I would maintain confidentiality.

It was a one-off conversation. She never brought the subject up again. And neither did I.

Looking back on it now, I can see that I was mirroring back to her everything that she wanted but didn't have. Her comment all those years ago about not being able to see the value I brought was untrue. It was her pain speaking. Decades went by before this memory popped up again, only this time, I really felt the pain, like a kick to my stomach, and I spontaneously burst into tears. I had defrosted and dismantled the tough skin enough to access the wound within. And even more than that, I now appreciated my own contribution to my family and the wider world.

At long last, I was happy to be the soil.

The Soul Speaks
of *Feeling the Call*

It is calling You.
You can hear its tune on the soft wind,
Like a song you remember from oh so long ago.
A melody that stirs you deep inside.

Not knowing where it comes from,
Not knowing why it came.

Yet, slowly, surely, the lyrics reveal themselves to you.

You feel your body responding.
Your heart flutters.
Your body begins to move to its rhythm.

The dance is expressing itself through you now.

The volume is getting louder.
There is no denying it now.

It's here.
It's pressing.
It's prescient.
It's tangible.
It's visceral.
It's loud.
Louder.
And louder still.

What do you choose?

The Labyrinth Speaks
of *the Mystery Within*

Deep within the symbol of the Labyrinth, there lies a mystery.

Find the mystery and you find your treasure.

The Labyrinth has hidden many secrets over the centuries.

What will it reveal to you?

Step inside and see.

The Labyrinth invites you to step onto the pathway and put aside the ordinary as you step into the extraordinary.

Re-store, re-balance, focus, gain clarity.

Here is a chance to take stock, reflect, be still and to allow the magic of the Labyrinth to support you.

Let the Labyrinth lead.

Come and experience the magic and the mystery of the Labyrinth for yourself.

Dive in, let yourself be absorbed, immerse yourself.

Immerse, immerse, immerse.

Deeply.

Fully.

Wholly.

Awakening '99

I went through a phase late into my thirties of feeling nervous about the whole concept of having a 'calling'. The notion came out of nowhere. I hadn't been thinking about it. It just landed in my consciousness one day as a thought. And yet, it felt more than a mere thought. It had a gravitas about it. It felt like a fully formed 'Thing' rather than a wispy, cloud-like thought. There was a great, big anchor attached to this notion. It was no pie-in-the-sky, lightweight notion. It held a significance that my body could feel even though my head couldn't make sense of it. Not yet anyway.

I didn't personally know anyone who had felt a calling, other than a friend who had entered a silent order convent in her late twenties. It landed with me both as a curiosity and as an anxiety simultaneously. I had only read about those in religious orders and a few celebrities who had felt a calling to totally switch lanes and change careers, move across the world, leave relationships, or join a convent. The notion of receiving a calling took hold and freaked me out at times. I found a book about the phenomena in our local new age shop. I was keen to learn more about it and the circumstances surrounding these mysterious happenings. The thing I was most worried about was what would happen to me if I received one. What might be the consequences? Seemingly, one couldn't refuse a calling when it came knocking. I was fascinated, enthralled and apprehensive for several months. The whole notion of it absorbed my attention. I didn't share this idea with anyone at the time. I didn't know anyone who might understand it. In any case, it struck me as a strange thing to be obsessing over.

Looking back, I can now see that I was picking up on what was about to happen. I was in some way being prepared for when the first calling would appear. It came later that year in the form of my first Reiki attunement.

It all began in the spring when I hired a life coach. A friend had gifted me a complimentary life coaching session with a coach. There was no specific challenge that I wanted to resolve at that time, but I intuitively felt that it would be good to experience some life coaching. Within a few sessions, I began to realise that this was a job that I would love to do, and I would be good at it too. I felt that it would also fulfil my emerging need to help others at a deeper level than I had so far had permission to do within a corporate setting. And even more than that, it might fulfil my new desire to make a difference to the world at large. I began to talk to others about my intention to work in this way, and within a week, I had three people wanting support with career changes.

Something else began to unlock. I had recently begun to question life. I had been pondering my purpose and what I was here to do with my life. I had begun to think that there must be more to life than I was experiencing. I was opening to the possibility that there was something beyond the tangible, physical realm. This wasn't new to me. I had always had a sense that there was an all-encompassing, loving presence and a purpose to life. I had always had a feeling that things worked out for the best, even when they didn't look or feel like it at the time. I knew that things happened for a reason. This had begun as an intuitive knowing which then got backed up by my life experience. I always got what I needed, even if it wasn't what I had wanted at the time.

The combination of the coaching and my coach's spiritual energy was potently powerful. He began to ask the questions that opened my perception and curiosity to explore more. As I did this, my senses began to change. My sense of smell and taste heightened, and I began to see psychically and clairvoyantly. I began to consider the concept of life purpose and what it meant to me. The Thing that I had felt was missing turned out not to be a Thing at all. It was all about connection. Connection to a deeper part of myself and connection to my Soul, and a more soulful way of living and working. I had been looking outside of myself, and it was all to be found within me.

Relaxing in the garden one day, I remembered how much I had enjoyed cloud watching as a child. It was a beautiful English summer's day, gloriously hot, and the clouds were high. The pure white of the cloud against the blue of the sky was a wonderful contrast. One cloud caught my attention. It morphed into a smiley face, then into a heart shape and finally angel wings. There was little transition between shapes – it went from one into another. And then the most extraordinary thing happened. A rainbow appeared around the angel wings, forming a circle. As this happened, I had an instant knowing that I was to investigate Reiki courses. I can't remember how I knew that, only that I knew. I immediately rang my coach and shared what had happened. He was just leaving a client session. She was a Reiki Seichem master, the symbol of which happened to link with rainbow colours. I rang her and booked onto the next available course, which was in three months' time.

Later that same day, I began to write a list of what I wanted next in my life. I allowed myself to dream way beyond my current horizon. I wasn't unhappy, yet I felt a desire to go beyond, to feel into what my heart and Soul were calling for. On my list were to start my own business, to have more time with my sons, and to have a second home by the sea. I folded the piece of paper carefully and put it in my jewellery box. I promptly forgot all about it.

What happened next, though, happened with startling speed. The next day was the solar eclipse event of August 1999. It was experienced strongest in the UK, and I remember being in one of the grottiest of offices in a meeting with one of the loveliest female commercial directors in the company. We both agreed that we would make time to experience this phenomenon, put on our safety glasses and waited. It was eerie beyond belief. I had shivers running through my entire body. It affected me viscerally. I had a sense of having experienced this somewhere else before, and that here was something so very sacred and special. It felt timeless. We looked at each other and both questioned what we were doing with our lives. It struck us both, instantaneously, that there was so much more to life than working in this organisation, any organisation, really. There was a big, wide world outside of the office that we both now felt a desire to experience.

As I was leaving her office, I took a call from the human resources director, who was clearly angry. She swore as she shared her displeasure at the report that one of my colleagues had produced for the main board finance director. She clearly didn't agree with its presentation and slant, even though we both knew that the numbers were correct. The combination of her tone, her foul language, the blame, and the deceit contrasted with the eerie, sacred experience I had just had was potent. I was unusually curt with her and closed the conversation. As I walked to my car, I burst into tears. In that moment, I was clear that I wanted to leave the organisation. Enough was enough. No amount of salary and benefits made up for being treated like this. I rang my husband there and then, and we agreed to look at our finances to see what might be possible. We agreed that we would take three months to explore the viability of my leaving, especially given that he was also wanting to find a new job with greater career prospects and security.

I had wanted to leave there and then, but he suggested that it would be better to leave under the right circumstances, having done some thinking and research first. He was right. What happened next was testament to that. For several years I had been riding a wave of success at work. After the birth of my second son, I was lucky enough to have been granted a part-time role. This was a first for anyone at my level of seniority, and due in part, I suspect, to the conversation that I'd had with the CEO just before leaving for maternity leave. I had been briefing him on a new director-level development programme, and he asked me how I found balancing motherhood and career and what I thought about the wealth scheme. I answered honestly. Money was always welcome. When my child is ill and can't go to nursery, money doesn't cut it. I explained that what I would value most would be to have a three-day week to bring greater balance. He nodded and understood. Several months later, when I asked for a reduction in my hours, it was granted. I was told that I would need to make it work as I would be watched carefully. My success in the experiment would determine whether they offered the opportunity more widely.

I had indeed thrived. I achieved a lot more in less time. I managed programmes and teams to deliver change across the whole of the head office function, which in turn meant that rapid change in response to market trends was now smoother and more coherent for those taking part in cross-functional roles. It revolutionised how big change programmes were resourced and brought an order and process into how those taking part were cared for. I was recognised and known across multiple head office sites and beyond and had received excellent performance ratings. I was in a team of people I loved and who loved me. It felt so very different. It came as a shock that I felt ready to leave. I could see that there was little opportunity to work at this level on three days a week, the company had made that clear. Although I loved the role that I was in, I was sensing that it was time to move on as there was little growth opportunity. We had also done the maths and knew that it would be feasible for me to leave and set up my own coaching practice.

During this time, I was receiving images and words and insights into the new business. The most notable of which was the name and an image which has stuck with me for over two decades. The name was 'Life Purpose', and the image came to me overnight in a semi-sleeping state. I was looking at a beautiful sandy beach surrounded by a cliff. The beach was full of people. As I moved my hand from the left-hand side of the beach to the right, the people turned from sepia to full colour. From this, I understood that my new purpose was to help people to live their life purpose and to live in a fully connected way that brought vibrancy. I was to help them come alive to life. I began to work on a logo that represented this and set up a company and website ready for the right time in the future when I could start actively living this dream.

The time arrived for my first Reiki course. As I received the attunement, I heard the words, 'You made it. What took you so long?' I was a little surprised. I had never experienced auditory messages before. Something was unlocking, unfolding. This environment felt like Home. The gentleness, ambience, values, and limitlessness of this way of working felt good. I could see and feel myself doing this work. It was soulful, and I was coming to terms that I needed more soul in my life. I knew in every fibre of my being that I wanted to do this.

I crafted my resignation letter that evening and resigned the following morning. Forty-eight hours later, I answered our home phone to a head-hunter. My husband was being invited to interview for a larger company with greater career progression, enhanced income, and more job security. Within a week, he had been through three interviews, and we had agreed it was the right next move for him and for us as a family. We were now going to move to West

Sussex. We sold our house to a cash buyer. Within a ten-day period, we had both resigned and sold our house. We were on the move.

I wrote another list. A list of all the qualities and features that we wanted in our next home. We viewed many houses, had three offers close to asking price rejected and were gazumped over the millennium period. We had, however, found the right school for our sons, and so we focused our search locally to the school. I began again. I threw away all the old estate agent papers and telephoned each of them with a very specific brief. I decided that I would make a personal connection with them. Three days later, I received notification of a house for sale just a ten-minute drive from the school. I recognised the house from a few months back. I didn't like the lack of symmetry in its style and had discarded it outright. This time I took a closer look. Internally, it ticked all the boxes on my list. It was within our price range. It had light and was spacious. The owners could move quickly. It looked like a house that we could work some magic on and create a lasting home.

Something told me to look at the back page of the details. I gasped. There was a photo of a bench in a field in the foothills of the South Downs. I had seen this very same photo in a magazine a few weeks beforehand, and my heart had jumped. I remember thinking, 'Wow, wouldn't it be great to have such an amazing view on your doorstep?' This bench with a view was in the field less than one hundred metres from the front garden of this house. I rang my husband and agreed to view it. As we drove closer to the property, my heart began to expand as I glimpsed the green, rolling hills of the South Downs for the first time. This place felt so magical. Now I could see why none of the previous properties had been right for us. We walked through the door of the house, and we both knew that this was our new family home. There was a lot of work to do, but we could take our time. And so, we put an offer in, it was accepted, and we moved lock, stock, and barrel within seven weeks. We were now in the semi-rural countryside of West Sussex, and it felt just like being on holiday. It was tangible just how much we all began to quickly relax into our new environment. Almost overnight. We had totally changed our lives within six short months.

Months later, I discovered the list that I had made the previous

August. I read it and smiled. Almost all of it was covered by our lifestyle and career change. There was one slight difference. Instead of having a second home by the sea, we now had our main home less than a twenty-minute drive from the coast. Life had delivered something so much better than my list. Perfect.

Our new adventure had begun.

Flow is the New Balance

Dear Moriah!

You will gain your balance and then you'll lose it again.

Balance is dynamic. It's not static.

Now this, now that.

It's cyclical.

FLOW is the new balance.

Focus on Flow and you'll be in a whole new vibe.

Wink, wink, nod, nod. X

I Need a Break!

This was the thought running in a continuous loop through my tired, frazzled head one Friday morning as I got ready to do the school run. I kept saying it out loud too, on repeat, as I busied myself and rallied the boys for the day ahead.

I was beyond exhausted. Bone tired. My body ached, especially my shoulders. I had one of those pressure kind of headaches behind my sore eyes. I hadn't been sleeping well, and I hadn't felt at my best for a while now. I had been grinding my teeth whilst asleep too, and that was always a sign that I needed to pay attention to my wellbeing. I had been on *full steam ahead* mode for quite some time. I was feeling wired and buoyant all at the same time, and whilst I still had physical energy, I could carry on. It never occurred to me that I could take some time for me. I had been so busy and wrapped up in activity that I hadn't allowed myself space and rest. I didn't easily take time out to rest back then. It was an alien concept. Rest had typically come only when I was ill or in the times when I sat down and watched a film or tv show. I would sometimes read a book, but that was my limit. It didn't compute with me that slowing down, resting, and doing no-thing could be a positive choice.

This week had undeniably been an exceptionally busy one with clients. In fact, it had been an exceptionally busy year. We had been through a lot of change in a very short space of time, to the extent that our lives were unrecognisable from nine months beforehand.

We had moved house and changed jobs. Our sons had moved schools and nurseries. We had left friends and family behind, and we were now building new connections. We had recently sold our home that we had bought brand new and moved over a hundred miles to the south coast into a bigger, less attractive, and significantly older and shabbier house that needed repair and some renovation.

We had moved from a busy, familiar, urban town environment with plentiful support systems around us and with business parks and an easy commute into London to a gloriously green, peaceful, rural idyll in the West Sussex countryside. In the desire to be more rural, I had totally underestimated just how little childcare would be available, let alone the quality of it. I had made use of breakfast and after-school clubs, holiday clubs, childminders, and a private nursery. There were none of these in our new area. There was no demand for it as most mums didn't work. It was an alien concept to me and took a while to adjust to.

I had underestimated how much I would miss my friends and my mum's hands-on support. We had underestimated how wearing it would immediately be for us to live in a house that had no wardrobes, a kitchen that didn't function and thirty-year-old bathroom suites which were avocado green and in need of repair. Whoever thought that would be a good colour for anything other than a genuine avocado needs their head testing. We hadn't been used to living like that, and we had no idea how stressful we would find it until we had moved in. We ran out of oil frequently in that first year because we had been so used to having access to a continuous gas supply for cooking and heating. There was no gas in our village at all.

Back then, we tolerated very little less than perfect, so it was a shock to our system on top of the unacknowledged but very evident stress of moving within such a short space of time. We were focused on our vision of how things could and would be, and we worked tirelessly towards that.

Within three months of moving, we had researched and fitted new wardrobes in three of the bedrooms, a brand-new kitchen, painted some of the rooms and cleared the gardens. I eventually found a playgroup that our youngest son was happy to go to. He had rejected six in that period, walking out almost as soon as he arrived because he didn't like the vibe. He liked the final one available, thank goodness!

We had three housewarming parties and all the preparation that went into those.

Several times a month, we had friends or family come to stay with us. Everyone loved our new location, and they were keen to visit us there. We were happy to have them. We enjoyed sharing our space with others. We missed them too. We had underestimated just how much we would miss the familiarity of neighbours and friends.

I missed my mum. I hadn't anticipated just how much until after we had moved. She was no longer a thirty-minute car drive away but was now almost two hours away. There wasn't room at my parent's home for us to stay overnight, and a four-hour round trip felt a lot with two young children, and so we saw her less often. My parents would come and spend longer with us when they could.

I missed my girlfriends. The friends I made in the early days after moving all emigrated and moved off to far-flung places, following their husbands' job relocations. I was putting a brave face on things as I often did; however, deep down, I felt very lonely and hungry for good quality female companionship. Saturday morning coffees, evening glasses of wine and occasional play days and birthday parties. When these were no longer a part of my life, I realised just how much I valued them. With this move, I was hoping for short-term pain for a longer-term gain.

My husband was getting used to a significantly bigger company with different values and discerning whom he could trust and whom he couldn't. That's often the bottom line of joining a new company, regardless of what people admit to. Who are you *safe* with? He missed his former colleagues and was adjusting to an hour-long daily car commute. This job at least provided greater job security and more interesting work. He wanted to be stretched, and this would give him that.

Our sons had adapted well and had seemingly settled into their new home. It seems that we had prepared them well. We had explained what we were planning from the very beginning and involved our eldest son in some of the choices too. He got to choose his new bedroom out of three offered. He chose the room with the view – the majestic South Downs could be clearly seen as they were just a five-minute walk away.

We had not had a holiday that summer, taking just one week to go exploring together. Our sons had had a week up with my in-laws, who had generously offered to have them stay. This was very welcome; however, I used most of that time working either on my business or in the house.

It was my first year as a full-time mum and part-time business owner. I had underestimated just how much I loved my new way of working and that I wanted more hours in a day to have client calls and to build my business. Unfortunately, I unwittingly super-imposed the 'try harder', 'grow it big' kind of mentality that I had wanted to escape from into my new hybrid part-time business and ways of working. It would take me two years to figure this situation out.

All of this, however, was outweighed by the joy of being in our new environment. At the bottom of our road was a large field where our sons could run free and play football, plus other fields full of horses and sheep. They were at last close to nature, and that made my heart happy. I had wanted this for them as they grew up. To know and appreciate nature. I hadn't realised that it was also what I needed too.

The tiredness had an accumulated effect on me. Despite this, I absolutely, thoroughly relished our school-run route. We had swapped twenty minutes of sitting in a queue of traffic, travelling three miles to school for the most glorious school run. We now spent ten minutes driving through country lanes, through a wood where we would regularly spot deer and their families, over an ancient bridge and alongside the most beautiful floodplain and wild brooks.

The sun shone through the tree canopies, and dappled light lit our way. It was early autumn, and the multi-coloured fallen leaves would rise into the air behind our car as we drove. This always brought a smile to my face and filled me with delight. When the boys were younger, squeals of 'whoa' came from the back seats as they turned to watch the dance of the leaves. Total joy.

Today was Friday, and I was determined to enjoy it. I dropped our eldest son off at school and then drove a further half an hour to our local city. I say 'city', however, in truth, it was more like a large town with a cathedral. Before running errands, my youngest son

Josh and I went off to find our favourite café. This was one of our Friday rituals.

It was the one day of the week that I didn't work, and he didn't go to his playgroup. He was still just three years old; however, he had a very clear idea even then of what he wanted, liked, and disliked. One of his favourite things was to have a snack together before we began our errands. I was happy to oblige. I enjoyed this special time together. He always had the same snack. Toast and jam with a glass of milk. He always headed for the same window seat too, so that we could look out at the people passing and the cars and buses.

I loved these times with him. I was aware of just how quickly he was growing up and changing, and I was keen to make the most of this time with him before he started school. He was such an observant child and had a quick wit too. He made me laugh and I marvelled at just how bright he was. He noticed details that many missed. He loved to 'people watch'. On this particular morning, we were making up stories about who the passers-by might be and where they might be heading off to.

I remember looking out of the window and noticing a young man who was making his way up the cobbled hill on crutches. It looked as though he had broken his right leg as it was in plaster from his toes right up to below his knee. I remember thinking, 'Wow! That must be difficult: crutches, cobblestones, and a hill to climb too.' It seemed like a very long time that he held my attention. It must have been a matter of a minute or so, yet it was like time stood still whilst I noticed the shape and colour of his plaster cast, the pattern of the words written across it, the colour of his crutches, the look of total concentration on his face as he carefully placed each crutch so that he could safely navigate the cobblestones of this old cityscape. I wondered what had happened to his leg. He seemed adept with his crutches, so he must have been used to using them. What struck me most was that he was able to go uphill, on cobblestones and on crutches. He had caught my attention, and I was aware of my prolonged fascination and curious as to why I was so moved by his plight. He didn't look in pain, I didn't feel sorry for him as such, it was curious. I was curious. The question in my head was, why was I so curious and why for what felt like such a prolonged period?

It was then that I heard my son talking to me; he had changed the subject and was calling my attention to something else. The broken-legged man, his crutches and the cobblestones disappeared from my awareness, and I was re-directed to the big, double-decker bus parked opposite our window.

Later that day, I remembered this fixation and wondered whether it had been a prophecy, a vision of what was to come. By the end of that day, I had broken a bone in my right foot, just below my ankle.

I'd had the repetitive thought that I wanted a break and said it out loud too, many times that day. The Universe, in its infinite wisdom and cooperative spirit, conspired to give me a break even if it wasn't the kind I wanted or welcomed!

It had been a long but happy day, and later that evening, after our sons were settling for sleep, I headed off to visit my friend on the other side of the village. I don't remember why I decided to drive that evening. It would have been just as easy to walk. I parked on a grass verge opposite and a little way up from her house, away from the main road.

She had prepared a lovely meal, and her daughters, who were five and three, had been allowed to stay up late to see me and say their goodbyes too. They were an absolute delight, and I always enjoyed their company. They were creative, curious, and confident. Just like their mum. I hadn't really allowed myself to admit just how much I was going to miss them. My sons would miss them too, as they had often played together during the summer months. We reminisced and laughed, and she shared some of the details of their new life out in Dubai. Her husband had been working out there on an assignment for several months and had now been offered a great job as a permanent employee, so they were going out to be with him. It was a great opportunity for the whole family. For her, it also meant that she would be closer to her birth family in Australia.

When it was time to leave, we hugged one of those long, heart-to-heart hugs and wished each other well, and I waved as I headed down the garden path to the gate which separated her garden from the thin pavement and the main road.

My heart was heavy. There was a lump in my throat, but I ignored it. I told myself there was no point in getting upset and that I would have to move on just like I always did. Crying wasn't going to solve the problem, and neither was feeling sorry for myself. I was grateful for our time together, and I was also sad at having to say goodbye to yet another woman. I had made friends with four great women, and all of them had now left the country. I didn't want to admit that I was feeling lonely even though I had my little family around me. I missed the hole that only quality female companionship can fill.

And then I was jolted out of my thoughts when I noticed just how very dark it was. It was late September, and the nights were drawing in earlier and quickly. It was our first autumn of living in the village, and I had only just noticed how very dark it was. I couldn't believe that I hadn't noticed that there were no streetlights in the village! How could I not have noticed that before now? I was mildly annoyed with myself too, because I was wearing slip-on shoes, which weren't the best for walking on a grass verge in the dark.

And then it happened.

SNAP!

I fell and broke my foot. Just like that. In a split second, I went from being upright to falling over and onto the main road in the path of oncoming traffic.

I felt my foot slip into what I could only imagine was a rabbit hole, my foot twisted in a rabbit hole, and I heard it 'snap'. I yelped in shock and sudden pain.

I felt myself fall sideways onto the main road.

Shit.

This was dangerous. I was in shock, in pain, and now I was in trouble.

I suddenly realised the severity of the situation.

I was lying on the main road. It was pitch dark. Drivers wouldn't have seen me until they were close enough for their headlights to have spotted me, by which time it would have been too late. I was genuinely concerned for my life by this point. This was a busy road, and drivers frequently exceeded the speed limit. I could be crushed.

The seconds it took to go from standing to lying on the tarmac felt like slow motion. I was lying there in shock. Time stood still. It felt like the longest time. I could feel the pain now, and my foot was throbbing. It was clear that I wasn't going to be able to stand or walk easily. I would only be able to drag and shuffle my way back to the grass verge so that I could decide on my plan of action.

It was a miracle that there was no traffic at all for around ten minutes. It was usually a busy road with cars picking up speed on that section as they had a clear stretch of road towards the next village. The Universe may have delivered my break as ordered; however, it was also looking after me.

I dragged myself back towards the pavement and managed to stand up. I realised that there was no way I could walk home, it was too far. It wasn't wise to go back to my friends either because that involved me crossing the main road to the other side. I had my mobile phone with me, but there was no signal. The only way home was to drive. So, I did. I drove home. In agony.

I hopped into the lounge and dropped onto an armchair. The shock hit me as I began to cry as I explained to my husband what had just happened. My foot and ankle were now swelling badly. I took painkillers and went to bed. I managed to get a few hours of sleep even though my foot was throbbing. At this stage, I still didn't quite believe that I had broken it. The following day my husband drove us to the accident and emergency unit at our nearby hospital. The bone beneath my ankle was broken. It needed plaster, and they gave me crutches. So, I was now the one gingerly walking across cobblestones on crutches with my leg in plaster. The same leg as the man I had been watching the previous day!

Did I sense that this was an event about to happen? I don't know.

Did I make it happen, will it to happen by incessantly thinking and saying, 'I need a break?' I'm not sure.

It was a salutary lesson. But what was the lesson?

I needed a break.

I needed a full period of quality rest. I'd been on the go for a very long time and needed time to adjust to our new home, way of working and living and having 'held it all together' for so very long.

Also, looking back, I wanted a breakthrough. I wanted the company of good female friends who were going to stick around, mums with whom I could chat on the school run and whose children we could have over to play, and someone who could pick up our eldest if I needed it. I also wanted clarity about my work which, of course, I got once I had the time and space to rest. I wanted a breakthrough badly.

The Universe, as it happens, dealt me a multi-faceted lesson which was very efficient in its design and delivery. Not only was this about me taking time out and pacing myself, but it was also about me learning to ask for and graciously receive help and to surrender my illusion of control over my life.

Once we got back from hospital, my husband and I set to work on a plan for the next six weeks. Our new life was heavily reliant on me driving our sons to and from school to after-school activities, food shopping and all the multiple 'nip to the shops' type car journeys when you live in a tiny rural village.

I was going to have to organise school runs for the next six weeks whilst I couldn't drive. I didn't know the other mums well enough to ask them. We were also the only family living right on the edge of the school catchment area, and it would be well out of their way to simply drop by. There was another reason too.

The mothers at the school stuck to their cliques, many of them had grown up locally together, and newcomers were not too welcome. They seemed to find me interesting until they had got as much information as they had needed to decide that I wasn't one of them and was no longer quite as interesting as I, at first, must have seemed.

I worked, which was a source of great curiosity for them. 'You poor thing!' one of them exclaimed. 'On the contrary,' I replied. 'I love to work. It's a great passion of mine.' I was met with some very strange looks. I didn't grow up around here, I hadn't gone to a private school, I didn't quite fit the social scene. Perhaps I was a bit too working class for their tastes. A corporate career background was also a very foreign concept to them.

I soon learned that many of them had left school, married, and had children straight away. From their conversations I gleaned that their social life was the thing they lived for. I was also almost a decade older than many of them as I had given birth whilst in my early thirties. I was as alien to them as their life was to me.

Once again, a familiar theme was building around me not fitting in. And I had to admit to myself that this time it was hurting. Standing at the school gates with other mums in their huddles and with no invitation to chat, no inclusion, was hard. Whenever I tried to engage with the mums, the conversation lasted only as long as it took for another mum from their huddle to arrive, interrupt, and take over the conversation.

I even joined the parent-teacher association to help behind the scenes to see if I could get to know my fellow mums that way; however, it turned out that they spent much of their time bitching. It was a valuable insight into their collective way of being. I realised that it was a blessing in disguise to be excluded in this case and I would just have to find friendship elsewhere or rely on myself. Perhaps the Universe had been protecting me.

It was clear to me that the school run was no longer the sociable delight that it had been before moving to Sussex. I had built up a lovely community of fellow working mums. We had met when our first and then second babies were small and had all gone to the same private nursery. Three of us had even given birth on consecutive days. We were a close-knit bunch, as were our children. I hadn't appreciated how much I would miss them, and I knew our sons missed their play buddies too.

It took a while – a few years to be exact – but thankfully, new families began to arrive in the area. I welcomed those mothers and their children with open arms, remembering how cold and isolating an experience it had at first been for me, and we developed strong friendships and alliances together.

And so, of course, when I asked the school to put out an appeal for help with school runs, no other parent stepped forward. Out of ninety children and a potential forty-five families or more, no one offered to help.

Thankfully my mother-in-law came to stay for the first week. My parents came for the first two days of each of the following five weeks, which left me three days a week to find lifts for. I relied on several friends who each came to stay for a few days each, plus taxis. Our youngest son often missed out on his playgroup days simply because it was in the opposite direction to the school, and it was too much to expect people to drive that far or too expensive on the days I was relying on taxi power alone.

I was grateful for all this additional support, and I was also very aware that it was coming from those connections and family we had left behind to make our move to Sussex. I was also aware of the added work involved. The organising and re-organising, the extra washing and changing of bed linen, food shopping, meal making, entertaining and so on. Some who helped also cooked and baked and played with our sons. Some came to be taxi drivers and expected to be waited on. It was a difficult balance, and I was also aware that I needed to rest and literally put my feet up. I was tired. My foot was sore, and it only improved through bed rest.

I had many ah-ha moments in that short amount of time whilst resting.

I recognised that I had been hopelessly bad at knowing when I needed to rest.

I was not adept at asking for support let alone gracefully receiving it.

I would even go as far as to say that I didn't always recognise that I needed anything nor that I could ask for support and expect to receive it. I was so used to pushing through challenges no matter how hard or uncomfortable they became. I had numbed myself to pain. Until now.

Independence had become a chronic, habitual response for me. It had swung so far on its spectrum that my independence was now distinctly unhealthy. I realised that it may even be a trauma response. If I can be as fully self-sufficient as possible, I won't be disappointed if things don't work out my way or if others let me down. I can't be disappointed. I remembered the words of my mum, who used to say to me, 'If you don't expect too much, you won't be disappointed.' I was resting one day when this awareness arrived. I spontaneously burst into tears. Weeks had gone by, and I hadn't cried other than when I first got home after the accident.

Now there were tears, lots of them. Uncontrollable sobbing for the 'younger me' who had kept on going through all the pain of doing it all alone and being bullied, the more recent me of working full-time whilst desperately wanting to spend more time with my sons and then the current me who didn't know when she had reached capacity and had to fall and break a bone to STOP.

And there were tears for the 'little girl' inside of me who often felt alone in the world. I called to her and held that part of me close as I rocked myself to sleep. I was exhausted and I had just opened the valve to the emotional healing that I so badly needed.

For so long, surrender had been a foreign concept to me.

It took a broken foot and being unable to move independently for me to appreciate it.

Enforced rest was a familiar experience and I felt the distant echoes of mystery viruses from my corporate days – especially as I often succumbed to illness during the times of either the spring or the autumn equinox. This break was just one week following the autumn one. In the future, I would have several falls off bikes and downstairs, and experience cars driving into the back of my car. Happily, this seems to have stopped now that I pay attention and pace myself more.

And so, with this enforced period of rest, I allowed myself the time I needed and wanted to lie on my bed and be looked after. I allowed myself to dare to ask for what I needed, however uncomfortable I felt, and most times I got it. I learned to be patient with myself and with life and to s-l-o-w down. For the first time in my life, I allowed myself to slow down. I was in my late thirties by this stage. Imagine. It had taken me so long to learn such a fundamental lesson.

I chilled on the bed, reading stories to our sons, napping, and considering what I'd like to do with my business. One day, whilst I was daydreaming, an idea dropped into my mind that it would be fun to create a career guide to help people choose careers which would be in alignment with their life purpose. As this idea was percolating, I received a phone call. It was my last boss. He was inviting me to write a proposal to win a bid to create a career guide for the cross-functional team members, the division that I had helped to set up. I, of course, said 'Yes', and a few weeks down the line, I was offered the contract. It was five times what I was earning doing one-to-one coaching, I loved every minute of it and got some great feedback from the early participants. It was a win-win situation.

Once again, I wondered, was I picking up on something that was 'in the air' and about to happen or was I creating my own reality?

Was it an omen or did I manifest it?

What I was certain of then as much as I am certain of today, is that I never utter the words, 'I need a break!' And I caution anyone else whom I hear say those four words. I am so much better at listening and responding to the needs of my body now. I rest as and when I need to. Daydreaming and regular naps are now baked in as standard.

This was the note that I found on the bedroom carpet early one morning as I got up to prepare breakfast and make sandwiches for our sons' school lunch. Our eldest son had written it and slid it under the door so that I would see it first thing in the morning.

He was seven years old and even at that age, he had a strong sense of fairness and honesty. I knew it was genuine. I knew that he was tired. I'd noticed that he was going through a growth spurt. His trousers now needed letting down and his school sweatshirt was becoming short of sleeve. This had all happened within the last week. So, his little frame was growing rapidly, and this would have used up a lot of energy. I could feel his exhaustion and I had noticed that he was lacking his usual tigger-like bounce. His eyes had lost their sparkle and his energy had felt *flat*.

I went to his bedroom and sat down with him. He hopped onto my lap and told me that he didn't feel like school today and wanted to stay at home. I didn't question him. I just acknowledged that he seemed tired and agreed with him that a day at home would work some magic. He smiled, kissed me on the cheek and thanked me. I gave him a hug and then left him to get dressed whilst I went downstairs to the kitchen.

Once back from the school run, I postponed my morning client sessions and let him lead the day. A favourite film, some stories, playtime, a walk through the woods and some gentle time together and he began to come back to his usual bouncy, happy self.

He needed a rest, he needed a break from the school routine, he needed to just be. He was bright, creative, sociable, and had a lot of physical energy. Most boys are like puppies at this age, I discovered. They need a lot of exercise, love, good food in plentiful supply plus some healthy boundaries and then they can flourish.

To be able to support my sons in this way when they were needing time out was one of the key reasons I left my corporate job. I wanted to be there for them at the beginning and end of the school day and to be able to give them space if they needed time away from school or if they were sick.

In truth, I loved the days when I had one of them at home for what I called 'wellbeing' days. They were both bright and caught up with their work quickly and the teachers understood my reasons for keeping them off school. Some teachers even confided that they thought it was a good idea and that they noticed the benefits. They acknowledged that they were happier in themselves and settled more quickly into tasks.

I loved having one-on-one time with my sons on days such as these. It gave us time to chill and connect. I felt like I could be present with them in a way that I couldn't when they were younger and I was working full-time. Was I compensating? Yes, probably. Did I benefit too? Absolutely.

They would share more of what was going on in their heads, in their school life and in their friendships. They would freely share their thoughts, hopes, dreams, worries and disappointments. It was like experiencing a window into their world and I got to feel what it was like to be them, and this gave me valuable information to understand how they were changing and growing. I understood better how to nurture and stretch them because of these conversations.

On these days, we got to snuggle up together to watch one of their favourite films or tv shows. They would often go back to an old favourite, and it brought them comfort in knowing the storyline, characters, and humour. They were changing so quickly, I guess this provided a degree of familiarity, security, and stability, of the known amidst all of the unknown.

Sometimes we would bake, paint, doodle, or simply curl up together and nap. I enjoyed their company so much. It reminded me of the days when they were just toddlers, and I was on maternity leave or at weekends. We would spend ages being creative, immersing ourselves in an activity for the joy of it and no expected outcome.

In these times together there was no timetable. There was nowhere to go, nowhere we needed to be and no agenda. We let the day unfold, one conversation and one activity at a time. Six whole hours. There was a wonderful freedom and quality of spaciousness to these times. If it were a food, I'd say that it was like a delicious, quality milk chocolate.

It allowed for a depth of connection that wasn't possible in the rush of regular school days. There was most definitely a quality about those days that I relished. And it worked its magic. We were more relaxed, content and connected by bedtime.

I could have left them to their own devices on days off from school, however, I saw it as an opportunity to slow down and relish time with them. It was time to bond, to connect and to enjoy each other's company. Work could wait. My clients understood. It all worked out.

It gave me a rest day too and at a time when I didn't easily or readily allow myself downtime. It gave me permission to go more slowly and to be more present with them in a way that was difficult on regular school days. Time stretched out ahead of us. It had a different feeling to it than a school holiday too. This was just one day. It was a rare occurrence. It was spontaneous. It was never planned. Their physical energy was 'low' on these days which more easily facilitated rest and renewal. And all of this fuelled my love of nurture, of a deeper connection with them.

To be honest, there may also have been a kind of delicious, almost *naughty* undertone to the day too, like we were skipping off whilst everyone else was at school and their dad at work. We were in our own colourful 'mum and son' bubble, doing our own thing, in our own way, in our own time.

There were some of these days when they wanted – and needed – time to themselves – and I encouraged them to lead the way on that too. This was especially true when they were teenagers. Privacy and time out became more the norm, and, in those times, I was present in the house and available when and if they wanted my company or input.

I am still so very grateful that I was now able to put them first and run my business around their schedule and needs. It made my heart sing, made me a happier person, and I'm sure that had a knock-on effect all around.

Everyone needs downtime, including little people as well as grown-ups.

And oh my, what I would give to go back to some of those times and to be with them as the me I am now – the wiser, more grounded, present, heart-led woman. And even as I type these words, I recognise that my sons have been instrumental to me becoming the woman I am today.

I am not yet a grandmother and I wonder if this is part of the magic and joy that I hear grandparents speak of. The opportunity to be the unconditional, loving, playful presence we always wanted to be as parents but perhaps were too busy, too tired, or just not fully able to be when our children were growing up.

And perhaps the Inner Child in us always needs such times of peace, space, play and permission to Be, to simply BE.

Beaming much love to the Inner Child within us all. May they always shine and show us the way.

The Soul Speaks
Passenger or Pilot?

Life unfolds.

It's a mystery.

We don't have all the answers

but we can learn to read the signposts.

Would you really want all the answers?

Where's the fun in that?

It's like seeing the end of a film before it has barely begun!

Sure, there is a sense of safety in the known.

But there is no growth in safety.

Only predictable routine dwells in that space.

Living life in the safe zone would be akin to living life in black and white.

Wouldn't you rather live a life of colour, where each day is different?

Where you respond to life and create your experiences rather than just react?

Do you want to be the Passenger or the Pilot of your Life?

And it's not about control either.

It's about engagement.

It's about engaging with Life and crafting your chosen experience of it.

It's about choosing experiences which expand you, fill you up with joy, inspire you, soothe you.

Until you are full, fuller, fullest.

How do you want to feel, Dear One?

How do you want to nourish and to invest your precious energy, this precious life?

It's about saying YES to people and experiences that chime with you, that match and support your personal vibrational signature and values, both work and personal.

It's about living life with a sense of purpose.

It's about coming alive with COLOUR.

And wouldn't that be wonderful!

Dive In

It matters not how the Creative Soul is fed. It matters only that it is fed.
Don't tiptoe around the edges of your creativity.
Dive in like a thirsty fish!
Engage. Get messy. Indulge yourself.
Follow your instinct, stay connected

It is so important to keep our creative juices flowing.

Do things you love, get inspired, do something different, meet new people, nap, meditate, keep a journal, write, sing, dance, move your body, cook, stare at the clouds, get out into nature, play, paint, do whatever you have to do to get yourself back into flow.

Quench your taste buds.
Come alive through the wild nature of your creative juices.
Sink, bathe, melt, gorge until you have had your fill and emerge transformed.

Creativity cannot be forced or squeezed to suit our whims and man-made timetables.
Instead it must be born, nurtured, and given the right ecology to thrive.
Just like us, the creative process has its own timing.
There is a time to seed, a time to germinate, a time to be born, a time to flourish, a time to die.

Dive in. Dive in. Dive in.

A Thirsty Fish

During the first two years of running my own business, I enjoyed the simplicity of being a life coach during the week and teaching Reiki one weekend per month. It was a good blend for me whilst I learned to balance my workload around school hours and settled into being a full-time mum and our new lifestyle. Except that something major had changed. My work no longer felt arduous, it no longer felt like 'work'.

It wasn't something I wanted to escape from, it was now something I looked forward to. I was now a round peg in a round hole, helping others, getting great results with a plentiful supply of new clients. I loved supporting them through the changes they were making. This fed the pragmatic, soulful parts of me. Reiki brought the mystical aspect of me to the fore. Having my first Reiki attunement felt like it had opened a magical portal into a whole new world that I had felt was missing but hadn't been able to name. And whilst I couldn't name it, only feel it, it remained a mystery.

So many of my clients' breakthroughs came from my intuition. I now wanted to give it centre stage. I wanted to serve my clients as me, fully me. I was not going to do this by half measures. I was going to be fully in. I had been a master and an apprentice during the sixteen years that I had spent in the corporate sector. I had trained and qualified in a wide variety of skills, techniques, and psychometric evaluation tools. I had benefited from accreditation in facilitation skills and coaching. I knew my stuff, and I was good at it. Now, I was feeling and trusting my intuition. I was finding my way home to my innate gifts that had been walled off and that I had mistrusted for so long.

I did my own thing, and it worked. I blended some key coaching models with my intuition, and I began each session with the client's immediate need and led with that. I discovered that one of the most valuable exercises to do with clients was to help them to understand their personal and work values. Once they had a good grasp of these, they could more easily discern what was in or out of alignment for them. It would help them understand how to optimise the success and fulfilment of their lives. It seemed so simple, and yet it was fundamental.

The Reiki weekends provided a good contrast in my working rhythms. I thrived on variety in those days, and I was totally enthralled and delighted by the positive changes my Reiki students were experiencing. So, whilst my intuition, deep listening and questioning skills were at work with my coaching clients, and with my Reiki students, it was the attunements that were creating the inner change. It felt like magic to me. There was very little to be done. My training to become a Reiki Master had been relatively quick, progressing through the four levels within a year to become qualified. I had assumed that I would offer in-person healing sessions – however, it didn't quite work out like that. I was receiving requests to teach before I had even completed the training. And so it was that I taught Reiki but rarely gave in-person sessions. Clients came from all walks of life and professions, and there was a blend of men and women.

After two years, I began to feel restless, and I became interested in the art of channelling spirit messages. I'd had several channelled readings. They all suggested that I had the capacity to be a great channel, but none of them could tell me when, how, or what I had to do to unblock or activate to experience it. I became a little obsessive, as was my way back then. I began reading books and listening to audio cassettes about how to channel but nothing seemed to be happening. In my daily meditation I would ask for help, sometimes bargaining to try to have my way. Of course, it didn't work. It was a long time before I learned that my agenda and timescales were not always in line with that of my Soul. When I pushed for something to happen, it rarely did. I'd push harder, exhausting all possible avenues until I learned to surrender and let go. I didn't know it at the time, but my Soul was teaching me the art of allowing, patience, and Divine timing.

I booked onto a two-day 'learn to channel' course in London. It promised that within two days, I would be able to channel my spirit guide. Great, I thought. Job done. I can let go now.

And, of course, that was when the magic happened. Three days before I was due on the course, I began to hear a clear voice speaking to me through my left ear. There was information for my grandmother which, when I passed it on to her, brought her to tears. She never explained what the message referred to or meant and I never asked her, but it was clear that it had touched her deeply.

There were some direct, detailed suggestions about how to re-invent my business, inviting me to blend my energy-healing skills with the telephone coaching. I wasn't sure that I was brave enough yet to reveal to some of my coaching clients that I was also a Reiki Master. At first, that seemed potentially too weird and 'woo-woo'. I did feel brave enough, however, to implement the suggestions two weeks later, and the results both surprised and delighted me and my clients. It took their transformations to a whole new level. It was also suggested that I pay special attention to how to channel messages for others when I was on the course because this was to become a third string to my business bow.

The course itself was pragmatic and well-structured. There was little mysticism involved, simply a step-by-step formula to follow to support us in being able to open to channel our spirit guide. I hadn't appreciated that I was facilitating my Reiki students to do this when I was attuning them; I was helping them to channel universal life force energy through their hands. This course was opening our ability to *hear* Spirit. This was new to me. I had seen colours, symbols, and faces, but I'd not heard messages, not up until that point.

The teacher came over to each of us to check how we were getting on. There were thirty of us and I was impressed at how she was teaching. I shared with her the messages that I had received that morning. Her immediate response was to say that it must be my mind, not Spirit, that I was engaging with. She suggested that I was too new to this to be receiving the content that I showed her. I then showed her a message that I had received for her. I couldn't possibly have known the content previously. She thanked me and apologised. She then received a message for me and passed it on. It confirmed something I had been told earlier that week by my spirit guide. I smiled and thanked her too.

I began to offer channelled readings within a week of the course, firstly to people I knew well and then more widely until they became a staple of my offerings. Within a year, though, I began to feel uneasy. I was already inviting clients to be discerning in the guidance I was offering, to take what resonated and leave the rest. There was a growing number of clients, however, who regularly and frequently asked for readings, and this didn't sit well with me. They were now relying on me to give them answers and to help them make decisions. They were giving their power away. I have always been passionate about empowering others. After some contemplation, I decided to phase out this aspect of my work. The readings were bringing in a third of my income, but something didn't feel right – it felt off.

I began to get curious about other healing modalities and very quickly booked myself onto training courses. Firstly, I qualified as a Resonance Repatterning practitioner. I had been having a challenging time with a particular situation and just one session from a practitioner had transformed it. I could immediately feel the benefit to me and knew that I wanted to be able to do this for myself and for clients too.

Resonance Repatterning is an emerging field of alternative therapy which focuses on clearing the non-coherent or limiting emotional and mental patterns which adversely influence our beliefs, behaviour, and quality of life. These non-coherent patterns are held within the physical structure of our body or aura at a vibrational frequency level. Through the repatterning process and the use of muscle checking, a practitioner can identify the limiting beliefs and memories of earlier experiences behind current-day challenges and causes of distress. These can then be cleared using a healing modality such as colour, sound, or breathwork therapy. Once the limiting or non-coherent pattern is cleared, a new positive, more life-enhancing one is anchored.

This was revolutionary for me and for my clients. It meant that there was a way of not attracting the same old experiences into our lives, that we could positively influence what we attracted. If we no longer resonated, for example, with the driver of 'try harder, be perfect', it could no longer have a grip on us. It brought freedom.

My 'not good enough' voice had been getting louder, and it significantly softened and quietened using this method. I was hooked. I loved it too because it gave me the clues as to what was going on in my unconscious self, where in my mind-body system it was stored, and a means to transform or dissolve it. It felt like a miracle. I was hooked, and my drive to find relief from all the beliefs that held me back had me doing sessions for myself almost daily. I became a little obsessed, as was my way at the time. My clients loved the system and the results they received from it too. They often referred to it as 'that magic thing you do'. I still use it today, and it has been the inspiration for many healing systems that I have channelled and worked with.

I was having fun. Work felt more like creative play than work. My curiosity and intuition led me to further train and qualify in colour therapy, colour puncture, Earth astrology and light-body activation. I became interested in esoteric practices too. I immersed myself into the stories of the Goddess. This was new to me, yet I felt a strong resonance. I went on to qualify in a system called Magnified Healing, which has the Goddess Kwan Yin as its leading energy.

And then everything changed. Again. I began to spontaneously draw symbols and receive information on a course that I was to create and run. I was being invited by my guides to create a whole new healing energy system based on the wisdom lineage of the Goddess, that of Sophia, Mother Mary, Mary Magdalene, Kwan Yin, and Isis. I was given the name 'Lumi-N-Essence' for the course. I had a real sense that the vibe of this new course emerging was very different to my coaching work. I took the bold step of putting the coaching on hold. I instinctively knew that I would need three months to fully channel and develop this new creative baby and that I would do it over the summer.

I was so confident that I could complete the design of the course within that time that I even booked a venue, set a date, and began selling spaces on the course before I had completed its design. Once I had created space and fully committed, the information that I needed landed quickly. It was to be a full daily spiritual practice plus a new method of sending remote healing energy to others. A level two course began to reveal itself quickly too, and within five months, I had a three-tier programme.

Level One served to connect women to the feminine Yin aspect within themselves and with the sacred feminine energy of the archetypal wisdom Goddesses.

Level Two helped to balance the Yin and the Yang energy within.

Level Three connected women to the fiery power of the dragon energy of the Earth and to the starry aspect of the Cosmos, above and below.

It was very popular and served over two hundred women over the two years that I ran it. It was only after the three levels had been written that I could see the intelligence at work behind the scenes. My mind could never have conceived such a course. Each piece of each level ingeniously building one upon the other.

It was my first experience of what I now call 'creative manifestation' where a new creative baby calls my attention and lands step by step in its fullest expression versus me deciding to develop something. It feels like a magical process. I have since created many courses and two oracle decks in this way. This book is another example of it. I hadn't set out to write a book of my own experiences however this is what wanted to be expressed through me.

My business was about to change again. Something new was on the horizon.

PS If you would like to know more about creative manifestation, I share more about this process through social media and on my website. It is also the focus of a new card deck which I am in the process of developing.

Three Male Catalysts

Moriah,

There will be three male catalysts in your awakening.
One will wake and shake you.
One will connect you with your fire energy.
One will help you over the finishing line.

You will meet the first and the last in a sacred garden.
They will both sing the song 'Yellow' to you.
You will recognise all of them from another time.
All are soul mates, none of them will be relationship material in this lifetime.
Their sacred contract is to catalyse you.
Nothing more.
Nothing less.

Love and hugs x

PS You will forget all of this until you remember.

You're Not Here to Fit In

Until I discovered The Numerology of Moses and the Soul Contract work that stems from it, I had been living and working pretty much blindfolded in relation to my purpose and destiny. That said, I had been doing pretty well, all things considered, and yet I hadn't been able to make true sense of my life, my purpose, the world, and my place in it. I hadn't yet been able to piece it all together. It was like I had the pieces of the mosaic and yet I couldn't fathom how they all pieced together to make the glorious, colourful, coherent design.

Finding the numerology and the soul contract body of work that stems from it, was like a bright light had illuminated my world. Things about my inner workings that had been hidden from me were clear for me to see. All at once, my blind spots were revealed, the context for my life made clear, reasons behind my motivations given. My struggles suddenly made sense even though there was still some pain in acknowledging them. I suddenly saw how I only felt at home in certain situations and roles and why I had tried so hard to fit in.

I recognised my talents as true gifts rather than oddities, and I could now appreciate how I could really hone them. My gifts were primarily associated with energy, creativity, alignment, emotional intelligence, and connection to Spirit – no wonder then that others in the corporate environment had struggled to see how I fitted. My gifts were needed but not yet acknowledged as needed. I finally understood what my purpose was for this lifetime. I could see how it all fitted together. How and where I fitted in relation to the greater scheme of things.

It had taken 44 years to understand, to reach this point of clarity.

I wasn't here to fit in.

I was here to bring something very old to the world, presented in a new, contemporary way. I would be ahead of my time in my thinking. I would have to totally disentangle myself from the karmic patterns of disempowerment, resisting intuition, ignoring the call of Spirit, and not trusting myself or life. I would need to find ways to allow and foster my sensitivity without tipping into overwhelm. I would need to find ways to ground my Soul's energy into my physical form and most of all I would need to recognise, finally, that my power lies within me. And that I am here to share my embodied learning with others as a teacher, mentor, facilitator.

It was revelatory for me. So much clarity, context and truth all rolled into one. In just one hour, it had explained what a lifetime of searching, musing, stumbling, and experimenting had not. Having my soul contract read was probably one of the most profound and revelatory moments of my life.

And all this information held within the numerology of our birth certificate name. Encoded. Embedded. It is the sum of the choices and contracts that we made at a Soul level prior to incarnation. All hidden in plain sight, just waiting to be discovered.

It all came about as a result of me seeing an advert in a magazine for a course on soul contracts. I had been magnetically drawn to book my place on it without knowing much of the detail. The course itself was not for another three months' time and I didn't think much about it until I got a call to come and have my soul contract read. I wasn't sure what to expect, and so I decided to drive the ninety minutes in person to listen to what they were going to share.

Having my soul contract read not only changed my life from a perspective of my own understanding of my Design, but it also significantly informed the work that I went on to offer. I trained and qualified in all three levels. To date, sixteen years later, I still regularly give soul contract readings to clients and enjoy it immensely. Their charts come to life as I immerse myself into the reading. I experience it now in a fifth-dimensional way. I can see the numbers and energies on their charts start to dance. I see all the interconnections. I hear, sense, taste, feel what their Soul is wanting to impart and transmit on the day of their reading. It really is quite magical.

I also love extending the work beyond the individual into relationship readings, business names, children's charts, and whole family constellations. I have developed a speciality in name optimisation work, in helping clients to create a new name for themselves that aligns with their soul's evolutionary path. I did this for myself several years after completing my qualification in this work.

I have lost count of the readings that I have done over the years, each one unique to the individual and all of them such a sacred joy to facilitate. It is still one of my very favourite things to do. I even had a whole year as an agony aunt for a national magazine, offering solutions to the readers' problems, simply by knowing their birth certificate name.

When my mum had completed several months of research into our family tree, I ran the names of the women and their husbands' names through the soul contract software. What I found astonished me. The women were all running the same karmic patterns. Six generations of my female ancestors in my maternal line, all of us working through issues around disempowerment and disconnection. With no daughters, I was here at the end of the line to transmute and transform the karma and turn it into ancestral gold. When I looked at the men whom I had been in relationship with, they all turned out to have the same soul destiny number. I could see how my Soul was wanting to work something through by being with these men. I could also see the opportunities and exchanges at a soul level that we each held for the other. I was totally fascinated. It still humbles me even after all this time.

Understanding my soul contract helped me to understand myself in ways that no other psychometric tool or channelled reading had ever done. It is still what I return to regularly when something happens in my life that I need some understanding and context for. It has informed my personal growth, explained my life choices and been a great source of joy and comfort.

I had finally understood how and where I fitted. I finally knew where I belonged. And there was a great deal of peace in that knowledge.

The Soul Speaks
of *Boundlessness*

You belong to the moon and the stars,
to the Earth and the Sky,
to the seas and to the wild winds,
to the elements.

You belong to no one.
No one can own you.
Just as you can own no one.

Pinning anyone or anything down is tantamount to a slow death,
Stagnation at best.
It drains the essence of life,
Squashes potential,
And blocks expressive flow.

Let your touch be light.
Let your love be without condition.
let your love be all it can possibly be.
And relish each day,
each moment,
as it happens,

when it happens,
and how it happens.

Boundless.

I Said YES!

Part Two

In the late summer of 2006, my parents came to stay with us to help take care of our sons whilst I was away. I was going to be flying down to the Pyrenees in southern France, to run a women's retreat, and my husband was going to be working.

My parents had been busy clearing their house for some time. They were selling their home of decades – the one my brother and I grew up in – and were heading north to be closer to other family members. They were downsizing and so quite naturally wanted to clear out anything they no longer wanted to hold onto.

Mum brought the only thing that she still had of mine – my wedding dress. I was stunned to see it. I hadn't thought much about it for years and it hadn't crossed my mind that they would need to hand it back to me when they moved. I have to say that I felt a little sick when she handed it over, and I remembered the strange knowing I'd had all those years ago that it should stay with her. I took it upstairs in readiness for it to go into the loft over the weekend whilst I was away.

It was the same weekend that saw a crack begin to develop in our bedroom wall.

'I Don't Like Who You've Become.'

This was the bolt out of the blue that my husband greeted me with one evening before bedtime.

He went on to explain that the previous three weeks that he had just taken off work were not due to job-related stress, as he had told me, but to the inner turmoil he had been feeling in relation to our marriage.

I was in shock. I had no inkling that he had been feeling like this. I had no idea that he was considering ending our marriage. In all the years we had been together, separation had never crossed my mind. I had felt settled and sure of the future, our future together. My whole body was shaking on the inside as I took in his words. My stomach was turning knots, and there was an intense pain in my heart. My head could not comprehend what he was saying, but my body was streets ahead and giving me feedback. I felt instantaneously sick and dizzy. My mind was racing. My head was thumping. I could feel the blood coursing through my whole body. My whole reality crashing all around me. I had not seen this coming. It was a true 'bolt out of the blue'.

My instinctive reaction was to ask what he needed or wanted from me for it to be OK. This was my default setting, if you will, back in those days. Pleasing others, bending over backwards to fit in, making things OK, being the good girl who didn't rock the boat and who put her own needs last. It didn't even cross my mind that his words were hurtful, confusing or had come as a complete surprise. My immediate response was that I was in the wrong and that I would have to change for things to be OK. Anything for a quiet life. Ultimately, as I only fully, consciously understood several years on, this instinctive response was to ensure that I could keep myself safe.

And so, I asked: 'How could we meet each other in the middle?'

He wanted me to go back to being the version of me whom he had married. A wife who had a corporate job, organised childcare for our sons, and who did not bring her spiritual beliefs and books into our home. And he wanted me to pull out of co-running the women's retreat in the French Pyrenees the following month. It seemed there was no middle ground in his eyes.

I could hear the pain in his voice and see the torment he was in, and I acknowledged this. I could see how deeply he felt this.

And at the same time, I knew in my gut that all these demands were simply not negotiable. I couldn't reverse the transformation that had been going on for these past six years. I couldn't and wouldn't. It was perhaps the first time in our marriage that I was not prepared to compromise.

I was stunned. I couldn't deny that in the nineteen years we had been together, I had changed significantly. Motherhood helped me evolve into an emotionally intelligent woman. I no longer led with my head. The complementary and spiritual courses and work I was engaged in had helped my soul-full self to flourish. I was now heart-centred, and Soul led. My husband didn't share my spiritual beliefs, which wasn't an issue for me, but I could now clearly see that it was for him. Things had to be tangible for him; he wasn't spiritual or religious, and so my transformation was a step too far for him to contend with.

I was now a more soulful, creative, empathic woman who was happiest nurturing our family and home and following my soulful, creative business path. I had also become so much more empowered and stood my ground more than ever before. I knew what I wanted. I was in touch with my intuition, and I followed it without hesitation. I had switched to a new way of navigating both my life and my work.

My husband was a practical, pragmatic man, and the stress of his emotional response to me was clouding the realities of our situation. I responded by pointing out the practicalities. There were no corporate jobs locally. A long commute was not a practical option for both of us, given he already had an hour-long drive to work. There was no local childcare available. I was the primary carer for our sons. I took care of school runs, homework, housework, food shopping, after-school activities, most of the cooking, and the practical and emotional running of the home. It wasn't a viable option for me to work full-time in a corporate role. We were living in a rural community now, not a large town close to business parks or an easy commute into London as was the case six years previously. I acknowledged too that I was so long out of that environment that I was out of touch and not tech-savvy enough. That time of my life had passed. That woman had left the building long ago.

I affirmed gently that the retreat would go ahead as planned. Everyone had paid, everything was booked, and my co-facilitator was relying on me. It was not an option to cancel.

I agreed that I would make a concerted effort to increase my income, although deep down, I knew that income wasn't the fundamental issue here. My 'spiritual' perspective was at the core of this dilemma for him. I agreed to remove a few items from around the house which hinted at spirituality which were offending him.

I could not and would not go back to being who I was 18 years ago. I was changed beyond measure. For now, the conversation seemed to calm the stormy waters. It felt like a big release had happened for him. He felt acknowledged, heard, and respected, and he thanked me, kissed me goodnight and switched off the bedside lamp.

But the nuclear bomb had exploded.

The Labyrinth Speaks
All of You is Welcome

Nothing to prove.

Nothing to declare.

Nothing to change.

Just as you are.

From the day you were born,

From the moment you took your first breath

And until you take your last.

All of you.

All of you is welcome here.

The Tale of The Labyrinth, The Void & Rennes Le Chateau

Part One

In May 2007, I ran a retreat in the beautiful foothills of Rennes le Chateau in the southwest of France. The sacred intent woven directly into the retreat was to connect participants more deeply with their Masculine and Feminine energies, both human and Divine. It ran over a four-day period from 4th to 7th May, at the time of Beltane and a full moon so that we could harness the energies of Union even more potently. We stayed at a beautiful retreat centre which was well situated for sacred pilgrimages and journeys around the region.

The combination of all these factors was heady and yet it didn't occur to me that it might be an immensely significant weekend for me too. I had every faith that the retreat itself would reap rich rewards for those taking part and that I would grow as a facilitator for holding space for their transformation. Yet I did not expect the magic of the unfolding that sent turbulent ripples through my life for a decade or more.

The clues were all there. I can see them as I look back now. I had always had big energy shifts when I ran workshops founded in spirituality and inner growth. I had already felt my nerve and commitment being tested on the weeks leading up to the retreat, with two remaining spaces to be filled just ten days before we were due to fly. We had four participants which paid for all our expenses. The final two participants would mean that myself and a friend who had offered to help run it with me, would receive an income from it too. The final two people booked just seven days beforehand, creating a flurry of activity right up until the final evening.

As we boarded the plane early on Friday morning, I heard a voice inside my head say, 'Your life will never be the same again.' I had a head full of details I needed to attend to on the flight and didn't think much of it other than a flutter of excitement in my tummy. I also think my spiritual ego was doing a little jig imagining a life of adventure and high demand for retreat goers. Little did I know what was about to unfold.

We all arrived at the retreat centre and settled into our rooms. We had allowed time for us all to explore the sacred spaces inside and out. I had co-run a women's retreat there just nine months previously, and so it was familiar to me. This time around, I was running the event with a new friend who had approached me to ask if she could co-facilitate. We had a strong connection with each other and the theme of the retreat, and I knew it would be fun and supportive to share the responsibility together.

This was a very special place with a strong creative and spiritual energy. As I walked around the perimeter, I could sense the energies of Mary Magdalene very clearly. I could feel a strong, grounded, deeply Feminine beauty permeating the air. The land felt intensely healing and it felt like I had come Home. The red of the soil was especially stunning in the hot spring sunshine. I could feel my body begin to relax and let go of the admin details I had been working on in my head, and I lay on the grass and let my body be held by the Earth, letting go of the stress of the previous few days and weeks, letting myself land here in this most sacred of places.

I would trust the weekend to unfold as it was meant to be for everyone's highest good.

I would trust myself and the process.

I would trust that I would be held and guided all the way.

The Tale of the Labyrinth, The Void & Rennes le Chateau

Part Two

We gathered for lunch together in the early afternoon. It was the first time that all of us had met and had a chance to chat. The food and conversation were nourishing, and everyone settled into the group well. Everything and everyone were in full flow. When lunch had come to its natural end, we moved into the large lounge where we would hold our group sessions. It was a beautiful space with high ceilings, wooden floors and natural fibre carpets, curtains, and soft furnishings. The fresh flowers added colour and aroma whilst the candles created a warm glow.

Once everyone was seated and comfortable, I led a brief meditation to help ground us all and bring our energies in to focus on the retreat. I then invited each person to introduce themselves, including their hopes and wishes for the weekend. Some wanted to attract a soulmate relationship, some to have a peaceful, soulful experience.

I moved anti-clockwise around the circle, beginning with the females and closing with the male. As I turned to face him and invited him to share, I began to have a very physical sensation of shaking in my body. Shivers were running head to toe, I turned cold as ice, and my hands felt very clammy. And then something quite extraordinary happened. In front of my eyes, I could see what looked like an old camera strip of negatives, except instead of being brown, it was in full colour. Tiny square-shaped visual shots of different times in my life, past and present, that I recognised and some that I didn't. It sounds cheesy, but it was as if my life were flashing in front of my eyes. It moved left to right and then right to left. It was all so very fast. It felt like this went on for a long time, and yet, it was probably no longer than sixty seconds or so.

I had no idea what was going on. I could still hear the male talking but I was barely able to hold his words in my head. I was, however, catching the gist and energy of what he was sharing. The images stopped as suddenly as they had started. I felt alarmed and confused. I didn't know how to make sense of what was happening. I'd had a similar experience during dream time a few years previously, but not like this and not in waking hours.

I could feel that my energy field had expanded. I felt like I was suddenly huge with a great wide-open space all around me that I was now filling. My heart felt more open, and I felt flooded with love. And then I remembered. I had felt this flavour of love before when the Magdalene energy came through me during meditation and for clients. This was Divine love. The colour I associated it with was pale pink and this was all around me like a blanket whilst the heady and fragrant rose scent filled my senses.

This man had openly talked about his connection with the work of the Mary Magdalene energy over lunch and I could only imagine that he was a conduit through which the energy was channelling, through him to me. It seems that he was a catalyst to help me grow in some way. The crown chakra at the top of my head felt as though it had been blown wide open, and one of the participants told me later that evening that they saw a bright white light shining down into it and through my body. As soon as he stopped talking, my body returned to normal, and it was as if nothing had happened.

The Tale of the Labyrinth, The Void & Rennes le Chateau

Part Three

The time had come to walk the Labyrinth. It was Sunday, our third day on retreat, and it was the highlight that everyone had been looking forward to. We began our day gently with a nourishing breakfast and then moved into the main lounge to settle into a deep meditation to meet the consciousness of the Labyrinth. Many received insights into the very personal reasons why they were drawn to the retreat at that time. Others received clarity on the sacred intent with which they were going to walk the pathways later that day. I led the meditation for the group, including my co-facilitator friend, so that she too could receive. The group fell into silence and stillness as the energies built during the meditation. It felt like we were all deepening, dropping downwards as if in deep, dark space. Spacious. Velvety rich. Fathomless. Expansive. Endless. Boundless.

It was an energy that I was becoming familiar with. The Void. It felt familiar, similar to the years of work I had done accessing the Cosmic Archive, and yet this was different. The Cosmic Archive felt literally that – cosmic – somewhere out there, above, beyond, but this felt different. It felt like a dropping inside of myself, as into a well. It felt personal and expansive all at once. I was very conscious of holding the space for the group, and at the same time, I had an experience of dropping down. Yes, that was it, a dropping-down sensation in my own body. Like a lead weight falling from my heart downwards. Dropping down deeply into my base chakra, my perineum and into my hips and pelvis. At this time, this experience of being or feeling energy in my lower body was quite new. It felt good. I could feel my body relaxing, shoulders dropping, face softening, jaw loosening. I could feel my feet tingling and buzzing in a way that I had never experienced before.

We stayed in this meditative space for around forty minutes, and then it was time to gently call each person back to their conscious awareness. It took a while for everyone to return to waking consciousness. They had gone so very deep that it took time and care to help them come back into their bodies. We had tea and cake available and allowed for an extra half an hour for them to journal, stretch, walk, and share experiences with their fellow Labyrinth walkers and us as facilitators.

It was now late morning, and we invited everyone to prepare for their experience with the Labyrinth. We talked briefly about how we were going to facilitate the afternoon and each person's walk. We invited them to write down their sacred intent and to help with the creation of the Labyrinth if they felt called to. Whilst my friend went out onto the field to begin laying the pattern of the Labyrinth, I remained in the retreat centre and answered questions, gave some individuals healing, and checked in on the arrangements for lunch.

In the early afternoon, preparations were complete, and we were all ready to begin the main event.

As was the sacred tradition of pilgrims, we took time to wash and cleanse our feet. Just alongside the retreat house ran *le Ruisseau de Couleurs* – the River of Colours. The name of the centre itself translated as 'the cleansing place', and there were tales of Mary Magdalene having lived and preached in the area after she had fled the Holy Land and landed in southern France. It was more of a babbling brook than a river, however, it was very picturesque. Imagine large rocks with smaller ones scattered on the riverbed. The tall, leafy trees overhanging the river offered shade in the warm spring sunshine. The birdsong accompanied us. We all stepped into the river and paired up to wash each other's feet, as was the custom in ancient times. There was much laughter and fun, and it created a lightness of being for everyone involved. As each person stepped out of the river, my friend and I took it in turns to dry their feet and to massage spikenard oil onto the underside of their feet, directly onto the chakra energy points. And then we did the same for each other.

Once complete, we walked barefoot back across the red earth of the land to the field where the Labyrinth awaited.

The order of walking had already been chosen by each participant drawing a piece of paper from a velvet bag which held a number, one to six. My friend and I would walk last.

Those not walking sat at intervals around the Labyrinth and bore witness to all that was unfolding.

My friend and I took turns in holding the space. As each Labyrinth walker arrived at the entrance to the sacred pathway inwards, we would ask them to pause and answer two questions.

'What is your sacred intent?'

'Are you ready?'

And then, one by one, each of the participants took their turn.

Some sang, some carried a special talisman or crystal with them, some had created a headdress of flowers that they had gathered from the garden and the wild hedgerows. Some had drawn oracle cards earlier that day and chose to bring these with them. One woman carried a letter that she had written to herself, which she later burned that evening. Although it was a group event, it was also a deeply personal experience for each of us once it came to walking the Labyrinthine pathways. Some hesitated at certain points, some had emotional releases, some had insights. It felt a very special and sacred initiation to witness and be a part of. I felt privileged and grateful.

As the afternoon wore on, it became clear that we were running later than we had planned. Understandably, each person was taking the time they needed for their individual walk. It was getting close to supper time, and it was clear that we were not going to complete our day before we all sat down to eat. We agreed that three of us would walk after dinner. It was all in flow, we trusted that implicitly. So once the five women had completed their turns, we returned to the main house to eat the food which had been lovingly prepared for us. There was a lot of talking and laughter during our meal. The sharing of experiences, the insights, the feelings all combined into a magical evening meal.

It was seven o'clock in the evening when we arrived back at the

Labyrinth. The light was already beginning to fade, and we had been given a handheld lantern each. There was something very mystical and magical being part of the procession of the eight of us making our way, one by one, holding our lanterns in front of us as we made the journey once more to the field. We had all agreed that we would walk to the Labyrinth in silence, somehow that felt important and significant. And so, our silent, candlelit procession to the Labyrinth began. The sense of anticipation was palpable. Magic was in the air for sure. Once we arrived back at the sacred symbol, everyone took their places, and we began the final walks. I was to take my turn last.

By the time it was my turn to walk, it was dark. It was a truly magical scene. There was a candlelit Labyrinthine pathway awaiting me. The lights up ahead on the mountainside from the village of Rennes le Chateau shone and flickered in the distance. The stars were out in the midnight blue sky, and there was a full moon. There was a chill in the air and yet I didn't feel cold. I remember feeling a deep sense of peace coupled with a hint of anticipation. I went at my own pace, paused when I sensed it was the right thing for me, felt the energetic shifts at certain points and felt elated as I walked out of the Labyrinth. I had goosebumps all through the experience. It felt a very sacred experience and I felt distinctly different by the time I had completed the walk. I felt expanded, altered, more grounded. Although we hadn't planned to still be walking it in the dark, I was grateful that I had had the chance to.

As I walked the sacred pathways, there was a familiarity to them, and I had a strong sense that I had done this before – or was it that I had already planned this before birth? It could have been one or the other or both. It was a little like the experience of déjà vu. I wondered what the significance was to be walking it in the dark as opposed to daylight. It only dawned on me much later that I was walking it in the dark as an initiation into the Void and that the darkness was a metaphor for the personal Shadow work that was on the horizon for me.

Once complete, we gathered in a circle, held hands, and said a prayer of gratitude for our day together, for the Labyrinth and for the transformations that would surely unfold. As facilitators, we closed the energy of the day and left the Labyrinth on the field as the owners had asked us to. They wanted the energetic imprint of it to take hold on the Earth there. We then gathered our lanterns and walked back to the main house together. Once inside, we were served cake and hot chocolate to help warm and ground us. Some stayed up to chat, some journaled, and some went to bed. It had been a beautiful day, a powerful day. Sleep would help us integrate the energetic shifts.

Only time would reveal the changes yet to manifest.

The Tale of the Labyrinth, The Void & Rennes le Chateau

Part Four

When I returned home from the retreat, I was not the same woman who had left four days earlier.

In just one look, one exchange, this male had given me such a powerful, soulful transmission that it had blown my heart and energy field wide open. There was something so familiar about his presence. I discovered much later that we'd had past lives together. It was the remembrance of this that had been sweet yet so utterly confusing all at once.

On the second day, as we were leaving the chapel in Rennes le Chateau, he briefly touched my shoulder, very lightly, gently and said the words, 'You don't have to do this alone.'

He had hooked into an unconscious need or desire of mine to have someone to understand me, see me and appreciate me and the work that I was being called to carry out in the world. At home, my husband referred to it as 'woo-woo', which on many levels, I lived with because I respected his point of view. This man had just revealed how I was feeling beneath all my logical, good-girl responses. He understood the work I was doing, and even more than that, I could see just how dynamically creative he was. He followed his Soul's calling. He trusted his intuition and acted swiftly upon it. There were no filters or brakes as far as I could tell as I observed him that weekend. He lived his life in full colour, and it reminded me of the vision that had landed with me when I first began my business just seven years beforehand. He was showing me just how magical and exciting life could be when you live in this way.

I didn't want or expect my husband to share my beliefs or to become 'spiritual'. Instead, I now recognised that I wanted to have the freedom to explore my spirituality. I also wanted to be loved and accepted for the woman I was becoming. And this was the conversation that I took back with me and opened with my husband. The very part of me that he did not value or welcome had been noticed and acknowledged by another. I wanted to know whether he could find it within himself to meet me halfway or whether it was just a step too far.

In the end, despite our very best intentions and efforts, the cracks became too pronounced to paper over, and we couldn't seem to find our way through. The emotional defence wall that had built up all around me had now been smashed wide open. The next level of emotional connection had been freed up and activated. This, coupled with the Labyrinth Walk into the Void, would indeed change my life but not in the way I had imagined or hoped. It was the beginning of a plunge into the deepest, darkest parts of me.

The voyage into my own underworld had begun, and there was no going back.

I Changed My Name

2008

Oh my, it was a BIG Thing. A giant step that felt exciting, slightly daunting, and at the same time, it felt like the most natural next step that I could take. It felt liberating and ever so slightly scary.

I was nervous about how others might react, whether I'd be seen as 'woo-woo'. I knew that this was a part of my unbinding from overly caring what other people thought of me. It was part of the letting go and shedding of the good girl programming and the part of me that wanted so badly to fit in and be conventional.

It's not that I didn't like my name – I loved the name Catherine, and my surname was my married name at the time, and I liked that too. It linked me to my husband, our sons and my in-law family as well.

In many ways, it was a curious thing to do, changing my name. After all, I had spent much of my life wanting to *belong*, consciously or unconsciously. I wanted to be a part of a tribe. My husband's family had welcomed me into their clan without hesitation, and here I was considering letting go of the name that I had happily taken on twenty years earlier.

Why did I do it?

The truth is, my Soul made me do it!

Ha, ha,

Well, in part, it's true.

Looking back, I would say that it was a complex and multi-layered decision-making process that I went through before I could feel OK with a name change. It was one of those situations that I found myself in then and since when I felt what I would now recognise and name as a *Calling*. It felt like I was being propelled by an energy not of my own making, or as if I were being pulled forwards by an invisible cord. It was powerful, insistent, and mystical.

Then there was *instinct*. It was an embodied knowing deep in my gut and in my bones. It felt like I was always meant to do this.

And finally, if I ever needed any more persuasion, there was an indisputable body of *evidence* that had been gently yet persistently amassing through my consultations with clients over the previous eighteen months.

I had fully trained and qualified as a practitioner of The Numerology of Moses two years earlier. I had trained both in personal and business numerology as well as in how to change and optimise a name. I had seen just how accurate and powerful the system was through my own personal exploration of the numerology. It was clear to see in my soul contract as well as in my work with clients.

Still, it took me three months or so to come to terms with the possibility of changing my name once the idea had landed. I wouldn't say I resisted it; however, I did allow myself the time I needed to let the decision 'arrive' rather than 'push' it. In many ways it was a 'no brainer', and yet it was a big deal. A very big deal. As much as I tried to get my head around why I felt this innate urge to make the change, I could also feel that, at some other level, the decision was already made. It was waiting for me to catch up and get fully on board with it. It was the human part of me that was trying so hard to make sense of it, bargaining with it even. If I were going to do this thing, I decided that I would be happy to change anything but not my first name, Catherine, which I felt very attached to. I really liked my first name and didn't want to give it up. So, I made a pact with myself – or perhaps more likely, my Soul – that I would change anything but not Catherine.

Of course, it didn't quite work out that way. I tried hard to find a name that worked, a name that had the right combination of numbers, energies, and possibilities, but it wasn't falling into place. I concluded that I was being invited to let go of my whole identity as Catherine. Forty-five years of embodying a name and, moreover, a name that I loved.

So, I set clear intentions about what I wanted to experience more of, less of, and a balance of in my life, together with a list of energies and corresponding numbers that I knew I needed. I was also very clear that I didn't want an overly 'spiritual' name.

And with that, I let go.

I let go of the worrying.

I let go of needing it to be a certain way.

I surrendered. I gently let it go and softened into a state of grace and receptivity.

And that's when the magic began to work.

Names began to appear, one by one, month by month.

Gently, gently, like the most delicate of feathers dropping out of the sky and into place.

In January 2008, my new surname made itself known. It came about during a conversation with a client one day. It was at the end of her session, and we were laughing about something that had emerged from our work together and she called me the archetypal optimist. I laughed and replied something along the lines of, 'Yes, I live in perpetual hope.' And there it was.

Hope.

I really liked this name. It felt like the most natural thing in the world to *adopt* this as my new surname.

My new middle name made itself known in February. I had a feeling for some time that my new middle name would be a *bridge* between the first and the last names. The names that I helped optimise for clients all had a middle name, and all sounded quite lyrical. There had been a distinct rhythm about them, with their first, middle, and last names all having a combination of one, two, or three beats to them. This was a distinct pattern, and I was aware that this was more than likely going to be similar for me.

At this time of my life, I was meditating every day. I kept seeing the beautiful face of Mother Amma in my mind's eye, the spiritual avatar who is also known as the 'hugging saint'. I'd received darshan from her at the end of the previous year when I was initially considering changing my name. When it came to my turn to receive a hug from her, she spoke to me in my right ear, rapidly and in her native tongue, and then released me. Unusually, just as I was about to move away, she called me back to her and hugged me close once more, speaking this time into my left ear, and then brought my face directly in front of hers, cupped my face in her hands, and looked into my eyes for what felt like a very long time. It was a magical moment in time. The love that she embodies and exudes is very special, and I could feel my own energy field responding to hers. The only word that I could make out was Amma. From time to time since that moment, I wondered why she had done that and then it suddenly struck me that perhaps this was the middle name that I had been calling in. I knew that I wouldn't want the same spelling as it would feel too presumptuous and ostentatious to use her name, and so I chose a slightly shorter version which felt just right.

I adopted Ama as my middle name.

It was a further four weeks before my first name made its appearance. I had been actively working with the numerology software, and I was close to losing my patience. My passport was expiring soon too, and I had to renew it so that I could travel in the summer. I didn't have a lot of time to wait for the new name to drop in of its own accord, in its own timing, so I was *pushing*. As always, when I tried to push anything like this, it pushed back, and nothing was happening.

So, I let go, again.

I booked time with another practitioner who was also a friend to see if that would help me land it. Perhaps it was good to have someone hold space for me rather than trying to do it on my own, which had been an old pattern of mine and one that I wanted to let go of. After forty-five minutes of being with her and both of us brainstorming possible names, there was still no new name appearing that I either liked or that worked well numerologically. She went downstairs to make us some tea, and I took the opportunity to sit back in my seat and give it and me some space.

I remember distinctly re-setting the process. I called to my guides, Soul, the Universe, whoever was listening and my ally in my name process, and I told them something along the lines of:

'OK, you guys. No more messing. I've paid for an hour, driven ninety minutes to get here and I need to leave soon to get home in time to do a school run. I am here to discover my new first name. I want to know it NOW.'

And then I heard it. Just like that. Immediately.

I remember the moment so very clearly. It was a male voice in my left ear.

'Moriah.'

The voice enunciated it so well that I understood the spelling even though I had never actually heard of this name before. I immediately tapped the three names together into the software, and there, to my delight – and, to be fair, sheer amazement – was a perfect alignment of numbers and energies, an even better combination than I had imagined.

Moriah Ama Hope.

When I saw the three names together, they looked right.

I have experienced this a lot with my clients ever since too.

It sounded beautiful.

They looked like they were meant to be together.

And in my body, I felt something like a 'penny dropping'.

Ka dunk.

Once home, I began to 'try the new name on'. I would write it out. I sang it. I wrote it on paper notes and had them in different places around the house, in my diary and in my journal. I wrote it on a piece of paper and placed it under a glass of water, speaking my new name directly into the water. I figured I could then drink the vibration of this new name, to get it into my internal systems.

I also began to type the name 'Moriah' into search engines. I learned that it is a derivative of the name Mary and specifically associated with Hebrew. This fascinated me as the numerology I work with is based on the sound of the twenty-two sacred letters of the Hebrew alphabet. There was also a Mount Moriah which had associations with King Solomon's Temple plus Calgary and a host of other biblical, sacred associations. It seemed too that in the USA, the two names of Moriah and Hope were associated with the Baptist movement. Moriah seemed to be synonymous with the quality of Hope. Curiouser and curiouser. In addition, it seemed that there were Baptist churches called 'Moriah Chapels' in south Wales.

It would be a further full twelve years before I discovered that my maternal great-grandfather used to preach in chapels around South Wales where these Moriah Chapels were. This was the same great-grandfather on whose birthday I was born and with whom I share the same soul destiny number and many other synchronicities too. During the writing of this book, a psychic told me, totally unprompted, that my great-grandfather and I share the same soul, we are one and the same. The same soul in two different bodies, for a short while. Who knows? Maybe. Maybe not. Could it be that he preached in the Moriah Chapels? Could it have been his voice that I heard? Was it all coming full circle?

As I began to accept the name, limiting beliefs and doubts appeared. I acknowledged each of them as and when they popped up. Sometimes I used my own transformational techniques to clear them, sometimes I simply allowed them to be swimming around in the mix of my thoughts.

Whilst all of this was happening, something else was bubbling away too. My husband and I had considered taking some temporary time apart. We wanted to give each other space to see if we could come to an agreement on how or if we could move forward together. We decided on three months as a reasonable period to be able to gauge how we both felt. He stayed away for three nights a week and was at home for the remainder. I booked a few weekends away during that time to give him time alone and time with our sons. When it came to the day that we had agreed on to discuss 'Us', I was clear that I wanted to go ahead and change my name. On something as fundamental as this was, I would normally have committed to finding a way to compromise or meet him halfway. On this occasion, however, I felt that if I did this, I would be compromising myself, betraying myself even. And so, I stayed true to myself and did not compromise.

My name change would need to come into the mix of topics to discuss together. This was already a delicate conversation, and my name change was probably not going to be welcome, given it reflected the more spiritual, soulful aspects of my beliefs and work, which had already brought us into conflict. He wasn't keen on the idea, but he agreed not to stand in my way of doing it. He knew that my mind was made up and knew me well enough to know there was little he could do to stop me from following through. He didn't like it, though. It was understandable. I got it. I wouldn't like it either if our perspectives were reversed. Our sons had already given me their blessing to change my name, saying that if it was what I wanted to do, it was OK with them. My husband and I did find our way through to a new phase in our relationship, agreeing that we loved each other still and wanted to find new ways of being together and rekindling our marriage. He never could bring himself to call me by my new first name. I have been 'M' to him ever since.

By early summer, the time had come to start telling family and close friends. I was particularly concerned about upsetting my parents, who had, after all, named and christened me Catherine. Their response was surprising to me.

'We had no idea what to call you when you were born!'

Well, of all the responses I had anticipated from my parents, I hadn't considered this one. I was in my mid-forties, and they had never mentioned that they had trouble deciding upon a name for me! It turned out that my dad had gone to the registry office with three potential first names for me and that it was the Registrar who had chosen my name. My mum didn't know what I was going to be called until my dad arrived home. When I rang them to let them know that I was changing my name, they weren't at all surprised.

In fact, they were delighted. I felt relieved and surprised all at once. How could they not have mentioned this before?

Unfortunately, my in-laws were less in favour of it, and I discovered later that they thought I had joined a cult and were worried that I would change our sons' names too. It wasn't a rational or logical thing to do in their minds, and no amount of explaining could help them get their heads around it other than by considering it to be a 'professional' name, a nom de plume, if you will. In some ways, I was, in their eyes, rejecting their family name. I gave family members an option of continuing to call me by my original name if they had trouble converting. I didn't want to create unnecessary tension, and I was sensitive to everyone's responses.

I sent an email out to friends, clients, and colleagues explaining what I was doing whilst making it clear that I wanted to be called by my new name. Everyone switched. Immediately.

And so it was that on 10th October 2008 (10.10.10) at 10 a.m., I legally changed my name to Moriah Ama Hope via deed poll.

The Labyrinth Speaks
of *Taking Your Time*

Take your time.
There is no rush.

Feel your mind unwind
and the coiled springs relax.

There is no time here, in this space.
Nothing else to do.
Nowhere else to go.
Only here and now.
It is just you and the Labyrinth.
No need for thoughts.
No need for decisions.
Nothing to do other than relax and unwind.
Allow the consciousness of the Labyrinth to do the work,
as it meets your outer edges and travels deeper into your psyche.
It will align you with your purpose,
unlock your potential,
reveal your wisdom,
re-balance your systems.
All you have to do is to show up and be here, now.

Can You See the Vole, Mum?

It was a beautiful, sunny, hot summer's day at the beginning of the school holidays. I had brought my sons to the local wetland centre. They were ten and eight and excited to see the recently released water voles.

We waited our turn and got into the small motorboat that was to take us through the wetlands. The boys loved it. I was trying, and failing, to be fully present, to be fully in the moment for them and for me.

My head was full of 'stuff' to attend to later that day. Food shopping, holiday prep, cooking dinner, the boys' swimming lessons, and an evening client. I felt edgy and fidgety. I tried to switch off the endless chatter in my head, to dial down its volume.

I focused on the voice of the guide telling us stories of the life of a vole and how the centre had reared the water voles to help guard against extinction.

I focused on the boys. I enjoyed the excitement glowing in my sons' eyes and the sheer anticipation of seeing one of these rare creatures. They were fully, completely, wholly engrossed. Captivated. How I longed to be that immersed. Was it a quality of youth, I wondered?

I brought myself back to the surroundings. I felt the sun on my skin, the gentle breeze, the birds singing. I looked intently at the reed bed for the signs that the guide had advised us would indicate a vole family being close by.

I heard his voice fade away, and my mind interrupted again. It was fussing over how I would ever have enough time to get everything done. It was re-scheduling. It was re-organising. Would it work if I re-jigged everything? Had a picnic lunch on the go in the car maybe?

And then I was brought back to Earth with a loud voice. My youngest son shouted.

'Muuuuum! Can you see it? Can you see the water vole, Mum?'

'Aww you missed it!'

He was right. I had missed it.

The 'must try harder' voice ran through my head.

My heart sank.

Fast forward five years. My eldest son was now studying photography. We had recently gifted him a top-of-the-range camera for his birthday. He asked to go to the wetland centre to take some photos for the project he was doing. We packed a bag, hopped into the car, and drove the short distance to the centre. It was a beautiful spring day. Crisp, bright, and sunny. On this occasion it was just the two of us.

We got into the waiting boat and immediately began to immerse ourselves in the wetland landscape. The colours, smells, the wind through the reeds and, of course, the promise of spotting a water vole. And there it was. Right in front of me.

'Look, can you see it?' I said to my son.

It was then that I realised that I had made it. I had made the journey from distraction to presence. From head to heart. And I was truly grateful. Truly.

The Labyrinth Speaks
of *Being Free to Fly*

And you will need to let down your guard,
knock down the walls all around you,
unbind all that has held you safe until this moment of now.
Let it go.
Let it be.
You are ready.
You always have been.

The cage door is open.
It is not locked.
You are free to fly, fly, fly.
Let it be so.

The choice is yours.
Your Life is in your hands.
You held the key all along,
deep within you.

The key to your freedom is waiting. Waiting to be claimed.
Will you claim it now?
Will you?

Dare you?

I Changed Beyond Measure

I changed beyond measure.
My priorities changed.
My relationship with myself and with Life changed.
Values shuffled. Identities fell away.

My heart began to lead the way, and then my Soul came a-calling.
I became a spiritual being rather than a materialistic being.
I placed quality over quantity.
I began to care less about what others thought of me and more about my relationship with myself.
I cared less about accumulating stuff and more about the quality of my inner state.
I came to appreciate what we had as opposed to what we didn't yet have.
I began to appreciate what was enough and to be OK with that.
I began to speak up and stand up for myself.
I began to take up the lead where I'd been happy to follow.
There were things I was no longer willing to tolerate.
I made choices for myself rather than defer to my husband.
I looked within for my answers.
I developed beliefs and perspectives that he didn't share.
I stopped trying to please everyone.
I found my voice.
I reclaimed my power.

I danced with my Shadows and invited them as welcome strangers.
I craved depth.
I craved something I couldn't even quantify.
A yearning so deep within me.
I felt it, yet couldn't quite name it.
A compulsion.
Something was missing.
A hole.
A deep hole.
My hormones began to run wild.
I wasn't the same woman.

I changed a thousand times a day.
Emotions blew through me like some crazy March wind.
I no longer controlled every detail. I had little control. I'd let go.
I relished change. Arms open wide. Heart ablaze. Soul hungry.
There were times when I longed to be broken open.
To feel. To heal. To feel ALIVE.
I changed my name. A Thing. A very BIG Thing.
A defining moment.

Deeply held patterns, drivers, engrained behaviours, and beliefs fell away.
Unlocking, unblocking, and freeing up.
Liberation at a rapid rate.
I couldn't have stopped if I'd tried. This process had a will of its own.
An impulse, a drive so deep within me.
To purge, transmute, transform, keep moving, to be in flow.
A solo dance.
At high speed.
Insatiable.
Unstoppable.
Unapologetic.

I Said YES!

Part Three

In the spring of 2011, I had a total compulsion to make bunting for the garden. It came out of the blue and held my fascination for weeks until I answered its calling and began to search in the loft for appropriate scraps of material to use.

I had a ball pulling it all together. I hadn't engaged in a creative project like this one for years, and it felt good. There was one aspect of the project that was going to require a sewing machine, which I didn't have. My mum, however, did have one and so I decided to combine the completion of the project with a visit to my parents during the boys' Easter school holidays.

As I busied myself with the stitching, I let myself get distracted just for a split second and then got firmly pulled back into concentration when I yelped and realised that the needle had pierced and gone right through the fatty part of my right index finger. I screamed for help, 'Muuum!' in the way my sons' might have done when they were younger.

I felt pathetic; the sight of the needle piercing through my finger had me feeling quite faint but at least I had the presence of mind to take my foot off the pedal that was powering the machine. And whilst all of this was going on, I also heard a very clear voice in my head that said, 'The spell is broken,' and as I looked up from the sewing machine, I caught sight of one of my favourite line drawings of my parents and its name leaped out at me. It was called 'Spellbound'.

I had no idea at the time that in a few short months, I would be bringing my marriage to a close.

It Was Time

August 2011

As I opened, my marriage closed.

It happened slowly over time.
A dissolution of sorts.
A gentle loosening and unravelling,
over five years.
Imperceptibly,
slowly but surely,
the glue holding our marriage together dissolved.
There were no dramatic peaks or troughs.
No reckonings.
Only intermittent hiccoughs, blips, and ravines.
Late-night conversations and weekends away,
reflecting, contemplating, seeking salve.
Neither of us wanting to let 'Us' go.
Both hoping, praying that the love was enough to prevail.
And that the invisible thread that had woven our stories together
in the beginning would continue to work its magic until our final
breath.
Yet it seemed our paths were diverging.

I could feel the pulling apart in my lower body and felt sadness
creep in where contentment had once been.
All our efforts to repair, replenish and refocus anew
could not gain the traction or momentum needed.
We shared our home, our beloved sons, and our history,
yet we no longer shared certain values, priorities, or outlooks.

Our Souls were calling time.

We had completed our contract.

The energy for our belonging was draining away.

The respect and the love remained

yet something indescribable had changed

and it felt beyond Us.

And for me, the only thing harder than leaving was staying because I could not tolerate staying in a marriage where I could not grow and where I wasn't loved for being true to myself.

It was Time.

'Smile, Why Don't You? It Might Never Happen!'

November 2011

This is what I was greeted with one early morning as I was swimming.

Driving to my local pool and completing fifty lengths became a daily ritual in the months after separation. I would stay until I had done the full fifty unless my body suggested otherwise – in which case, I would stop when she was ready. I loved being in water. It was my morning swim that helped to strengthen me not only physically but emotionally too.

I would repeat an affirmation on each stroke. I would do it mindfully. After a while, I began to forget about the sadness and the fears that had kept me awake at night, and I came into a state of presence, which felt such a relief. Looking back, I would say that it felt like an inner state of grace.

One morning, as I rested at the end of the swimming lane in between laps, a woman in the adjacent lane to mine, shouted at me. 'Smile, why don't you? It might never happen!' And then she swam off. Even if she had stayed long enough for me to respond, I don't think I could have done, as by that point, I was in a state of shock. I wanted to scream at her of the pain, the fear, the grief, the guilt, and the confusion that flooded me daily.

How dare she!

That's not my style, though. In any case, I couldn't have responded fast enough even if I had tried.

And then a miracle happened.

I noticed an elderly lady stepping gracefully down the steps into the pool. She was very slight of frame with silver hair. I was drawn to her face. She was looking directly into my eyes. I experienced what I would now call a 'transmission'. Her eyes were gently shining, and all I could feel was immense love, understanding, and compassion.

And then she winked and swam off.

I felt my body relax, and I smiled through my tears. I instantly felt seen and held. On reflection, it may have been the first time I had experienced such true compassion since the breakup. At that time, everything felt so very raw, like a deep flesh wound. In a single moment, she had brought me relief and perhaps even hope.

Although I looked out for her in the weeks that followed, I never saw her again. I had wanted to say thank you and explain just how precious her look and wink had been to me that day.

An Angel in the Supermarket

It was one of those days when sadness was sitting heavily within me. I decided to nip to the shops to get some groceries. At the checkout, I was in a queue behind a man who was dressed as if it were summer even though it was late winter transitioning into early spring. Shorts, open-toed sandals with no socks, open neck shirt and no coat. He was chatting away to the cashier, which suited me fine as I was in no real rush to get home.

He then turned to me, smiled, and introduced himself. 'My name is Michael.'

We had a chat. And then he repeated, 'My *name* is Michael.' Although I noticed how he put an emphasis on the word *name*, I didn't really think any more of it.

He began to tell me about his trip to Egypt and his spiritual awakening. He unbuttoned his shirt even further and lifted a necklace to show me – it was an Egyptian Ankh that he had hand-carved from locally sourced wood. As he began to explain the spiritual significance behind the symbol, I smiled and nodded. He had no idea at that point what I did for a living and that I was familiar with the symbolism. The cashier cast me a knowing look as if to say, 'This one is crazy.' I smiled, listened to his story, and asked questions about his experience. By this point he was paying for his groceries.

Just before he left, he turned to face me once more, looked directly into my eyes and repeated for the third time, 'I am Michael.' And then he left.

That's when the penny dropped. Three times he had told me his name. On the third time of telling me his name, I had shivers running through my whole body. I felt SO cold. I just knew that it was no coincidence that I had bumped into him. He appeared as a messenger. My knowing was so visceral, it was like a penny dropping down through the core of my being into my lower body. Boom! In my work as an energy alchemist, I have come to recognise this cold energy as an angelic presence.

And his eyes looked so very different to earlier in the conversation. They were electric blue and shining, almost piercing.

Earlier that day, I had been meditating and asking for healing and hope. It was a particularly difficult point in our separation, and I was feeling distinctly unsupported. I had forgotten about my request until that moment of realisation in the supermarket. One of the guides that watches over me and works with me is Archangel Michael. The colour most associated with him is electric blue. The joke was on me. And I laughed.

Michael appeared several times afterwards, and we would stop and chat. He always appeared when I was feeling low, and he always made me smile. On one of these occasions, I made a point of thanking him.

After several months I didn't see him so often and I came to realise that I was feeling so much better by that point. Perhaps his healing presence was no longer needed and the hope I had prayed for had worked its miracle.

The Labyrinth Speaks
of *Navigating Blindfolded*

There are times when we must navigate life blindly.

We may not know what we want or what our next step is.

Being 'blindfolded' in this way teaches us to rely less on linear thinking and our need to be in control and to trust more in our intuition and feelings to navigate life.

In this way, we become more empowered and better equipped to be in flow with life's twists and turns.

Take time in stillness, ask for clues and signals, and stay open to stay alert for messages.

Listen to your intuition and to your gut feelings.

Act when you feel that you have enough information and when it feels right to do so.

Ultimately, all will be revealed in right ways and in right timing. For now, you are learning to trust yourself and life's unfolding.

A Financial Resolution

It has taken me a while to write this chapter. It is deeply personal, and even though I feel vulnerable sharing her, it is pivotal to my story of belonging, of coming Home to myself, and so I include it.

There comes a point in every separation or divorce where money and the division of assets are discussed and agreed. It is never an easy process. Nothing is easy about separation and divorce.

Every situation is unique. In my case and without going into detail, only one of us could afford to buy a home post-divorce. And it was unlikely to be me.

I was now fifty and had been out of the corporate, higher-paying sector for a decade. I had been the primary carer for our sons for all that time, and my business had always worked within and around school hours. When they were very young, I would work for two hours a day and two evenings a week whilst our youngest son attended his playgroup. When the boys jumped into their next school stage, my business immediately responded, and my client base increased proportionately. My income covered all the expenses that I was responsible for. Clients were mostly referred and recommended. I was earning enough, however, it was not enough to secure me a mortgage, and my age had me at a disadvantage too. I had to face a stark reality that, for the first time in my life, I would have to rent. After twenty-eight years of home ownership, it was a shock. And whilst I recognised that I had been privileged enough to have been a homeowner for so long and from such a young age, this was little comfort to me as I faced the future.

I was very clear that I wanted our sons to have at least one secure home. That was non-negotiable.

My solicitor advised me to go to court and fight my husband all the way. I knew that this would have an emotional toll on the whole family and that going to court would be financially costly too. So, it didn't make sense and moreover, it didn't sit well with me. I didn't want to fight my husband. He didn't deserve that. Neither of us deserved to have to go through a court battle. We had known each other for thirty years and been married for twenty-three. We had two wonderful sons together and had had many happy times. Fighting wasn't my style, despite what some of my friends were advising me to do. I did, though, have to check in with myself that I wasn't giving my power away, as this had been a pattern of mine.

It also wouldn't be a good foundation for how we wanted to be able to co-parent our sons moving forward. We wanted to be able to put their needs first and to be flexible if needed with our week on, week off arrangement. This would mean trust and respect needed to be inherent in our new arrangement.

I had been lying awake at night turning the variables over and over in my head. I feared not being able to financially support myself. I wanted to be able to give a secure and loving home to our sons. I had been brought up to believe that renting was a waste of money, and that home ownership was the only secure way to have a home. Renting a home in the UK is more expensive than buying. I bought my first home at the tender age of twenty-two, just nine months after graduating from university. I had owned two properties before my husband and I married. How could it be that I was now in this situation? I had worked hard all my life. I didn't have extravagant spending habits. None of this made sense to me. My life had always made sense up until this point. Now, very little made sense or felt fair. All I could feel was this intense maelstrom of emotion tearing through my body.

And of course, looking back, it didn't make sense. Good things happen to bad people and bad things happen to good people. Life isn't always fair in that sense. But this was a new concept for me to get my head and heart around.

For what felt like the first time in my life, I felt like a victim of external circumstances. I hadn't felt like this before, even when I was experiencing the bullying at work. I didn't feel like a victim when I miscarried, I felt sad and hopeless. I always considered that I had made my own luck and that things always worked out for the best. I couldn't see how this situation was going to shift any time soon.

To clear my head and calm my emotions, I decided to drive to the beach. Whilst there, I felt calmer and more grounded. I had spent weeks wrangling with the decisions I needed to make, and to feel a degree of peace, even for a short while, was a blessed relief. Being by the sea always helped.

As I lay on the sand, it occurred to me that I could ask my heart what she wanted and needed in this situation. I placed my hand over my heart and focused my attention there. As I did this, I could feel my body relaxing, letting go of the tension that had been storing up, sinking a little deeper into the sand.

'I want to be free,' was her reply.

And I instantly knew what I had to do. It became so clear.

I would not go to court. We would discuss and agree as fair and equitable a settlement that we could muster. My husband would buy a home. I would rent. I would take my chances. I would trust. If it was right for my heart and was aligned with my core values, then it would be OK. I would be OK. We would all be OK, no matter how it might look on paper right at that moment in time.

My solicitor sacked me as a client. I was prohibited from engaging them in the future because I hadn't taken his advice. He advised me of all the things that could go horribly wrong and that I was sabotaging my financial wellbeing. Perhaps he was right, perhaps not. Only the fullness of time would reveal the plan for us all.

Eventually, the house sold, we moved into two new homes and began a new way of relating.

Within a few weeks of moving in, I began to have some very strong emotional responses.

My head and my heart were often at war.

My head knew that we had agreed on a solution that was as fair and as equal as it could be, considering the constraints we were working within.

I knew that I couldn't afford to buy. I had to rent. I appreciated the additional temporary financial bridging my husband was providing.

I knew that I had done the right thing by our sons.

And, at the same time, I also felt the emotional fall-out from my decision.

I often felt sad as I returned home from dropping our sons at their dad's newly built house. I frequently cried for quite a few months. My rental was always cold regardless of how high or how long the heating had been on. It turned out that the boiler was twenty-five years old but because it was still deemed 'legal' by its annual service, I was told that it would not be replaced. The house was very grubby in places. There were stains on many of the carpets, which did not come out with elbow grease and carpet cleaner. Some of the windows didn't open and there was mould in several rooms. I was paying a lot of money for low-quality accommodation. I felt resentful. I felt powerless to change the situation. And for all of this, I felt sad, frustrated, angry and ashamed.

For the first time in my life, I fell into victim mode. I felt life had dealt me a harsh blow. It felt unfair. How could I have been able to buy at twenty-two and now I couldn't at fifty? Why should it be that being a full-time mother leaves you so financially vulnerable? How is it that I had worked hard for more than twenty-five years, paid my taxes, and now when I was in most need, I was entitled to a small amount of money per month from the government benefit scheme? How could that be fair? How could we call ourselves a progressive country?

I could rationalise it all by telling myself that I had chosen to leave my corporate job and we had together decided to move to a rural location. I could rationalise it by saying that our sons were mid to late teens and so the financial protections of the main caregiver were limited or non-existent. And sometimes, when I caught myself in a self-pity fest (my own words), I would also remind myself that I was still in a very privileged position and there were billions who could not afford the comforts of a home.

In the cauldron of unfairness came all manner of feelings, including shame, guilt, jealousy, self-pity, and utter terror at how things could unfold financially for me.

I was surrounded by people living very comfortable lives in big houses with expensive tastes and holidays. I was sad about not being a family of four. I missed many of our daily family routines. I felt sad seeing how difficult it was initially for our sons to adapt to having two homes and being semi-nomadic. Everywhere I went, all I noticed were happy family units, and for a long time, I felt sad, and I sometimes cried too.

It probably didn't help that, at the time, I was also going through menopause, and I was in chronic pain from osteoarthritis. It felt like my life was shutting down. It felt like I was boxed in. Night sweats and night terrors were frequent visitors. I didn't know what was up and what was down. It felt like I was in a permanent spin cycle, and I didn't know how to stop it. I was exhausted.

I had to ask my parents to stop telling me what a shame it was that I couldn't afford to buy a home of my own. They couldn't get their heads around it either. They meant well but it poked at my own shame and sorrow each time they voiced it. It was still a wound, not yet a scab. In their own words, they just wanted me to be 'sorted'. I felt a very long way from being sorted.

It would, in fact, take me around a decade to fully recover emotionally from that time and the major shift I was in the process of making. It was colossal.

On reflection, I made matters worse in many ways by not fully taking responsibility for my own decisions and for focussing on what I had lost, rather than what I had gained.

I decided I wanted to leave my corporate job and set up my own business.

I decided I wanted to be the main carer for our sons whilst building my business around them.

I decided that I wanted a more soul-led life and business, which meant that my income might temporarily take a financial hit.

I said that I wanted to separate.

I chose to put our sons first to ensure that they would have at least one secure home.

I chose not to go to court.

I participated fully in the discussions about money and how best to apportion it, and I had agreed to the financial settlement that we had formulated together.

And still a little voice loudly cried, 'But it's not fair!'

And this rumbled on for quite some time, not helped by my utter fixation on home ownership and that, for the very first time in my life, I was now feeling like a victim. A victim without hope of things ever getting any better.

It took years for this to unhook, unravel, unlock.

It was all tied up with my journey of understanding what 'Home' really meant.

It would be a decade before this internal dynamic would fully unravel and resolve and for the experience of what Home really means to me to be felt and known.

'I'd Rather Walk on Hot Coals Than Do That!'

Summer Solstice, June 2012

This was my instinctive response to my dear friend Sue, one morning.

I don't remember now what it was in response to; however, I smile at what happened next every time I think about it!

Earlier that day, I had completed another section of my new vision board. I was just six months into a separation from my husband of 23 years and had been going through some deep grieving AND some true clarity of wanting to experience more joy and passion in my life.

So, I added an intention around inviting more fire energy into my life.

Later that afternoon, I felt a call to go into a local tea shop with my journal.

On the wall, I noticed a flyer for a fire walk. I laughed out loud.

It was to be in two weeks' time on the summer solstice, and it was being held in a school field at the bottom of the road where I lived. A big proportion of the fee was to be donated to our local hospice charity, which was a cause close to my heart.

The irony and speed of this synchronicity were astonishing. How could I refuse?

I sent a text to tell her. She immediately replied, saying she was going to join me. Within an hour, we had both signed up.

I absolutely LOVED the experience of the fire walk. I did three fire walks across hot coals in total, relaxing into the experience each time. My feet didn't get burned; however, they tingled all night and for a further two days.

It was exhilarating and grounding all at once.

The FIRE element had heard my call and had begun its return.

Three Wise Women

The number three seems to appear a lot in my life.

It was true of my pregnancies, the three leading men in my life, three months to write a book, develop new programmes, and now when I needed additional expert support, three wise women arrived.

They also say, whoever 'they' really are, that it takes a village to raise a child.

Well, in my experience, it takes women to support fellow women through significant change. Women need midwives to help them through major life change. We need each other not only for helping us give birth to our babies but also for helping us give birth and rebirth ourselves and our creative projects into the world.

Having been that midwife to so many women over the previous years, it was now my time to be supported. I didn't set off with the intention of the magic three, but it is what I manifested.

They didn't quite bring gold, frankincense, and myrrh; however, what they did bring was priceless. They brought their gifts of unconditional love, wisdom, and healing.

Soon after separating from my husband, I recognised that I was going to need some professional support. My intention was to move through the transition ahead with as much self-awareness and grace as I could muster. I acknowledged that I was not just dealing with our separation and everything that entailed, but I was also perimenopausal, moving into menopause, and had the early signs of osteoarthritis. Our house was taking a while to sell, and we were all still living in the same house and whilst that provided a degree of stability and continuity, it also brought its own challenges. I wanted to be a steady, calm, loving presence for our sons and I was crumbling inside and struggling emotionally. I frequently felt overwhelmed and coped with it better some days more than others. After twenty-three years of marriage, it is very difficult to let go and move on.

Whilst I was well equipped to hold space for myself with all the techniques, insights, and experience I had in my kit bag, I also recognised the value of having others support me on a one-to-one basis. I pared back my spending and created the budget. I figured that having professional support would be a wise move.

And they arrived, one by one.

A shamanic journeying practitioner

A homoeopathic practitioner.

A a craniosacral and Bowen practitioner.

I worked with one of these women every three to four weeks. Their three modalities worked well together. One worked at a physical and energetic level, one on the inner planes, and the other on my constitution. All of them brought their own special brand of magic. Together they produced an effect like an aromatherapy synergistic blend. The work of each of the women was supporting and enhancing the other two.

Aehlah helped me to journey deep within me to my inner landscape, the middle world where I gained valuable insight, context, and transmutation. There was rarely any comfort in the session other than her familiar and caring voice at the end of the phone. There was no sugar-coating; the sessions cut right to the core of the truth of what I was feeling – or not feeling – and the Shadow behind them. They brought all my Shadows to light, and it took me a while to truly welcome them as friends. I wanted answers. I wanted to know why I felt the way I did. Even more than that, I wanted to know how I was going to *fix* things. I would have to feel everything. There was not going to be a quick fix. It would show me my blind spots. The journeying would illuminate all my deepest, darkest fears. The parts of me that I had closed off from and disowned. Terror of being shamed, rejected, homeless. Terror of being judged. The disempowerment, the fear, the lack of safety, the loss, the disappointment, the confusion, the disillusion, the futility, the helplessness, victimhood, the lack of hope. Hope had always been a bright beacon in my life. The hope that things would always work out and always feel better soon had been an ever-present sense in my life for as long as I can remember. It was one of the reasons why I chose Hope as my new surname. I didn't expect that to embody it, I would first have to lose it.

I was learning to let go of my compulsion to figure things out with my head, to put my trust in myself and let go of the need to look outside of myself for answers, and I would also learn how to let go of my need to get stuff done, to be constantly *do*ing and to come even more into presence and *be*-ing.

Alice in Wonderland figures would often appear and the command 'off with her head' frequently featured in my sessions. Transformational magic was also afoot, and I lost count of how many times I was invited to step into an imaginary fire. The transmutation process was endless until one day, I found myself as Alice, sweeping away all the ashes, and there was no fire to step into anymore. It would be a year or so before the physical manifestation of all this transformation would make itself known in my life. One thing was clear, though, and it became a bit of a joke. Merlin was the guide who often showed up on these journeys to guide me. He would ask the question: 'Where are we off to now, Moriah?' And the answer that always came to me was 'Home. I'm going Home.' I didn't know exactly what this would mean or look like, but I did feel it to be true and what my heart most wanted. Home.

Through this period, my first oracle deck, *The Magician's Toolkit®*, appeared. Many of the messages, shamanic techniques and insights presented themselves during the sessions for me to consider and to practise, contemplate and apply in my life until they eventually became embodied wisdom. I love this card deck. It has such a potent, compact, quirky, and simple style. It reflects the individual inner journeys and magical energies that work with me and through me.

I learned so much about myself through two years of journeying in this way, and I also learned how to support other women in this way. It is still a go-to technique for my clients who want deep, lasting change and who love the mystery of shamanic inner journeying.

Lynne helped me in a different way. Firstly, she would come to the house to treat me, and that was invaluable. It felt honouring and meant I felt very emotionally safe. She would ask me questions. I would talk, and she would listen to both what I said as much as what I wasn't saying or was even aware of. It helped to get things off my chest, to speak out loud the words that were swimming around inside my head. I felt seen and heard. I felt validated. She would then prescribe a homoeopathic remedy. I can't say I fully understood each remedy, yet I always felt the benefit. As luck would have it, she was also a specialist in menopausal symptoms, so we were covering off the impact of several life transitions all at once.

Carol held a very steady, safe space in which I could let go and be fully surrendered on her couch whilst she worked. It felt physically very nurturing, and I always felt grounded and calmer as I left. The sessions helped me to feel safer and more at peace in my body and in life. It calmed my anxiety, and I felt soothed and nourished after these sessions. My mind-body system relaxed and let go of the tension I'd been carrying. One whole hour of lying down and receiving this form of therapy felt wonderful.

All three wise women helped me find more pieces to my puzzle. The sessions helped me to come back to myself and to be more centred and present, and this helped me deal with the day-to-day reality of the separation, house sale, work, and taking care of our sons.

I am so grateful to all three of them for their support through that tricky time. A big benefit was that I felt less alone. I felt held. I knew that I was never more than five weeks away from working with one of them, and I could hold myself amply in between sessions. There came a point where I began to feel I no longer needed such regular support, and the intervals between sessions lengthened until we completed our work together and we signed off.

Women need midwives, and now I am a midwife to women moving through inner and outer change and who are re-inventing themselves and birthing their creativity. It is a sacred privilege to hold a woman through such times and having been through so much change and gone so deep within myself, the space I can hold now is so much greater.

I am grateful, truly grateful.

And now, as I write this book, I find myself with another set of three wise women.

I hadn't planned it that way; however, that is exactly what has magically manifested.

One is the founder of the Unbound Press.

Another is a story-telling expert.

And the shamanic practitioner.

All bringing their gifts. All magical. All showing up in perfect timing, in perfect ways.

Life moves on.

Life unfolds.

Old chapters end.

New ones open.

And at certain points we complete a whole book, and an era of our life ends.

We may face similar challenges, yet we will experience them differently, from a new perspective and it will be less loud, less pressing, a fainter imprint and echo.

Having others hold space and witness us in such unfolding is priceless.

Dear Home

September 2012

Dear Home,

I have been putting off making decisions about what to keep and what to shed. I have been putting off legal documents that need writing and agreeing, and today, just now, I have felt the reason why even more acutely.

You have been at the very epicentre of our family life for thirteen years now. Life as we have known it is about to crash all around us as we prepare to leave, go our separate ways, and create two new homes.

We have lovingly restored you, we have laughed and cried within your loving embrace. Our baby boys have grown into teenagers. We have welcomed friends and family here, partied here, and made so many family memories. Happy times and sad times, laughter, tears, and some wonderful celebrations. So much to cherish. So much love has filled this home, and you have been the steadfast container for us.

I feel so sad, so desolate. I don't want it to be real. I will miss you terribly. I have always felt welcome here, I have always felt at home here. You didn't look the way we had expected, and yet you felt so right. As soon as we crossed the threshold, we just knew in our bodies that you were 'The One'.

And now, as I pick through pieces of furniture, our sons' childhood teddy bears and photo albums, it is like sorting through the house of someone who has died. A lifetime of possessions and treasured memories, now forever changed, and the life force that gave them meaning has gone. Whilst I know that our memories will stay with us, this ending has such a brutal finality to it.

You are soon to be sold to a cash buyer who is keen to get in and get on and assumes that we are just as keen to get on and get out.

And yet, at a deeper level, we are holding on and attempting to delay the inevitable day that we leave, and our separation will be even more real than it has ever been so far.

Some of our furniture has been with us since our very first home. This makes it at least 25 years old. There are photos and christening outfits, teddies, and shared memories in some of the most mundane things. And we must make decisions on all of them or simply divide them in a broad-brush agreement.

On a practical level, we can't take it all with us. I want to live more lightly on this Earth, and yet I now find myself wanting to hang onto books and things 'just in case' they might have a home in the next house.

I have cleared clutter all my life and don't normally have a problem with it, up until now. The clutter no longer feels like clutter. Each piece is a piece of our shared history and going through it now with a house move looming makes it even more painful. It feels as though we are being ripped apart. And of course, this, in many ways, is exactly what is happening, however gentle we try to be with each other. The reality is stark.

And no, no one has died. But our marriage has died. Our dreams have died. Our family unit is no longer. The home that we have so carefully crafted, nurtured, and adapted and in which so many happy family moments took place is about to be sold so that two new homes can be created where there was once just one.

Hopes and dreams for what could have been, now dashed and in pieces.

New life to be born from the ashes.

Before any new beginning, there is an ending. In dealing fully with this ending, I know that we will eventually be able to create the most glorious of new beginnings, however hopeless and desolate things feel right now.

And so, the paperwork, decisions, clearing, heartache, and tears all have their role to play, and the process must be allowed to unfold so that the new can emerge.

This is the way of all things.

The pain that we feel now will surely fade.

And in the meantime, our hearts break wide open, chaos reigns, and we bring as much love, forgiveness, tolerance, and compassion that we can muster for ourselves, each other, and the process.

As we prepare to leave, it blows my mind that our leaving date is exactly thirteen years to the day since we arrived. Such a synchronicity. This gives me a degree of comfort and a sense that all is in Divine order.

And so, Dear Home, we thank you for all that you have held us through, for the sanctuary you have provided and for all the memories that we will carry with us in our hearts.

Forever grateful,

Love always,

Moriah x

I Said YES!

Part Four

It was spring of 2013, and I was making the final preparations to leave our family home and needed to decide what to do with my wedding dress. The box itself was huge and I knew that I didn't have room for it in the next house. I had no daughters, and my sons naturally had no real interest in it. I decided to do some research online and discovered a charity shop which specialised in selling second hand wedding dresses. It was in the next town to where I would be staying whilst I waited for the rental house to be available. I had a plan: I would take my dress to the shop and donate it. It felt like a good choice.

The day after I moved out of our family home, I drove with my friend to the shop and handed over my wedding dress, in its original box. I was invited up to the showroom but declined. I suddenly felt nauseous and wanted to get back outside into the fresh air. I wasn't feeling victorious or happy to hand it over. I felt sad and heavy-hearted. For me, it represented yet another symbol of my married life coming to an end. The end of an era. The end of a dream.

As I crossed the threshold of the shop, I received a call from the solicitor saying 'Congratulations, the sale has gone through, and your share of the funds have been transferred to your account. You are now free.'

I felt a long way from celebrating. The book had closed and a new one was opening, but not now, not today.

Perfectly Imperfect

Everything is perfect. Perfectly imperfect. Life can be messy. Seeking perfection can cause delays and stop us from enjoying what is already here for the taking. Being OK with what is allows us to enjoy all that we already have. Every moment tenderly holds the potential for us to begin, to begin again, to take action towards our dreams and desires. Don't wait for the conditions to be perfect; they already are.

Be bold. Jump right in. It's where the magic is.

From *The Magician's Toolkit®*

The Soul Speaks
on *Being Deeply Rooted*

To truly thrive as the creative beings that we are,
we must learn to be deeply rooted within ourselves,
so that we can flourish wherever we are planted.

In this way, we always know what it is to belong and to feel whole.
Until that point, it will always feel like something is missing.

We must find that w-hole-ness within ourselves.

Only in this way can we call off the search and come Home to ourselves,
to come Home to the seat of our belonging.

And that is precious, beyond treasure, it is the very nectar of life itself.

The Day the Sun Broke Through
the Clouds

April 2013

It was the week after I had moved into my rental house, and I had begun to worry about the knot in my stomach. It had been forming for a week or so and was getting bigger and denser with each day. I had assumed it was just anxiety until one day I began to wonder if something more sinister might be afoot.

It felt as though this thing in my stomach was a rag being twisted, turned, and wrung out.

It was mighty uncomfortable and had kept me awake some nights.

I was contemplating this troublesome internal knot one morning when I was cleaning the bath. Or should I say, scrubbing the bath. I had spent five minutes on my knees scrubbing away, trying to remove the previous tenants' stubborn stains, when I just stopped in my tracks and sat back on the bathroom floor.

Exhausted. I was exhausted. Who was I kidding? I had zero energy for this. And I sobbed.

I sobbed for the loss of a clean house, the fact that I was still making my way around the house clearing up the mess that was supposed to have been covered by the previous occupants. I was tired from the conversation earlier that morning with the managing agent on my questions about the standard of presentation of the house when I took it over. I was bemused and angry that her response was that it was acceptable that the tenants left it in the condition they found it. How was that a good standard to go by, and surely they had to provide receipts that carpets had been professionally cleaned? I had found dirty kitchen cupboards, cobwebs everywhere, tea stains on carpets and a bathroom that hadn't been cleaned thoroughly for some time. And in their opinion, this house was in 'good decorative order'.

So now it was mid-morning, and I was sitting on the floor, sobbing, again.

'If I don't have enough energy to clean a bath, how on Earth am I going to rebuild my life and business?'

This was the thought ringing through my head.

I got up off the floor and rang the doctor's surgery for an appointment. After a brief chat with a doctor, I was booked in the following day with a practice nurse to have blood tests. Great. Something I could do. Some degree of control over my own life. I could act on my health. I could at least do that.

I arrived for my appointment at the doctors' surgery the following morning and sat in the waiting room. It was my first time since registering here, and I was enjoying looking around at the décor and the layout, taking it all in. It was so much more welcoming than my last doctors' surgery.

I turned around as I heard my name called, and there she was. A vision in orange. Top to toe. Literally. Her hair was a stunningly bright auburn colour, and she was wearing a tangerine-coloured dress. This was the nurse. It was my turn.

Once in the private room, she introduced herself as Bridie, and I smiled. I asked where in Ireland she was from. Dublin. How wonderful. I loved the fact that this woman was Irish, called Bridie and in orange. She reminded me of the Goddess Bridget. I rolled my sleeve up, ready for the blood tests. Just as she began drawing my blood, she began to say that she had noticed my address and that she recognised me as being 'our new tenant in the close'. I asked her if she were a neighbour. 'No. I'm your landlady,' she replied.

This was a little surreal. I was having my blood drawn by a woman in orange who now turned out to be my landlady. She had access to my medical records and knew that I was having blood tests because of the tension knot in my stomach. I wasn't sure which way this was going to go – however, I was about to be pleasantly surprised.

Once Bridie had finished with her needles, she looked at me directly and shared with me that she had a good feeling about me. She said that she could tell I was going to be a great tenant and winked at me. She asked me how I was settling in, and I shared some of the pleasures and the frustrations with her. She said that I was to leave things with her, and she would see to them. She gave me a hug, wished me well, and then we parted. I have to say that I was a little stunned. What were the chances of that happening?

It was still early morning, and I decided to go to my favourite local coffee shop. I settled into writing in my journal and treated myself to some artisan baked toast and local honey with my coffee. I spent an hour or so there just writing and people-watching, and as I wrote, I noticed how my body was beginning to sink into the chair and relax a little more. I could feel the tension dropping and my shoulders too. The tension in my thighs was loosening.

I was softening once more.

And I let out a big, deep, long sigh.

As I headed out of the café, a thought flashed through my mind about just how much I loved the purple raincoat I was wearing and how I'd love the same raincoat in a jade colour. This raincoat was about six months old, had a lapel, big buttons and came to just above knee length. It had a belt that finished it nicely and gave my waist more definition. I loved it.

And then I forgot all about it.

I was about to have another lovely surprise when someone I hadn't seen for around four years stepped off the bus. He was the guy who used to run a crystal shop locally. It was so good to see him. We stopped and had a quick catch-up chat before he headed off to a meeting and I headed into the charity shop to drop some books off.

And there it was. A jade-coloured raincoat almost identical in style to the one I was wearing. In its pocket was the original ticket. It was from the same high street shop as my purple one. It was being sold for ten pounds. I could not believe my eyes. Within thirty minutes of thinking about it, there it was. And so, I bought it.

I reflected on my extraordinary morning on my walk back to the house. I appreciated all the surprises and the deliciousness of connection that I'd just experienced, and I also noticed a great tiredness in my body. When I got home, I decided I would go take a nap. This was a first; I hadn't allowed myself to do this during the day for fear of not being able to sleep at night and because it had been difficult to sleep with the knot twisting in my stomach. It seemed to have unravelled a little, so I took my chances and went to snuggle up in my bed and promptly fell asleep.

I was fast asleep when I heard the doorbell. I looked at the alarm clock on my bedside cabinet. I'd been asleep for four hours!

My landlady was at the door with flowers. She offered them to me as a housewarming gift and asked if she could come in. I made her tea, and we chatted a little before she asked me which jobs around the house and garden needed attention. I gave her what I thought was a reasonable list and she agreed that they were priorities. She said that she would get onto the managing agent straightaway. She thanked me for the tea and left for home.

What an extraordinary day. The so-far impersonal, less-than-perfect rental experience I'd had with this house had suddenly changed. It now felt more personal, more human, and I felt acknowledged by this woman in orange who had taken my blood and my to-do list. Even more than that, I felt like she had seen me, truly seen me, and she had responded to me and my needs. The fact that she had cared enough to introduce herself, come to the house and had taken away my requests warmed my heart.

It felt like the sun had broken through the clouds that had been hanging around for months.

She had cared and that had made all the difference to me and how I felt about this house.

Maybe, just maybe, I could begin to settle in and make it a home.

Come to the Beach

May 2013

'Come to the beach,' she said. 'It's my friend's birthday, and we're having a picnic. Come join us. It will do you good.'

My friend meant well. She knew that I'd been feeling flat and sad since moving out of our marital home and into my rental. It had only been six short weeks. Barely any time to adjust.

I considered her invitation and decided that it might well be good to be on the beach and meet some new women. A change of scenery and some sea air might be exactly what I needed. I gathered up some beach gear, chose a few things to eat from the fridge, packed a bag and drove across the South Downs to the beach.

It was a beautifully warm day in May. The lavender alongside the beach was just coming into bloom and the scent of the nearby wild rosemary was in the air too. I could feel my body relax as the sun kissed my skin. It had been a long, cold, damp winter. It felt good to be out and about.

The picnic was fun. There was a great blend of laughter and deep conversation. We all shared similar interests. It felt good to be in company again and to be able to switch off from the worries that had been plaguing me.

When we had finished eating, we packed away the remaining food and blankets into our cars and set off for a walk together along the water's edge.

As we walked, one of the women approached me and asked if she could walk with me. She began to ask about my work, how I knew our mutual friend, and then dug deeper and asked why I'd been quiet during the picnic. I wasn't aware that I had contributed less than anyone else. I was puzzled but let it go.

She then launched into a long monologue about how my low vibration was going to impact me negatively, could make me very ill and keep me stuck in a rut. She said that unless I shifted into a high vibe, I would manifest all manner of bad experiences and I would spiral down in vibration even further. She explained how I needed to get myself into a better feeling place and how getting into a vortex of high vibrational energy would lift my spirits and help me to manifest all manner of happy things including a new partner, more money, and a new car. I didn't want a new man or a new car right now, thank you, but extra money would always be welcome!

By this time, I had guessed that she was a fan of The Law of Attraction. Whilst I understood the principles, I didn't agree with all of them. I had a different way of working and engaging with Life.

She carried on giving me her advice. And on. And on.

I could take it no more. Enough was enough. And this was a bellyful of her own opinion and unsolicited advice that I was most certainly not going to be digesting!

I stopped in my tracks, raised both hands to signal 'No' and began to shout.

'I think I'm entitled to feel *everything* I'm feeling.

I'm just six weeks into living apart from my husband of twenty-three years and I'm missing family times.

I'm letting go of the dreams we had.

I'm doing the best to hold it together to support our sons.

I'm not sleeping well.

I feel anxious a lot of the time.

My income has dropped because I don't have the energy to hold space for clients.

And I've just been told I have osteoarthritis and will need major surgery to fix it.

'I think I'm entitled to feel however I want to feel right now. I don't want to ignore, repress, or suppress my feelings. I won't do that. It's not healthy. It's probably the worst thing I could do right now. And chanting mantras and trying to think my way into a "better" feeling state is just not going to cut it right now.

I'm allowed to feel sad.

I'm allowed to feel anxious, and I'm allowed to stay in this state until I naturally come out of it or until I feel ready to take some inspired action to change things.'

She looked stunned. I was stunned too. As I finished speaking, I was aware that the other women had stopped chatting and were watching us. I was so angry that I said thank you and goodbye to everyone, saying that it was probably best I leave and return home.

And as I drove away from the car park, I could feel a change in me. I could sense that I felt lighter. I had a big smile on my face. I felt proud of myself. I had spoken up for myself. I had just given myself full permission to feel everything that was coming up for me. I had felt angry and had expressed it clearly and cleanly. This was new to me. It felt good.

And in that realisation, I also gave myself permission to take a month off from work to take really good care of myself.

It was time to put my own oxygen mask on first.

The Soul Speaks
of *the Presence of Love*

What is possible

in the presence

of LOVE?

Three Months' Grace

June 2013

Once I gave myself permission to feel everything, I began to relax more. I could feel my shoulders drop, the tension in my body ease, and I found myself sighing peaceful sighs rather than sad ones. My head had been trying to figure out how my life was going to unfold and how I was going to build my business back up again. My head couldn't figure it out, I knew that deep down, but it didn't stop me over-thinking and beating myself up.

I had tried figuring it out and I had put time and energy into creating offers that my head thought were good ideas and much wanted in the world. It all came to nothing. And, of course, my heart wasn't in any of them. And I was running on empty.

Time to put my own oxygen mask on first. It was time to prioritise me first. My wellbeing, perhaps for the first time in my life, would now take priority.

In those times, I often had quotes or phrases drop into my head and the most frequent had been an *Alice in Wonderland* one.

'Off with her head!'

Indeed, off with my head. I could not think my way through this situation. I was going to have to *feel* my way through it. I was going to have to trust that there was indeed a higher purpose for all of this and trust too that my Soul had my back. I would have to trust all of this even when I couldn't see, sense, feel or hear its presence. My feelings and intuition would be guiding me. I would be doing this blindfolded.

As soon as I acknowledged this fully, I fell into a state of what I can only describe as grace.

My singular strategy now became to take really good care of myself. In fact, I gave it the name radical self-care. That was my only job. To take exquisite care of myself. I would use some of the money that I had from the house sale as backup if I needed to, and I would trust that in looking after myself, Life would look after me. After a few days I realised that I was still putting expectations on myself and the outcome and making taking care of myself a means to an end, a conditional exercise. I was bargaining.

It was time to take care of me, fully, exquisitely, and *unconditionally*.

And I gave myself full permission to do just that.

I prioritised nutrition over the cost of my food bills. I began to seek new recipes to try out. I wanted to experiment with new tastes. This was the first time in over twenty years that I had cooked just for me. At first, I made different pasta sauces and then moved onto vegetarian curries. I wanted to see how many types of vegetarian curries I could find and make. I found thirty that I liked.

This was all such a revelation to me. I had never considered cooking to be something I was good at, and even now, I would say a creative cook is someone who can create a great meal without reference to a recipe. I wasn't that kind of creative, not yet at least. Maybe given time. What I did discover, though, were my taste buds.

I became a little obsessed with low-fat coconut milk, turmeric, and aubergines, albeit not always in the same recipe. My tastebuds were returning to life after years of being seemingly switched off. I discovered that I responded better to hot foods than cold food. Going 'raw', I realised, was never going to satisfy me. I didn't limit cooking to the evenings either. I began to experiment with breakfast, lunch, and dinner. I looked forward to cooking in a way that I never had before. I could feel my body getting excited as it got closer to the time for me to go into the kitchen and cook.

I noticed that the more I cooked in this way, with fresh ingredients, trying new tastes and textures, the less I longed for sweeter things. My sugar craving dropped completely.

After a few weeks, I acknowledged that I was an OK cook and that I enjoyed the process of creating a meal and nurturing myself through food. This was new to me. I may never be a great cook and that was OK. It was enough.

I began to invite friends over for meals and remembered just how much I love to host and create the ambience within the home as much as around the food. It was such a beautiful summer that we would often eat outdoors in the garden.

My love of food was a new joy to me. I had never fully enjoyed eating, let alone cooking. And now, this new appreciation of both was stirring within me, and it felt good. Delicious, in fact.

I also began to spend time in the two small gardens. One was a courtyard design full of cottage-style plants. It hadn't been loved for many years. It was very neglected and over-grown, but I could see the original design of the planting, and I felt a great curiosity growing inside of me to discover what I might find, what it might look like once I had restored it.

As I chopped, weeded, and pruned, I got a sense of the woman whose garden this had been for thirty years. I could almost feel her with me as I worked. A neighbour had told me in conversation that the garden had been this woman's pride and joy and she only stopped when the dementia had really set in.

She was clearly a woman who had loved plants. I could see how much care had been taken to make sure that each plant was in a position within the garden where it could thrive. And I smiled. I had forgotten just how much I loved to garden and just how great a gardener I had been in my youth. I had styled, re-styled and dug two gardens, grown flowers from seeds, taken cuttings, laid turf, and so much more. I remembered how I used to get home from my corporate jobs feeling grubby from the day's stresses, and I would spend hours in the garden until the sun set. I would get everything that felt 'toxic' out of my system. Perhaps I was doing the very same here and history was repeating itself.

It felt good to be looking after this little plot of land now and to be restoring it to its original design and beauty. The whole experience gave me so much pleasure. Each day I discovered a new plant hidden beneath the undergrowth. It was like finding little jewels. It often amazed me just how they managed to survive with so little oxygen, light, or water. They were little survivors. And once discovered, they thrived.

In the warm summer evenings when my sons were at their dad's home, I would work in the garden until sunset. Once I had finished gardening, I would sit at my little garden table and chairs that I had reclaimed, restored, and painted Mediterranean blue, with a chilled glass of rosé wine, enjoying the fruits of my labour. Listening to the evening birdsong became one of my most favourite daily pleasures. More birds had arrived in the garden once the undergrowth began to clear. We now had a robin who arrived every morning and evening and perched on a chair, singing its heart out. There were goldfinches, bluebirds, and wrens too. The garden was throbbing with life and colour and scent, and this made my heart very happy indeed.

There was height, depth, colour, and movement now. The design showcased the changing seasons. There was always a new delight to enjoy. As one plant faded from bloom, another one opened and flourished.

It was now a *beautiful* space. I felt very fortunate. It was small yet it was so perfectly designed and compact. It was a joy to behold. It brought me immense pleasure and a sense of satisfaction that I hadn't felt in a long time.

The other garden was set to lawn and had a long, winding bed brimming full of old English roses. The colours and scent were delicious, and I was lucky to have roses in the house throughout spring, summer and into early autumn. I was so very grateful for the roses. The remainder of the garden was set to grass which I did my best to bring it back to its former glory. Years of neglect had taken their toll, though, and it recovered a little but never fully. It was perfect as it was. I was happy to see the new growth.

My landlady kept her word and all the repairs I had requested were swiftly carried out. Several rooms were redecorated in the colours and style I wanted, and she had a tree surgeon cut back the dead branches of a large tree in the courtyard garden which brought much-needed space and light that had been missing.

When my landlady visited to check on the work, her delight at seeing the courtyard garden was palpable. She gasped. She looked me directly in the eyes and said, 'Thank you', and I knew that she truly meant it. She began to show me some of the plants that she had bought for her mother-in-law and relayed some tales about how the garden had been tended over the years. She told me it was now restored true to its original design and that gave me and her much pleasure. I offered her tea and she accepted, staying a further hour. I was grateful for this personal connection with her and, through her stories, to the woman who had so tenderly cared for this house and its gardens. It somehow softened the feelings of disempowerment that I had experienced on moving into this, my first rental home.

I wondered whether I would have met her if I hadn't been referred for blood tests and if I hadn't felt so anxious that I needed the blood tests? I'll never know. I did however know that I was truly, fully, deeply grateful for this connection.

My morning tea became a ritual. I would make tea in my favourite mug and take it back to bed with me. I would prop myself up against my pillows and bring my full focus inwards, into my body, imagining myself filling up with light. I would focus on someone or something I loved, feel the feeling, and then expand it through my whole body until I was full, fuller, fullest. Mostly I would begin with my sons. It was so very easy to feel love for them. After a while, there were so many things to love about my life and to feel grateful for that it became a sumptuous way to start the day.

I also began journaling again, sometimes first thing in the morning and always at night. In the mornings, I would write whatever came into my head, a stream of consciousness, if you will. I would keep writing until I ran out of words. Sometimes it was gibberish. Sometimes there were helpful insights that came through. And often, there were some core truths or realisations, and these were the gems. Many of these gems went on to feature in the work I did with clients in addition to supporting me with my next steps.

Evenings also became a special time of the day. Bath time became a sacred ritual. Dropping essential oils of geranium, rose, and lavender into the steam and running water of the bath was a delicious act. I would sometimes bring some of the flowers and rose petals from the garden and have them float on the water too. Candlelight added even more ambience. It felt a wonderful luxury to have each evening. I would reflect on my day and look for the moments, big and small, that I was grateful for. I would again get into the *feeling* of those moments and then amplify the feeling until it ran all the way through my body and filled me, head to toe, in love and gratitude.

I would then capture the day's special moments through writing. Sometimes it would be funny things I'd experienced, new insights or ways of looking at old things. Sometimes it would be things that were bothering me. I would journey within when I felt stuck, and I would write up what I saw and felt in those journeys. I kept the most beautiful notebooks for this. My favourite was a gift from a dear friend. It was a very thick, beautifully bound journal with rich, intense magenta silk cover and a ribbon to close it. I absolutely loved everything about it. In this journal, I would write with a fountain pen in black ink. It was beautiful to the eye and to the touch.

Once complete, I would settle into bed, appreciating the white Egyptian cotton bed linen and feel immense gratitude that I was finally beginning to sleep so much better. These simple things became my luxuries. Simple, beautiful, daily sensual rituals helped me to deeply rest and unwind.

Life was feeling brighter. I was feeling more hopeful.

I joined the local gym. I returned to swimming. I sold the pieces of furniture from our marital home that didn't fit in this one and I created a clear, clean sanctuary space in my bedroom.

I made sure that the house and I were ready for the alternate weeks that my sons were with me. The house was clean, tidy, their bed linen fresh, and food in the fridge and cupboards. I aimed to make myself available to cook, nurture, listen, to drive them, to be present physically, mentally, and emotionally.

And it came to pass that at the end of the three months I felt so completely different. So much happier and healthier. You could say that Hope had been restored. At the very least, Hope was in the process of being restored, together with Joy.

I had begun to fall back in love with life, and in the process, I was falling back in love with myself too.

And as my inner shift in state took hold, I began to see the shifts in my life too

Love Hearts Everywhere

Suddenly, one day, they were everywhere I looked.

Love hearts.

Heart shapes.

Everywhere.

It began by me seeing the outline of a loving couple in the fur of my friend's cat.
Strange but true.
There they were as clear as day. To me, at least.
She couldn't see them.
The couple were walking with their back to me, hand in hand, clearly very much in love, together as a couple on a long walk together.

Then it was puddles.
Following rain showers I would see puddles in the shape of hearts.
Everywhere I looked.
In the high street, in the car park, in my courtyard garden, outside my front door.

It was June and the first of the roses were just beginning to shed their petals.
And yes, you've guessed it, they were heart shaped.

Heart shapes appeared everywhere for around three weeks.

In the swirls of the aromatic oil in my bath.
The light as the sun shone through the leaves of the trees.
Shadows on walls of the rooms in my house.
Confetti on pavements in town, miles away from a church.
Cake decoration toppings when I went out for tea and cake with a friend.
A heart-shaped chocolate topping to my cappuccino.
Hearts already drawn in the sand on the beach.

Heart-shaped stones on the benches where I paused to sit.
A friend sent me bright pink, heart-shaped sticky notes.

On the radio, there was one song that seemed to pop up at least once a day.
'Are you ready for LOVE?' Elton John.
I would shake my head and laugh it off at first, and then I would be singing loudly and dancing around the lounge and affirming, 'Yes, I'm ready. I'm ready!'
Hearts and love popping up everywhere, every day.

I was curious.
I was intrigued.
I felt flirtatious.
It made me feel happy.

What was going on?
Was Life teasing me?
Was Life giving me a message?
I enjoyed the *feeling* of this time, luxuriating in it, affirming the signs each time they appeared and enjoying the playfulness of it all.

And I felt lighter, joyful, energised, and hopeful without assuming it was to do with a man coming into my life. It felt like I was ready to love myself and life once more.

I didn't feel ready.
I didn't feel ready for a new relationship.
It had only been eighteen months since the breakup,
and just a few short months of living independently.
I wanted longer to heal.
I wanted time to be on my own, in my own space.
I wanted to get to know who I'd become, who I was becoming.
The Me who was newly single.
I didn't want to be in a relationship just yet.
I wanted to taste this newly created freedom of mine.
I wanted to be independent.
I wanted time to explore.

I wanted more time.
I wanted to be *ready*.

Or at least that's what my head was telling me.
My heart and Soul were telling me something altogether different.
Magic was in the air.
And life as I knew it was about to change.

I Wrote a List

The trails of heart-shaped signs had piqued my interest.

My curiosity was aroused.

It got me thinking.

If I were to be in a relationship with a new man, what qualities would I most value?

I tore a sheet of paper out of my writing pad and began to fill the page with qualities, descriptive words, feelings, values. All randomly scattered on the page.

The page was yellow. All yellow.

It was surprisingly easy and fun.

It was complete within ten minutes.

I folded the paper into a neat little square and placed it beneath the pair of small, black, iron birds sitting on my bedroom windowsill.

I forgot all about it.

Literally, totally, genuinely forgot.

But magic was afoot.

'Are You Blonde?'

December 2013

I was reflecting on the year I'd had. The highs and the lows. The choices. The beauty and the ugliness. The sadness and the joys. The shocks and the delicious surprises. A memory floated into my mind of a psychic reading that I had sought in the summer of 2006. It was my first one. I was looking for some answers to questions whizzing through my mind, and on reflection, I guess I was also looking for hope. Hope that my marriage would survive and that we would find a way to reconcile the differences emerging.

The psychic reader opened with, 'Are you blonde?' 'No. I'm brunette,' I replied.

'Oh,' he said. 'I see your husband with a blonde woman. And I see a large diagonal crack in your bedroom wall. It represents the crack appearing in your marriage.'

The reader then went on to say, 'You will recognise your soulmate when the mist lifts. When the mist lifts, you will know him.'

There was indeed a crack in the bedroom wall, and a crack had recently been revealed in my marriage too. I wasn't sure what to make of the reader's other comments, though. I didn't get a sense that my husband was in a relationship with somebody else. I trusted him. And I knew that my husband was a soulmate. This hadn't felt at all helpful. Now I had more questions than answers.

Fast forward to March 2013. Our marriage had come to an end, and we were preparing to leave our family home for the last time. That same week, my former colleague and friend, Ian, was coming to terms with the breakdown of his long-term relationship.

We met up for lunch in June. It was the first time we had seen each other for several years. We had both changed, as you do when you have been through life's major transitions. We shared some of what had been happening and reminisced over our time working together more than twenty-five years earlier. We met up several times that summer. Sometimes lunch, sometimes a coffee or picnic, sometimes a beach walk.

This was around the time that I was taking three months' grace, noticing love hearts everywhere and writing a list of all the qualities that I wanted in a man.

One August day, we agreed to meet at a halfway point between our homes for a beach walk. When we arrived, the weather had turned. A dense sea haar had descended and was now obscuring the water's edge. We could barely see the sea, which was just several metres away. We set off towards the café further along the beach. Our conversation flowed easily, and we laughed together.

I remembered noticing how easy it was to be with him. And I also sensed a gentle soulfulness about him that I had not experienced quite in this way before. He spoke more of his own personal values, and I gleaned a deeper insight into the innermost world of this private man that I had known for decades. I was both surprised and intrigued. I began to feel a deeper connection with him. I felt his tender heart. I saw the depth in his brown eyes. I felt the hum of our energy fields connecting. I felt the rich texture of his voice vibrating through my bones. I had always loved his voice. I could listen to him speak for hours. I sensed the sheer depth of his wisdom. I had not experienced him in this way before. We had always shared what I would call a natural chemistry and had a mutual respect as colleagues too. I would say too that there was a fondness of him on my part.

As we neared the beach café, I became aware that the weather was changing.

The mist was clearing.

And now, on the Winter Solstice 2013, I remembered the psychic's words:

'You will recognise your soulmate when the mist lifts. When the mist lifts, you will know him.'

And I did. We gently yet powerfully shifted from being friends to lovers. It was surprising, tender, fun, exciting, joyful and, at times, challenging. I did *know* this man. When I first touched his skin, I knew him. His skin felt familiar. Isn't that an odd thing to say? And yet it was true. We had a natural chemistry, and our connection went beyond the physical, the mind or even the heart. There was a very strong soul connection.

He saw me. He got me. He respected and appreciated me. I could be fully myself with him. There were no hiding places, and it helped me to loosen the final layers of conditioning and hiding that I had been harbouring.

In him, I found the depth. In him, I found an edge to myself that hadn't manifested in any other relationship. I trusted him completely, and so I was able to let go, fully, wildly, joyously. There were complications too. Like any two fifty-somethings in a new relationship, we had histories to reconcile, a few wounds that weren't quite scabs, let alone scars. We didn't know whether our relationship would last or whether we were simply together to help each other heal from our previous relationships. And for now, that was ok.

And the blonde woman? My former husband met a lovely woman in late 2013, whom he later married.

And yes, she is blonde.

Bring Me Sunshine

Summer 2014

I was sitting in the garden one summer's morning having breakfast when the most beautiful thing happened. As I began to eat, I could feel a familiar presence all around me. It felt like a warm, loving hug. It made me smile. I felt happy and was surprised to feel tears spontaneously rolling down my cheeks.

And then, from the kitchen, I heard my eldest son, Will. He was whistling the song, '*Bring Me Sunshine*'. How on Earth does he know that song? I wondered. And then, in that very moment, I recognised the familiar presence – it was the energy of my favourite grandad.

I hadn't felt him around for such a very long time that I sat and basked in this glorious moment. I was glued to my chair; I didn't want to move a muscle. I wanted to drink it in, to feel it through my whole body for as long as I could. A memory dropped into my mind of the letter I wrote to him when he died. And then, the penny dropped. Today was 16th August and it was sixteen years ago this week that he had passed.

With goosebumps running all through my body, so many memories began to flood back. Will was just four then and Josh was eighteen months old. I remember the deep grief of losing my favourite grandad. Reflecting now, I can see just how lucky I was to have had him as a male role model, as well as the joy to have known him as my grandad. Immense privilege. What a truly wonderful man.

He was loved by so many – he was immensely kind, generous, loving and fun. As my way of honouring him, I'd had the idea to write him a letter. I wrote it on blue-tinged parchment paper and curled it into a scroll, securing it with an ivory silk ribbon from a box of wedding day memorabilia. The scroll was placed over his heart and went with him to be cremated.

I had kept a replica copy and now had a real desire to go find that letter so that I could re-read it. A mild panic set in. I hadn't seen it in years, and we had moved house recently, so I wasn't sure I knew where to find it. Instantly, in my mind's eye, I saw the box it was stored in and when I went to look for it, there it was. It was still rolled up into a scroll with the beige ribbon I had tied around it. Perfect. I settled down to read it once more.

A Letter to my Grandad

Dearest Grandad,

Why is it so difficult to say what really matters when it counts?

I am sitting in the garden surrounded by geraniums and roses. It is very hot – just as you would have loved it to be. The scent from the flowers is really quite heady and the bees are humming all around. Butterflies are dancing around the buddleia and the scabious, and the pink scented rose you gave me as a cutting from your front garden is now healthy and abundant with rose heads in a pot by the garden seat.

I want you to know that you were the best grandad I could ever have hoped for and that I love you very much. You will always be in my heart, and I am so lucky to have some very special memories of you and our time together.

~ I remember how special it felt to dance the waltz with you on my wedding day.

~ Thank you too for making our wedding cake all the more special for us.

~ I loved seeing you hold William, your first great-grandchild, when he was just three days old, the pride in your face and the tears in your eyes.

~ I remember how when you smiled, your nose would curl up and wrinkle.

~ How you used to say 'Ta-Ta!' as your way of saying goodbye.

~ The lilt of your soft Welsh accent and your laugh.

~ Your very special hugs and the way you winked at me – I knew always meant 'I love you'.

~ The special times at the farm, the donkey rides, feeding the pigs and collecting the chickens' eggs.

~ The geraniums and roses, snapdragons, and grapevines in your garden and battered greenhouse.

~ Saturday nights spent with you and Nan out ballroom dancing.

~ The scent of whiskey on your breath in the evenings.

~ The smell of freshly mown and gathered grass.

~ And the comfort and hope of watching you dance with Nan and seeing the love you shared.

I remember you most of all for being fun, loving, kind and always willing to help others.

I am sure that you are happy and well now. If you can give me a sign that all is well, that would be wonderful, and if not, that is fine too.

May you have a ball in heaven – save a dance for me when my time comes!

All my love x

I sat quietly for quite some time after this, feeling quite numb. My mind went back to the week that he passed. Grandad had a history of heart problems. He had been in and out of hospital so many times. Each time felt like it could be the last and yet still he came out, fit and healthy. We didn't expect to say goodbye to him that last time. We assumed he would come out again. But it wasn't to be. Over the period of three very hot days, we sat by his bed. Different family members were with him at different times, spontaneously dropping in as and when we could. My cousin and brother had the longest journeys, and they both managed to get there just in time before he passed. Sadly, my other cousin was in Canada and couldn't get a flight home in time. She and I shared a special kind of connection with him. I was devastated for her. I knew that she would have wanted to see him one last time before he died and to say her own goodbye in person.

On the third day of his hospital stay, as I was leaving, he took my hand in his, looked directly into my eyes and said, 'Goodbye, Catherine.' I *knew* in that moment that he was dying. He knew he was dying, and he knew that he was saying goodbye to me. Tears welled up. He smiled through his eyes. I felt what I can only describe as a 'transmission' from him. I felt a strength come through me. I don't know how long we continued to hold each other's gaze. It felt like a very long time, however, I imagine it was only a matter of seconds.

My heart felt so very heavy as I left the hospital and drove home. Robbie Williams' song 'Angel' came on the radio, and I turned the volume up as loud as it would go and sang my heart out, crying tears of sorrow and joy. Sorrow for the grandad I was never going to see again and joy for the love and gratitude that I felt for having had him in my life for all this time.

Later that evening, my husband and I decided to go swimming. We had a babysitter already planned and figured it would help me clear my head and process all that had gone on that week. I was swimming avidly up and down the pool when I suddenly started to get palpitations in my heart, and I had to stop. It was difficult to catch my breath. Simultaneously I had a vision of my grandad's face smiling at me. It was so real. It was like his face was right in front of me, as if he were there with me in person. I looked up and happened to notice the time. It was 9.20 p.m. I signalled to my husband that I was getting out and made my way to the changing area to get ready to go home.

I slept well that night. The phone woke me around six o'clock the following morning. It was my mum. My heart sank.

'I'm sorry to ring you so early, but I guess you already know and that I don't need to tell you?' she said.

'Grandad?' My mum replied, 'Yes.'

'Was it a heart attack? Around twenty past nine last night?' I asked.

'Exactly that. He had a fatal heart attack. He was in no pain. Nan was holding his hand, and there were five of us there with him. It was very peaceful. And yes, he died at exactly twenty past nine.'

And then I cried. Big gulps. My husband held me. Our sons heard me and came running into the bedroom. They climbed onto the bed and snuggled up and we explained that 'old grandad' had died. His heart had been poorly, and it had stopped beating. There were so many questions. Such sweet responses. I wish I could remember them all now.

On the day of his cremation, my husband brought our sons over to the gathering that followed. If the cremation itself hadn't invoked tears to fall, then what happened next saw everyone well up.

Will had chosen a special helium balloon that reminded him of his great-grandad. It had Winnie the Pooh on it. He held tightly onto its string and asked, 'Do I do it now? Is it time yet, Mummy?'

'Yes, I replied, it's time. Are you ready?' He nodded.

'Goodbye, old grandad. I love you,' he said.

And he released the balloon into the air, up into the warm summer sky.

Looking back, I always had a feeling that my grandad's passing had a link somehow to my awakening, although I can't quite put my finger on exactly why. One year on from his death and on the day of the solar eclipse in August 1999, as I shared earlier in the book, I had what some might describe as a spiritual awakening.

As I began to weave the pieces of this story together for this chapter of the book, I felt his presence with me. His smile and warmth arrived to be present for me and the words here.

Thank you, Grandad. You were The Best! I loved you then, I love you still.

And if you are wondering why the song 'Bring me Sunshine' immediately reminded me of my grandad, here is why. Partly it was because he was often visiting on the evenings when the British TV comedy duo Morecombe and Wise were on television – their signature tune was 'Bring Me Sunshine'.

And also because Eric Morecombe used to have a home next door to the smallholding where my grandad used to work. I spent many happy hours there having donkey rides, collecting the chickens' eggs, and feeding the pigs. Such happy memories.

And I never did ask Will how he knew that theme song.

The Labyrinth Speaks
Here I Sit

Earth beneath me.

Sky above me.

Here I sit.

I am part of the web of life.

Part of the whole and whole within myself.

Microcosm within macrocosm.

As within, so without.

As above, so below.

As in yin, so in yang.

Earth beneath me.

Sky above me.

Here I sit.

Funk Rocks!

Dear Moriah,

Give yourself permission to be in a gloriously messy, grumpy, tearful, sloth-like funk.

Wallow in it for longer than you think is healthy.

Shake off the 'shoulds'.

Defy the inner voices that tell you it's lazy and self-indulgent.

Have fun with it. Relish it.

Sink into it. Deeply. Ask questions of it.

Invite it closer like you might a lover.

Give it space, give it time, give it permission.

Let it be.

You won't get lost; you won't get swallowed up.

Here's the thing, Moriah.

You'll find yourself, your voice, and your rhythm.

You'll find your vibe, your groove.

Funk rocks!

Love from your funky, groovy Soul x

I Had a Rant!

Voice Note, Journal Entry, Easter Sunday 2015

I feel like a rabbit in the headlights.

My breathing is shallow.

I can't seem to get enough breath.

My chest is tight.

My head hurts, infernal, eternal spinning.

I haven't slept well again.

It's been months since I slept through the night.

Three night-sweats last night.

Flashes of searing heat like I've never experienced them before.

My body felt like there were waves of heat soaring through her.

Lying awake.

Feeling helpless.

Hopeless.

I don't understand why everything I'm trying comes to nothing.

I'm trying herbal remedies, changing my bedtime routine, I'm well-hydrated, physically rested, nourished by good food.

Nothing is working.

Nothing is helping.

My business is slow, in a dip.

Less clients showing up.

I'm trying everything I know to fix it but to no avail.

I hired a coach.

She misled me.

She changed the goalposts.

She wanted me to do it her way, not my way.

And I listened to her.

I changed my approach.

It alienated clients.

I ignored my intuition.

I didn't value my approach to work and how I like to work with clients.

I listened to her more than I listened to me.

Clients don't like the new way and I don't like the new way either.

When oh when will I ever learn and trust MY way is OK?

Why didn't I hold her to our contract?

Why did I let her change the goalposts halfway through?

I feel sick.

I feel weak.

Why don't I trust MY way?

I want to be free to work with clients in the way that works for me and them.

As needed, in the moment, raw and real.

I want to liberate them, empower them, and support them.

Not box them in or box myself in.

I don't want a one-size-fits-all programme.

I want to go deep.

I want to touch the Shadows.

I want the 'grit' as well as the 'grace'.

I want the light and the dark.

I don't do superficial.

It doesn't work for me; my Soul wants something else.

Why oh why am I in this situation?

It's not fair.

No matter what I try, nothing works.

All that I'm trying with my physical wellbeing and my business, all coming to nothing.

My body and my emotions keep me awake at night.

My head keeps me awake at night.

Menopause, chronic pain, recovering from divorce and now a business that I've lost my way with.

A business that feels as though it has abandoned me in my hour of need.

I need a hip replacement, but I'm told that I'm too young.

How does that work, you need it, but you are too young?

And now I must move house – again!

The landlady has broken her promise.

She is selling the house and the buyers want to move in fast, and I must move out.

Money speaks louder than promises, it seems.

And Josh will be part-way through important exams.

I've got less than eight weeks to find a new home and move.

The rug has been pulled from beneath my feet, again.

It's too much.

I can't do this.

It's not fair.

I'm exhausted.

WHERE ARE YOU?

Why do I feel so ALONE in all of this?

I'm on government benefits to bridge the gap between bills and income.

I've never had to do this before.

I've always paid my way.

I'm too old for a mortgage, and now I'm not earning enough.

I sometimes choose between heating and eating.

I've been working like a crazy woman to reinvent my business, to find a way of financially re-building so that I can feel good about myself and my ability to provide for myself and my sons.

It's not happening.

I've even looked at getting a job.

That won't work either.

I'm too long out of the corporate workplace to ever get back in.

I'm too qualified to work in a supermarket and my arthritic hip wouldn't allow it anyway.

The minimum wage or living wage still wouldn't pay the basic bills.

I can't believe that that is the Divine's plan for me.

I'm not feeling this is the right way to go.

But neither do I know what to DO or what is the right action.

There must be a way to break out of this downward spiral.

What is my life coming to?

I can't go on walks anymore and barely walk into the high street to pick up essentials because my hip is so painful.

I feel like I'm in a washing machine whose spin never stops.

No matter what I do, nothing is working, nothing is making any difference.

I don't know which way is up anymore.

The arthritis, the menopause, divorce, money squeeze, business dip has all come at once.

Is this some kind of crazy cosmic joke?

I feel powerless.

I feel wholly trapped.

Penned in.

There is no way out.

I can't see any way out of this unholy mess.

I'm grateful that we have a roof over our head – but for how long?

What happens if the money runs out, if it all tumbles?

If life comes crashing down and there is nothing?

Nothing?

What then?

What becomes of me then?

I feel wholly ashamed that it's come to this.

I can't believe that with all my experience, the skills I've honed, the thousands of people I've positively impacted, that I have come to this.

I can't believe that I can't make this work.

I've always made it work.

Why is this not working?

I don't understand.

Menopausal night sweats,

Pain through my hip and leg

Anxiety about my health, about money

And now I'm being kicked out of the house.

Even sleep doesn't bring me peace and respite.

I'm

Anxious

Sad

Scared.

I feel

A failure,

A victim,

Helpless

And hopeless.

I feel very alone.

It's not fair!

How can this be fair?

Why me?

I've followed all my callings, all the inner work, helped so many.

So much LOSS.

And like a volcano,

a wail rises through my body and out of my mouth,

a cry and then I scream.

WHY HAVE YOU ABANDONED ME?

Why don't I hear you, feel you, or see you?

WHERE ARE YOU?

And then a clear, calm, loving voice invites me to get pen and paper and to write down a message.

I would like to share this message with you in the two chapters that follow. It made me stop and think and take more responsibility for my choices. It helped to bring me out of 'victim mode' and feel more empowered. And most significantly, it reminded me to look within, always.

The Soul Speaks
of *the Power of Looking Within*

Dear Moriah,

We are all born into this world, and our orientation is outward facing because we are primarily dependent on others for our safety. The world keeps us this way. If we are not taught from a young age to reorient back to ourselves, our own needs and desires, then we continue to look outside of ourselves for our needs to be met.

Although some, if not all, our needs are met by being in right relationship with the world, they cannot be met by others – this is a very precarious way to live and spurns pain, fear, and disappointment. We must look within for our own inner compass. Our job, as we evolve and mature, is to find our way Home – home to ourselves.

Think about Dorothy in *The Wizard of Oz*. She travelled far and wide, looked to the wizard for answers, and the power was within her all along – she discovered this when she returned home. And think Alice in *Alice in Wonderland* – she had to experience so much before she grew into the Alice they were expecting – the Alice who could kill the Jabberwocky. This message is all about self-responsibility. It's about Mastery. Look within for your answers. Follow your own path, your own set of coordinates. It will bring you greater peace and contentment in the long run.

Living by someone else's rules, someone else's coordinates can never bring us peace. It takes us further away from ourselves.

In the same way, any comparative practice or habit can have a similar effect and denies us of the joy of who we are and what we are experiencing right now. So, comparing ourselves to who we were, what we had, who we thought we would become, who we think we should be or should have, who others want us to be, the norm in society, the perfect mother, girlfriend, wife, lover, employee, daughter, sister and so on is only going to bring us pain.

Who we are right now is where the magic is. It cannot be anywhere else. How could it be? Now is where it's happening. Now is where the alchemy is working. The circumstances, the opportunity, the thoughts, the feelings, and the intuitive nudges are all here in the present moment. You cannot step into the river at the same point with the same water flowing, ever. It is just not possible. Each new moment, each new day, each breath is an opportunity to embrace what is right and true for you. Your circumstances externally may initially look the same, yet your relationship with them will almost certainly not; it will have changed.

You cannot be self-responsible and be a victim. Who you are is love and if you honestly can't feel that, then your singular job and responsibility is to find your way home to that. At the end of the day, will you be content, truly content with anything less? If you are self-responsible, you can be in relationship with a man and not lose yourself. Know yourself. Self-knowledge is power.

A new guidance system is needed that isn't based on external values or others' values or coordinates.

Here is my offering to you today.

Love from your ever-present, tender loving Soul X

PS I step back so that you can grow. I am always here, with you. Always.

PPS Consider the following ten principles.

I'll be cheering you on.

It might take a few years for all ten to fully land, perfect, and embody, but it's all good.

What's a few years between friends, eh?

The Soul Speaks
of *the Ten Guiding Principles for Life*

Dear Moriah,

Here are your 10 Guiding Principles for life.

Be your own reference point
If you look outside of yourself, you will lose yourself and become disorientated. Look within for the answers you seek.

Decide how you want to be loved and give it to yourself first
No one else can love you in the way that you want to be loved. If you look to others, you will always be disappointed.

Feel what is real and true for you and stay with that
If you look to others to get a sense of what is real or true for you, you will always be disillusioned. Others' stories are not yours. You need to feel what is real and true for you and stay with that. Keep checking in with yourself because your story will change through time. If you live with someone else's story, you will always feel disorientated. Your story and someone else's story can be compatible and sometimes similar, but they will never be the same. How could they be?

Dance to your own rhythm
Dance to your own rhythm. If your rhythm is slow, be slow, honour slow. If your rhythm be fast, then be fast. Change it only when circumstances require you to temporarily step into a different rhythm. Do not entrain permanently or for long periods of time with someone else's rhythm. It won't work. They won't thank you for it. You will lose connection to the You they fell in love with. Stay true to your unique rhythm. Your Dance is precious and is needed in this world. Cherish it above all else, for it is Life itself.

Your truth lies in your body
Do not buy too blindly into the views of others. You do not have to agree with others, only give them a fair hearing. Check in with yourself regularly on what resonates and what doesn't. Chances are that you will feel it in the body anyway. Your truth lies in your body – your truth will be felt here first. What is true for you may not be true for another. Do not judge your own truth nor that of another. There is nothing to judge anyway.

Love everyone
Love everyone. Love yourself in the way that you want to be loved and love everyone, unconditionally if you can. The love will rebound many times over. Just don't expect it to show up in certain ways. It will show up in a myriad of ways.

Never hurt yourself
Never hurt yourself. Look at the thoughts and actions that cause you pain and stop them. Now.

It is an act of self-harm and serves no one, least of all you. Be self-compassionate with those parts of you that would rebel. They need love too. They will heal the hologram. They will heal your Whole.

Nourish yourself
Look at how you are feeding yourself – on all levels, physical, emotional, mental, and spiritual. Is it nourishing? If not, drop it.

Be your own sovereign being
Look within for your answers. Be your own sovereign being. Follow your own path, your own set of coordinates. In this way, you will never be knocked off-course, and you will always remain orientated, empowered, and free. You will be a stronger support for others but more importantly you will maintain your sense of self and be able to strengthen your energy on all levels. You are far less likely to feel drained. Living by someone else's rules and coordinates can never bring us peace. It takes us further away from ourselves. Being your own sovereign being will bring you greater peace and contentment in the long run.

Be in the moment
This is where the magic is. It cannot be anywhere else. How could it be? Now is where it is happening. Now is where the alchemy is working. The circumstances, the opportunity, the thoughts, the feelings, and the intuitive nudges are all here in the present moment. You cannot step into the river at the same point with the same water flowing, ever. It is just not possible. Each new moment, each new day, each breath is an opportunity to embrace what is right and true for you. Your circumstances externally may initially look the same, yet your relationship with them will almost certainly not, it will have changed.

With Love X

It is true to say that my rant had been loud, messy, and rambling. This message was calm, clear, and neutral. I felt a little taken aback. I had hoped maybe for a breakthrough in my work and finances or similar and yet my Soul did what it often does and gave me what I needed and not what I wanted. It was sound, practical advice. There was no sugar coating. Little reassurance, but sound wisdom. It stopped me in my tracks and gave me food for thought. It took a few weeks to digest it. It has, however, influenced me greatly over the months and years that have followed to the point that the guiding principles are now what I aim to live by, as well as being core to my philosophy of client offerings too.

How do these guiding principles resonate with you?

White Flag

Every angle.
Every route.
Every attempt.
Worked at it.
Pondered it.
Analysed it.
Examined it.
Thought long and hard about it.
Given up on it.
Tried some more.
Felt it.
Lived it.
Embodied it.
Sought help over it.
Talked about it.
Shared, simmered, and sizzled over it.
Shouted, screamed and ranted.
Puzzled over it.
Consulted and journaled about it.

Smiled, laughed, and fretted over it.
Joked about it.
Lost sleep over it.

And then, when I had tried every which way, when all the possibilities were exhausted, I lay down and I let myself rest.
And I began to surrender.

I began to let go of the chasing and the trying and the fixing of it, and I just let it be.
Time was on my side. There was no rush. I could afford to wait a while. I could let the solution come to me.

And I began to let it go.
Gently at first, with a sigh, and then with a l-o-n-g out-breath.

I felt my head begin to clear and my body relax.

I felt my jaw soften and my hands unclench.

I noticed the tension in my tummy and my hips, and I breathed that out too.

And I relished the glorious feeling of sinking down into my body and into my bed, deepening into the letting go.

I let go of berating myself for forgetting how powerful it is to allow rather than to push.

I let go of the tiredness that all this chasing and angsting had generated.

It was time to let go and to b-r-e-a-t-h-e.

'I surrender. I really do. I hand it over. I surrender.'

And I smile to myself, fully knowing that each time I remember to do this, I am less likely to go round the same loop again. And next time, just maybe, I will remember earlier that no-thing is an option.

Sometimes it's the only way.

The only thing to do.

The only thing I can do.

To do no-thing.

And to allow myself to trust in the mystery of this extraordinary experience that is Life, allowing the magic to unfold, in its own time and in its own way.

I surrender. I surrender. I surrender.

Come and Stay for Three Months

'Come and stay for three months.' This was the invitation from my partner. He knew that I was having difficulty finding a new rental home to meet the needs and criteria I had. He could feel the stress building in me and wanted to give me some respite and some peace. He knew that I was in physical pain and the toll that it was having on my overall wellbeing. He knew that I also had the added uncertainty of not knowing what my son would choose to do post-exams and which area it would be helpful to rent in. He wanted to give me some space and time to chill and to think about my next steps. And I loved him even more for that.

Me being me, I resisted. After all, it was only two years that I had been living independently, and I wasn't sure that I wanted to move in and live together, albeit for a short period of time. I enjoyed having my own space. I was also concerned for my younger son, who was fast approaching revising for and taking significant exams. Moving over to stay at my partner's home would mean that I would be an hour away, and I wouldn't so easily be able to support him in his revision. I knew that I would miss not seeing my sons, the informal chats, hearing about their day and what was going on for them, the small details. They had been with me constantly for twenty-one years. It felt a wrench to not be seeing them regularly. My eldest had already moved into his father's house to be closer to good transport links for work and socialising. I understood and accepted that as a good practical solution. I wasn't sure I was ready to have my younger son do the same. It felt like I would be fleeing the nest rather than vice versa, and looking back on it, maybe there was an uncomfortable truth in that. I recognised that I was afraid of being judged.

I had conflicted feelings. On the one hand, it would indeed be a blessed relief not to have to pay any bills for three months. I could save a good chunk of money for the next period of renting. I could rest in his home. He would be away working during the week, and we would spend each weekend together. I, in return, would be taking care of the house. Ever since we had got together in relationship, we had both referred to the house as 'The Sanctuary' or as 'Number

Ten'. It was, in many ways, a refuge for both of us. We had gotten together after we had both come out of long-term relationships and were in different stages of completion. Our relationship and this house had given us both space to breathe, to love and to heal. We were very aware of this when we got together. We knew that it was a risk, and we also recognised that it was an opportunity too. Our hearts had led the way.

However, I also felt guilty for not providing a home for my sons and for staying at my partner's home. I felt guilty for seemingly choosing him over them, and even though I knew that wasn't the case, I still felt it. I was judging myself. Could I really let life be this *easy*? Could I allow myself to be supported? Could I even trust that I was loved, no matter what choices I made? Fully, entirely supported, no strings attached.

Clearly not, initially, as I resisted it. I thanked my partner graciously and said I'd consider it. We agreed it would be my safety net if nothing else and that having it as an option would in and of itself help me to relax into choosing my next step. I wrote a list, as I often had done in these situations, listing everything I wanted in my next home. I made connections with all the local estate agents and visited many properties over the course of two weeks. I put my business on hold for those two weeks so that I could give our home search my full attention. I knew that I always got better results that way. Each house that I saw was a nice proposition and yet there was always a deal breaker. A house that was marketed for non-smokers reeked of cigarette smoke. A house that was great on the inside turned into a very noisy proposition when I opened a window and heard the busy arterial road at the bottom of the garden behind the bushes. The beautiful house in the nearby village, which had a river running alongside it, had swarms of mosquitoes hovering over the garden, and it had just a six-month lease available whilst the owners were abroad. And so, it went on. I was refused access to three properties because I was, and I quote, a 'single mum'. And this by female landlords. So much for women looking out for women. After viewing around fifteen properties and with just one week to go before timings would reach anxiety-inducing levels, I sat down and took stock.

I sat on the sofa and got myself comfortable, feeling my feet on the floor and my body supported, letting myself sink into the hug of the furniture. And I closed my eyes. I called to my mind the four potential properties that I would consider renting, including the option of staying at my partner's house. In my mind's eye, I saw them all in a line, one next to the other. I cast my eye over each one, working left to right, scanning them energetically. I had developed this technique a few years beforehand. I was looking to see which ones were optimum for me simply by looking at the energy around them. They all lined up, a little like an old photo negative reel. Side by side. I was puzzled and perplexed when the visual appeared. I decided to shake it all up again, to scramble the properties, a little like a magician moving around the cups on the table, hiding the shiny object beneath the domes. And then I invited all four properties to reveal themselves once more. Same result. One more time, I shuffled. And there it was. The only property in the line-up that was glowing was Number Ten. The Sanctuary was glowing so much, in fact, that it now had a beautiful golden aura all around it. All the other properties were in shadow, all black and white. So be it, this was the pathway ahead. This was the choice of my Soul, and although I wouldn't be going kicking and screaming, I still had some concerns.

I rang my partner to accept his invitation, and he was delighted, if a little surprised, as he thought I would choose an alternative. I began to talk with my sons and their father about this potential plan. Everyone agreed it made sense. My son would stay with his father and brother until he knew what he wanted to do post-exam results. We would visit each other and keep in touch by video calls in the meantime. I planned for my belongings to move into storage. All was organised within a day. Everything fell into place quickly. I could now relax and enjoy the last month in the beautiful town where I lived and catch up with local friends before I moved an hour further west along the coast. It also meant that I could focus on supporting my son in his exam preparation, even if it just meant that my role was one of ensuring he had good nutrition, was hydrated, and slept well. I could now put him first and let go of the worry around a home hunt.

It seemed that I was beginning to allow myself to be supported and for life to be easy. Getting my head out of the way of this decision had opened a clear pathway that I might otherwise not have chosen.

In the days leading up to moving day, I put aside the few things that I wanted to take with me to The Sanctuary. My work gear, my summer clothes and gym kit, a few fragile items, some books, my own oracle decks, plus toiletries. Everything else was going to be packed by the removal company, leaving me with just the cleaning to do. By this point, the osteoarthritis had progressed, and I wanted to be able to minimise discomfort and conserve energy, and so it felt wise not to be doing all my own packing for the sake of a few hundred pounds.

I helped my youngest son pack up the day before I moved out. His father came to pick him up. As he walked down the garden path towards the car, there was a finality that I felt in my heart and my body. I had a very strong sense that this was the end of a chapter in my life. It felt like the end of an era, with me handing over the baton to his father to be their main carer now. It wasn't a thought. It was a sense of what was happening, like reading the subtext to a plot in a story. A sense that this had been agreed at some other time and that I was following an invisible thread.

I didn't have time to process any of this because my friend arrived at the house just as they were leaving. She too had the sense that the 'baton' had just been handed over. She and I walked into the village and had afternoon tea together as planned. It seemed like a lovely way to mark the end of my time here, and I wanted to say thank you for all the love and support that she had given me in the years leading up to this point. It was a celebration.

Looking back, there were so many signs that this part of my life was ending, doors closing, and yet although I noticed the shifts, I still believed that I was coming back and that this change was temporary. I might not have chosen these changes if I hadn't been in this set of circumstances. I wasn't ready to live with someone else and certainly wasn't ready to let my sons go. Life had conspired to move me out of my own way so that my Soul's plan could play out. And being soul-led, I followed the energy signature, however hard it felt at the time.

As I got back from the tea shop, my partner was at home getting on with cleaning the bathrooms. He had also brought wine and a picnic for the evening. It had been such a bittersweet two years in this home. I had been to the depths of sadness and fear. I had fallen in love, created a new home, brought the gardens back to life, and helped my sons through their own transition following the separation. I had found a renewed sense of self-love and *joie de vivre*. Hope was returning. New chapters were beginning everywhere for all of us. Life was beginning to blossom once more. It was time. It was *my* time.

The day after I moved over to my partner's house, I began to bleed heavily. I had been peri-menopausal for a few years, and this had happened periodically before, noticeably three months earlier when I bled for three long, exhausting weeks. The build-up to moving, watching my youngest move out, cleaning, organising, driving two hours to padlock the storage unit where my belongings would be stored, and now this onset of bleeding all began to show up in my body. I ached from head to toe. My hip and leg were painful, and I had a headache. As I dealt with the final paperwork and invoices from the house move, I began to feel very tired. It was then that I decided that I would take the remainder of the week off from client work and release all expectations of myself. In this way, I could just be in flow with my body and give her what she needed most – rest. We had a holiday booked already for the following week so this would give me time to prepare for that too.

It turned out to be my very last period, and at the end of that week, I went into full menopause. The end of an era and the beginning of the next phase of my life story was just beginning.

PS In case you are curious, I am still here, living with my partner at Number Ten. The Sanctuary became my home.

Head in the Sand

September 2015

'You have osteoarthritis. You will need a hip replacement within five years but will have to wait longer because you are currently too young to qualify.'

My doctor gave me this news whilst staring at her computer screen. She didn't sugar-coat it; she didn't look at me, and she still didn't look at me when I began to ask her questions. She clearly either wasn't interested in me or had better things to do. She told me she would give me a referral for physiotherapy, and I could expect an appointment in six months' time.

I was in shock. Although I had suspected as much, I had not wanted to hear this news at all. I was way too young. I was just fifty-three. I associated arthritis with older age. And what does she mean that I'll need a replacement but can't have one? I left her surgery and went back downstairs to the reception desk. Remarkably, I had the presence of mind to ask for a second opinion and someone who could explain the prognosis to me. Luckily, another doctor was on hand and gave me fifteen minutes of his time. I left the doctors' surgery still stunned but with a little more information.

This had been building since I was forty-six. It began with not being able to sit cross-legged in a yoga session, to pain in my hip whilst sleeping, to not being able to open my hip fully, to pain whilst walking and now to limping. It took all that time before I had plucked up the courage to have a second X-ray. I had the first one a few years earlier but with moving house and my state of denial, I didn't go and ask for the results, and the doctor's surgery didn't contact me, so I left it, hoping it would disappear.

The reality of surgery, having my hip cut away and a new one positioned to replace it, the recovery and being left with a large, fifteen-centimetre scar horrified me. And my ego was jumping up and down like a child saying, 'NO, no way! I'm way too young.' It was the beginning of my needing to surrender and to accept to the fact that I was maturing, and my body was undergoing as much physical change as my life was. Change was going on within me and all around me, and at times, I was terrified. There was no safe anchor to drop, nothing that seemed constant or stable. And moreover, I had little or no control, it seemed.

Having qualified in so many vibrational and complementary therapies, I also believed that I might be able to heal it. I threw everything I had at it. I also spent a fair amount of money on sessions that seemed to promise the miracle cure but never did. It was a bit like pregnancy or parenting – everyone seemed to have a view and quite often they were conflicting. So, I stopped listening and instead followed my own route and began to listen to my body.

I began to tune in more deeply to my left hip. I would take myself into a shamanic inner journey and zone into the energy of my hip to see if I could learn from what was going on. My inner work over the previous few years had mostly been about healing the disempowerment felt either in my own life but also from my maternal grandmother's line. It seemed that part of my purpose in this lifetime was to resolve the issues they faced around themes of survival and sacrifice, how they had no voice of their own and how they couldn't stand on their own two feet and had to rely on their husbands to support them. It was a lot to do with the patriarchal society that we have been living within for centuries. A lot of my healing took place in these journeys and whilst I had hoped that they would clear the symptoms and heal my hip, it wasn't to be.

It all came to a head when my partner and I were on holiday in Greece, the week after I had moved over to stay. He asked me one morning, as we were on our way to the beach, what the prognosis was for my hip, and for the first time, he asked me what I was going to do about it. That shocked me out of my comfort zone. It played on my mind, and I felt defensive. He was right to ask me, challenge me even. He could see that I was in denial. I needed to face this reality.

When we reached the beach, he offered to carry our bags so that I could focus on walking. It seemed a simple thing to do, to focus on walking, however, it proved more difficult than I expected. The sand was very fine and with each step I took, my feet would sink deeply into the sand. This meant that I had to exert a lot of effort to lift my foot up each time to take the next step. This was easy enough with my right hip but difficult and excruciating with my left hip. It took me more than twice the amount of time to reach the spot where my partner had settled. By the time I got there I was close to tears and feeling embarrassed. I had noticed people looking at me, no doubt wondering why I was making such a meal of things. I felt so ashamed. No one could have known the pain I was in because osteoarthritis is such an invisible condition. It got steadily worse as the day went on. I went for a gentle swim but realised that I couldn't climb up the shore to get out of the sea and had to call my partner to help me. I felt even more shame at that point and resigned myself to lying on the beach until it was time to go back to our villa.

And then the most extraordinary thing happened.

I noticed a couple playing volleyball together just over to the left of us, on the sand. They were probably in their late fifties. She was in amazing shape, very toned and fit. As she moved around, I noticed that she had a scar on her left hip, exactly the shape and length of scar produced by hip surgery. Wow, I thought, *she's had a hip replacement*. I mentioned this to my partner. Just at that moment, she turned again, this time she was even closer to where we were sitting, and I could see that she had the same scar on her right hip too. She'd had two hip replacements.

I have sent that woman so many blessings since we saw her that day because she gave me the confidence to face the decisions and take the action that I knew needed to happen but that I had been putting off for so long.

When we got home from holiday, I booked in with my new, local doctor. I was immediately put onto a waiting list and referred to a surgeon who specialised in 'young adult' joint replacement. At the ripe age of 53, this made me smile! It seems that many surgeons won't operate on the under-60s. I had the surgery within seven months. It was life changing. I wish I had listened to my mum and others who had told me to have it done. I was scared. I had to work through the feelings of shame and inadequacy. I needed to know that it was OK to have this condition at such a young age and that it wasn't my fault. It was genetic and it happens to younger people. Thank goodness that I had a surgeon who specialises in 'younger' hips. By the time I had the operation, the surgeon told me that it was 'bone on bone'.

If you or someone you know needs a hip replacement, please gently encourage them to act sooner rather than later. It is a modern-day miracle. I wish I had had the courage to have it done sooner.

As it turned out, I only had two years of pain-free living before my right hip began to deteriorate quickly.

I Let My Belongings Go

December 2016

I remember thinking when I first began living independently of my husband that I wanted to *tread lightly* upon the Earth. I even wrote it on my vision board. It was a faint, *felt* feeling as such and without any thought or anticipation of what that might mean. Some might call it a romantic notion or a sentiment. For me, it felt like a desire, something to aspire to, perhaps. I even remember writing about it at around that time. Looking back, I would now say that it was my Soul speaking.

I had no way of knowing that less than four years later, I would be taking a major step toward this desire.

I had been staying at my partner's house for over a year and had recovered well from hip surgery. My sons had now settled fully into their dad's house and had made it their permanent home. It made total sense in so many ways. It was closer to their friends, amenities, and job opportunities and had good transport links. Their dad had by this time settled into a new relationship and was away from home more often and so this gave them all a good balance of time together and time alone. They were in their early twenties now and had transitioned into being young men and having their main hands-on influence as their dad was going to be helpful to their development. There seemed little point in moving an hour closer to them. I saw them regularly and we kept in touch via video calls and text messages in between visits. They were living independent lives and didn't need me in the same way that they once had.

It was time for me to take a step back.

I had also grown used to staying at Ian's house. He was still away working during the week and home at weekends, and this balance suited us both. I had joined the local health club, met new friends, explored the local beauty spots, and, of course, there was the long, expansive, stunning, sandy beach. I felt at home here. My Soul soared in this place. The beach had become my happy place. As much as I missed having my sons around, I also enjoyed having a newfound sense of time-freedom which brought with it more energy too.

Paying for the storage unit was expensive. It was now time for me to decide what to do with my belongings. It had been eighteen months since I had last seen or touched the contents of the storage unit. I knew exactly what was in it because I had packed and unpacked it so many times within the last few years. I also knew what was there because the items were the reduced remainder of my married life, having sifted through them and retained a smaller quantity when we moved out of our family home. A five-bedroom sized set of belongings had shrunk to three-bedroom size. And now it was about to become a whole lot less.

Without delay, I set a date and drove the hour-long journey to the storage centre. Once there, I located the storage unit assigned to me and opened the chunky padlock and heavy, barred doors.

It was an eerie feeling when I opened the big, heavy, bolted doors to the unit. So much had happened in the eighteen months since I was last here. My sons had grown into young men. Ian and I had decided to live together. I'd had a hip replacement. My business had finally begun to pick up again. I was once again feeling like Life had my back.

And here they were. My life's possessions, sitting just as I had left them.

I stepped into the container and began to familiarise myself with where everything was, and as I did so, I realised that I no longer felt any connection with so much of what was there. The shabby chic hall table, so many ornaments and pieces of furniture. These didn't feel like mine at all. The woman who had so lovingly and carefully packed all these things was not the woman I had become. I was forever changed. Again.

I had brought large bin bags with me plus pens, sticky labels, and all manner of things that I thought might be helpful. I decided that my first job would be to sort through the many boxes. It wouldn't take long. I could quickly make my way through them and sort easily into what to keep and what to give away. At least, that's what I thought.

I worked through ten boxes in six hours. A disproportionate amount of time for what could have been a very speedy job. It was evident right from the outset that this was going to be a very emotional process. I was making decisions about what to keep and what to throw away, sell, or give away forever. There was no middle ground here. There was no going back. My life's possessions were about to be scattered to the four winds.

When I initially moved over to stay with my partner, it was for a short three-month stay. I didn't anticipate staying any longer than that. I felt responsible for providing a home for the boys and I certainly wasn't emotionally ready to let go of them just yet. It was June when I moved, and so I brought with me only summer clothes, plus the financial and legal documents I might need, client notes, my jewellery box, plus my desktop computer and laptop. Everything else was packed and stored.

So, when I opened the boxes, I was, in effect, opening a lid on my past. The joy, the pain, and all the tears came flooding back.

The first box was full of cookery books. Some were old, dating back to university days, some quite recent. Some had been given as gifts. Some were so well-used that they had splashes of oil and messy, sticky fingerprints over their covers and on the recipe pages. Some still had barely been opened, let alone used.

I decided that I would keep only the ones that I would use now and into the future, namely healthy eating and/or vegetarian. This ruled out a lot of the books and made sorting a much simpler activity. The messy ones were sent off for recycling. I kept six out of the forty books, and the remainder went to charity shops. This was not an activity that I had ever anticipated being particularly difficult. I didn't think I would be so attached to recipe books. But of course, it wasn't the books that I was attached to. It was the memories of the experience of preparing family and celebration meals, the gatherings, everyday meals, my sons' favourite recipes, the people who had gifted me the books, and, of course, the golden threads running through all of this were the feelings each of these books evoked. It was potent. I could almost smell some of the ingredients and recipes. I could hear my sons' laughter. The clamber to get downstairs ahead of dinner time. The chatter of the day and the conversations shared over meals. These were the times when my sons often talked more openly about things that really mattered to them, and it was precious. Yes, there were ordinary days and not-so-great days when there was some conflict brewing or bursting, but overall, my memory is of happy times.

I closed my eyes and saw my sons as they were back when they were six and four. Their smiling faces, cheekiness, their eyes shining with the anticipation of their next scheme or play time. I saw the meals and the aromas, the noise, the chatter, the noise of the chairs' legs on the kitchen floor as they arrived. And I imagined scooping it all up into a ball inside my open hands and placed the ball inside my heart. Here is where the memories would live on, and the books could be set free to nourish other people, other families.

All of this was gut-wrenchingly tough. I thought I had dealt with the feelings of loss and sadness, and yet here I was again, sobbing. Another layer of the proverbial onion was peeling off.

It was whilst I was in a teary state that a man appeared at the entrance to the storage unit and asked me if I needed any help. He could see my tear-stained face and offered to make me a cup of tea. I smiled and accepted gratefully. Luckily, I had brought tissues with me. He was the manager for the storage site, and he offered practical help. He could pass on the items for charity to the local hospice shop that he supported. How wonderful. 'Yes, yes, please,' I responded. He told me it was rare to see anyone sorting through the contents of their units. Apparently, some units had remained unopened for up to five to ten years after items were originally stored there and doors locked. It seemed that folk generally did not return. He was so happy to help me, and I was grateful for his help and for his cheery company. I suggested that regular mugs of tea would be very welcome.

After our chat, I moved on to the next box and then the next. The process became so much easier with each box that I opened. I gave myself some parameters to work within. I would keep items that had true sentimental value, were practical and needed at home, beautiful, or would fit into the loft and I would use again. Preferably each thing would answer to multiple criteria. To this day, very little enters our home via me that isn't both practical and beautiful.

I let go of bed linen, clothing, curtains, lampshades, ornaments, books, DVDs, CDs, jewellery, furniture, kitchen utensils, cushions, electrical equipment, stationary, and shelving. On future visits, I sold the three-seater brown leather sofa that I'd loved and hoped I could keep but was just too big and didn't fit our coastal home style. I sold the washing machine, the tumble dryer and the dishwasher, the dining room table and chairs, a footstool, and a tall lamp. And I sold them all from the storage unit itself. The man who made tea gave me the go-ahead to invite buyers to pick up from the site itself, which made life so much easier.

I discovered that he had delivered the artificial Christmas tree, lights, and the decorations I was happy to give away to the local hospice, which made my heart very happy. I had a bizarre thought that it was like organ donation – all our treasured possessions that we now no longer needed or wanted were finding new homes and a renewed purpose. This brought me a great sense of acceptance and contentment. It felt right somehow.

Friends helped me on some occasions too. One friend helped me for the day, and I offered her the white crockery and cutlery sets for her daughter who was just setting up a new home on a budget. Another friend helped me clear the final bits. Ian helped me bring home the selected pieces that I would keep. All in all, four visits in the space of seven weeks. The last thing to load was my bed. And then it was all gone.

I set to work to clean the floor of the storage unit, signed the papers to release it back to the centre and gave the guy who had helped me a heartfelt thank you and a bottle of wine. I also gave him a box of tea bags to help replenish his supply! His presence, kindness, and tea-making service had made the world of difference to me in this letting-go process, more than he could possibly have known. It was good to have such steady, grounded, helpful male support and I was very grateful.

As I drove away, I felt a huge relief. It was like a weight that I didn't know I was carrying had suddenly lifted from my shoulders and from my heart. There was just a hint of sadness that I wouldn't see some of the items again and yet I also knew that I had made the right decisions. It was time to move on from the past. It was time to let go and I had certainly done that and in spectacular style.

The one thing that I found very hard to let go of was my bed. I had bought it new just over three years ago and it was exactly the size and style I wanted. A sled bed in oak, king size and with white Egyptian cotton bedding. It was the one luxury item that I had bought. In fact, it was the only item I bought at that time. My bedroom was my sanctuary. Sadly, there was nowhere to house it at home now and the individual pieces were too big. It came home with me and lay on the lounge floor for a few days until I could find a new home for it. It was a very big and visual reminder of the enormity of what I was letting go of.

There was now what felt like an emptiness inside of me. I had experienced so much loss and yet this had a different quality to it, and I couldn't find the words to describe it. I could feel it though, in the pit of my stomach. Perhaps it was just a new space rather than an emptiness. I guessed it would reveal itself in the fullness of time.

In those four visits, I had let go of *over ninety-five per cent of everything I owned*. Ninety-five per cent. I wonder if you can imagine doing that? Perhaps you have experienced this too? I had at least done this voluntarily, even if it was a good practical and financial decision to make. For others who let go of everything, it might have been taken from them, and I imagine that to be very shocking to their system.

Looking back, it was a mammoth task and not one I would have contemplated or achieved if I hadn't been in the unique set of circumstances that I found myself in. Yet again, I could feel the influence of my Soul guiding me in the direction that I needed to go in. I remember getting back to the house and sitting down with a cup of tea and feeling a little stunned, numb even. I was quite possibly in shock, but I didn't recognise it as such until much later on, several months to be exact. It was done now. Time to move on.

Time to let go and let be. Time for the new chapter to begin.

I had let go of almost all my possessions.

I no longer had the option of owning my own property.

My relationship with the concept and reality of 'ownership' was changing.

My relationship with the value I placed on the external, material world was rapidly transforming.

This seemingly simple task of clearing my storage unit had turned out to be a giant step in my journey to belonging.

In letting go of my belongings, I was coming home to myself. What was once extrinsic was becoming intrinsic. What once took up significant space, now occupied less than a single, small box room and a portion of the loft. And this is still the case today, several years on.

I think very carefully before I buy anything these days. Do I really need this thing? Is it beautiful? Will it enhance our home or life? Is it sustainable and will it last?

Unbelievably, my lingerie, for example, lived happily in a recyclable 'bag for life' for around five years before I got around to buying a set of drawers to store them more elegantly. This would have been impossible for me to imagine prior to my divorce, let alone accept or tolerate. Somehow it no longer mattered to me. I had previously had a full bedroom suite of matching furniture with a place for everything and everything in its place. I frequently marvelled at my new underwear home. I was very curious. It became a point of regular fascination. Was I lazy? What was going on?

 The stuff that was important to me was no longer important. It was that simple. Period.

A lifetime's conditioning had so utterly and completely unravelled. I no longer cared so much about what other people thought or what I felt I should be doing or how things in my life should be. What became more important to me was my relationship with my space and how I now chose to use my energy. The quality of my inner space and the quality of connection with others took on more value to me.

My priorities had shifted. I had let my belongings go and in so doing, I had come home to myself even more. I was gradually re-aligning to my new inner values. After all the years of transforming limiting beliefs and releasing layers upon layers of 'shoulds', 'coulds', and other peoples' expectations, my outer world was undeniably shifting to align with my inner world.

And I was gradually, imperceptibly, consistently unravelling the moss and freeing myself up.

And it felt foreign, new, and liberating all at once.

I was coming home, and Home was where I longed to be.

Home.

Home to Myself.

Home to my Soul.

Home to my Purpose.

Home to my Body.

Home.

It wasn't until I was forced to stop that I learned the value of the PAUSE.

It wasn't until I'd had to let everything go, that I learned to value everything I had.

And it wasn't until I had changed beyond measure that I discovered the peace so deeply within me that I had been seeking for so very long,

silently calling me into presence,

like buried treasure,

Home,

Home at last.

Glastonbury Tor Labyrinth

Journal Entry, 5th May 2017

Morning

Today's the day that I am walking the Glastonbury Tor Labyrinth with a small group of friends. I felt inspired to organise this last autumn and I had also had a full-bodied knowing that it needed to be at Beltane, in early spring.

I'm sitting in the breakfast room of the guest house I'm staying in. I can hear the church bells ringing as I eat my breakfast. I chose three cards from my own *Creative Manifestation Deck*.

Innocence, Visibility, Transformation.

What do they mean to me right now, ahead of today's Labyrinth walk?

An invitation to be myself, to show up and be visible as the true me.

An invitation to reclaim my Younger Self who knew about devas and nature spirits and how to communicate with them.

It is an exercise in Trust and Perseverance.

An invitation to put one foot in front of the other and to trust.

I am a cocktail of nervous energy, anticipation, and curiosity. I can feel my spirit of adventure kicking in. It's an endurance test for me and those who have booked to walk it with me. It's a seven-hour, arduous walk up, around, down the Labyrinth all around the mound that is the Tor. It's not easy. I'm told that many don't attempt it, let alone complete it. I am here to complete it. This feels important.

Evening

I did it! We did it! Feeling very satisfied that I managed to complete it. Wow, what an experience. It took over seven hours. Feet are very sore. I feel incredibly tired and wired. Just an hour before meeting up with the group again.

What has felt true to me today?

Walking the Labyrinth is like turning the end of a kaleidoscope, with each turn on the Labyrinthine pathway, our energy field or matrix shifts. Our internal reality begins to change first and then our external reality follows.

Everything feels like it's *shaking up*. Today it feels chaotic. We are walking just before a Scorpio full moon. I'm feeling very *jumbled*. I just need to *know* that it's all changing on the inside whilst *feeling* it all, *trusting* that a new, more coherent order will emerge in time.

The Labyrinth heralds in change. We cannot walk the Labyrinth and not experience change. The more we engage consciously with its energetic blueprint and archetype, the more profound a shift is possible. In this way, the Labyrinth brings us closer to our truest self. It can be no other way. It seems to me that whilst our minds were so focused on the physical challenge of climbing and walking, it may have allowed for our unconscious and superconscious minds to be at work with minimal interference.

Today was tough. There were times when I might have given up and stopped part way through. The old me would have done this for sure. I managed to keep going partly because I wanted the experience of completion and partly because of the support I received, encouraging me on. I allowed myself to just be me, the imperfectly perfect, messy me. I didn't need to be in control. I hadn't done it before. I had hired a specialist guide to help us navigate and so I didn't even have to do that.

I'm glad that I have maintained a high level of fitness. It's just a year since my hip replacement. This is a big achievement for me. I am proud of myself.

I just realised too that it is ten years ago this weekend that I led the Labyrinth walk at Rennes le Chateau and all that has happened since that time. There were many times that the physical nature of today's walk brought back memories of the last ten years. Somehow it feels like I have completed a loop or a circuit. Something is completing but I can't put my finger on it. Perhaps I have now completed what was initiated at that time?

Reflections.

What have I learned today?

Put one foot in front of the other. Stay in the present moment of 'now' and don't look back.

Keep things simple. Look for the simplest route forwards.

Be gentle and compassionate with myself. I can judge myself harshly. Be kind to me. I count too.

I don't have to prove anything to anyone, ever again, including me.

I trust my body to support me.

I can keep going even when I'm tired or I think that I can't carry on.

I can ask for help from both men and women when I need it *and* I can receive it.

I don't have to do this on my own.

My needs matter.

None of the above are new to me and yet the walk was so very physically challenging, I wonder if these lessons are now embodied because of the physicality of the experience.

Walking this Glastonbury Labyrinth was like a simulation of Life. For example, just as you thought you were reaching the end, the pathway doubled back on itself, and you realised that you had so much further to go. As it's three-dimensional and involves height, you can't see what's ahead.

Would I walk this again? Probably not. Not in this lifetime! Once was most certainly enough.

PS Seven toenails were badly bruised and fell away in the week following the walk. When I began compiling my stories, I looked up what Louise Hay has to say about toenails. She wrote a book called *You Can Heal your Life* in which she outlines her philosophy that at the root of all dis-ease is a mental, emotional, or spiritual issue. She suggests that toenails represent safety and that a helpful mantra to counteract any feeling of lack of safety is, 'I reach out safely'. It seems to be appropriate given my reflections and learning.

The Labyrinth Speaks
of *Being True to Self*

Be bold, be brave, be wild if that be your current impulse.
If it matches your emotional weather for the day, for the moment.
Be bold, be brave, be wild.

Be still, be pensive, be alone if that is where you are at right now.

Be sociable, colourful, full of life and *joie de vivre* if it's the emotional
colour of the hour.

Be whatever you need to be.
Be whoever you want to be,
but be YOU,

for Heaven's sake,
for all our sakes,
and for your precious, beautiful, delicate, fierce, timid, joyous Soul's
sake,
be YOU.

Gloriously messy, tumbled, crystalline, clear, muddled, directionless,
focused, visionary, formless, full-bodied YOU.

All of You is welcome here.
All of *You* is invited.
Invited to the party of life.
All of you is welcome.
All of you is invited.
All of you is welcome and invited to this party that is Life.

All of You.

I Walked Out of Counselling

Just as I was beginning to feel that I had solid ground beneath me once more, as my business was re-building and I had been feeling so much better, life began to shake things up again.

It had been quite a year.

And it was only halfway through.

In January, I had emptied the storage unit and fully let go of my belongings.

In February, I started training for a cycling holiday in the south of France.

During March, I began to feel nervous and anxious whilst out cycling and later that month had a major panic attack whilst out training on a main road. I took the hard decision not to continue with the training, or even to get back on a bike. I also noticed that my friend had started to behave oddly again, signalling a return to her mental health difficulties.

In April, the brakes of my car gave way on a major motorway, and I said goodbye to one of the last remaining material things from my life pre-divorce. It had served me well but really was on its last legs! I part-exchanged my old car for a jet-black sporty Mazda MX-5 convertible. Although I loved it, I very nearly took it back, feeling that it was too powerful and sexy for me! I noticed the lack of congruency in how such a beautiful, powerful, sexy car had shown up in my life versus where my inner state was at that time and decided to keep it and allow myself to grow into this new identity.

And then, heartbreakingly, at the end of the month, I lost my close friend and ally. She had taken her own life. It was a terrible shock. It took me days, possibly weeks, before I could cry. I felt numb and so very sad and empty. My dear, big-hearted, funny, wise, sweet friend. She was one of those people who could light up a room by her radiant energy and big smile. She was one of the kindest, most thoughtful, and generous women I had the privilege to know. She was like a burst of sunshine.

Sadly, as I discovered later, she felt very far from sunny on the inside. I began to get a sense of this a few years into our friendship. She rarely spoke of her difficulties. I tried to support her the best way I could; however, it was difficult because she would not speak the words to describe what was going on, believing that if she were to speak them out loud, her situation would worsen. Sadly, not talking may have compounded the sense of aloneness that she felt.

No one knew just how deeply she was suffering until the signs and symptoms of her mental health difficulties began to re-surface.

In addition to completing the Glastonbury Tor Labyrinth, May saw me going on holiday with my partner and his cycling friends, with me facing being the odd one out by not cycling. Neither my own myriad of techniques nor a series of hypnotherapy sessions could get to the bottom of the panic attacks nor cure it. I missed Sue's funeral. There had been an investigation following her passing and her burial was delayed by six weeks. Unfortunately, it fell part way through our holiday. Although I felt deeply conflicted, I decided to continue with our holiday as planned. I wrote a tribute, and it was read out before her burial.

In June, the panic attacks returned and an appointment with my local doctor confirmed that I was also experiencing low mood and anxiety, with borderline mild depression.

In July, I began my first counselling sessions.

I talked a lot during these sessions. It felt like I was going around in circles for much of the time. My childhood, early adulthood, divorce, and events earlier in the year. The 'not good enough' issue was loud and clear. Difficulty sharing my feelings too. Yet none of these were new to me. I had been working on them for years, decades even. They were an echo of how they used to be for me, and yet during counselling, it was like they became very BIG and very LOUD. I came to realise that I had to keep Wednesdays clear as I was fit for nothing after sessions. All sorts of emotions emerged and got amplified. Sadness and anger were the most prevalent. My head wanted to understand how this would help me with the panic attacks. The counsellor couldn't give me an answer. She kept asking the same questions on the same topics, week after week.

I was confused. I had so wanted this to help me and yet it seemed to be making it worse. I wasn't learning anything new about myself. I wasn't learning any techniques to help me. Nothing was shifting. I didn't feel any lighter. I wasn't clear how this was helping me manage or lift the anxiety. We hadn't got to the bottom of why I had started getting panic attacks whilst cycling. And I was feeling even more anxious than before I had started the sessions.

Anxiety was now a near constant companion, gnawing at my stomach and my self-confidence. It churned away in my belly like a washing machine on a repeat cycle. It was there in the morning as I woke up and it was still there when I went to bed.

My counsellor had begun to empathise with me, sharing stories about her relationship with her mother and about her previous profession, and she had made comments about aspects of my relationships which felt judgemental and inappropriate. I could tell that she wasn't filtering her thoughts and was, at times, projecting onto me. She was also looping back to the fact that she and I shared the same birthday. On more than one occasion, she mentioned that she would have liked to have been friends if I had not been her patient. I began to lose faith in her ability to cleanly facilitate my healing.

Despite this, I did complete the first series of six sessions and agreed to another, thinking that I might need more to resolve it. Several sessions in, I was still feeling no better, and I decided to stop. I decided that I would take matters into my own hands and find peace outside of counselling. I shared how I was feeling, thanked her, and left part-way through the session.

I could feel anger rising, so I took myself off to the beach to give myself some space and time to process and to think.

Instead, I simply let myself feel *everything* that was bubbling.

I was angry with my friend for dying. How could I be angry with her?

But at least I was honest with myself; right then, I was angry with her for leaving me behind. It wasn't her fault; she had several bouts of mental illness over the previous four years. I blamed myself for not doing enough, for not seeing her more frequently. And yet, I had spotted the signs early and spoken to her and another close friend and a family member. I tried to organise time out together. I had done all that I could have done in the circumstances. She went downhill rapidly, and none of us ever imagined that she might die. I missed her terribly. We had been so close, enjoying so many happy times and supporting each other through some difficult times too. In addition to the sadness and the anger, I also felt guilt. Guilt for not going to her funeral. Was I selfish? Had I been a lousy friend? All of this felt like an angry bee, buzzing around inside my head, leaving no room to think. So instead, I let myself feel it all. It felt messy, confusing, discombobulating. I needed a lot of time alone to process everything, and I turned to the beach for soothing.

And just when I began to feel calmer, I felt more anger rise, only this time I was angry with my partner for feeling disappointed that I didn't cycle with him on holiday. He had every right to feel what he felt. For me, it was a challenging time. I was away on holiday with the friends he had known for decades, doing something they all loved and were very proficient in. I had been a leisure cyclist and loved it until I started to get the panic attacks. By not cycling, I was going to be the odd one out, again. Although they always took care to include me in their conversations, I sometimes felt like an outsider looking into a cornucopia of their memories, experiences, and banter. And of course, I was grieving.

And then a hot, volcanic-like eruption of different emotions began to rise to the surface.

I was angry with Life, the Universe, my Soul, anyone out there in the great beyond who might be listening, that I still couldn't afford to buy property. It wasn't that I was unhappy living with my partner – I still saw property ownership as the only way for me to feel safe again in the world.

I let myself feel it all as I walked along the beach. It went on for several hours until I had finally exhausted the feelings rising and had exhausted myself physically in the process. Away from other people, I had screamed and shouted, ranted, and cried. I missed my friend so much at times, my heart physically hurt.

I began to return to the healing modalities that I had created and blended them into a morning ritual for an hour each day. This hour was for me to be in stillness, to journal, to transform the limiting beliefs that were popping up, to heal, to journey within.

The strong feelings didn't resolve all at once; however, they began to abate, to quieten, and to soften over the space of a few days. Intuition then prompted me to work with Ho'oponopono, what I call the 'Hawaiian Prayer'.

I'm sorry.
Please forgive me.
Thank you.
I love you.

Each morning when I woke and at night-time before I slept, I created a little ritual of saying the Hawaiian Prayer, either in my head or out loud. If I had a strong emotion about a situation that was current in my life, I would use that, and the person or people involved. Sometimes, a memory would surface, and I would bring those people or the situation itself to mind. Sometimes I worked with the prayer for myself. I would bring my attention to my heart chakra and breathe into it, inviting it to expand. Sometimes it did and sometimes it didn't, either was OK. The invitation and focus were always enough.

First, I would visualise the person, people, or situation I wanted to heal. Then I would repeat this beautiful prayer over and over until it felt complete, until there was no longer any emotional charge or until I felt myself become empty.

Each day, I felt almost compelled to come back to the prayer. It seemed to work well with my choice to FEEL everything that was coming up. Slowly but surely, the feelings of anxiety became softer and less frequent. The combination of techniques and the magic of time was beginning to work.

One morning in early October, I received a phone call out of the blue from an experienced psychic inviting me to take a stand at a psychic fair the following month. Giving psychic readings was easy for me but not something that I enjoyed. However, it seems that she had read reviews about the soul contract readings I gave and wanted me to offer those instead. I agreed and thought no more of it until a few days later when I started to get intuitive nudges to complete the writing of the oracle deck that had been bubbling for the past year. It was almost fully written and so it wouldn't take long to complete. It seemed to be wanting to come with me to the fair to have its first outing.

I spent two solid weeks completing the writing, sourcing a local printer, and getting the packaging just right. Everything fell into place beautifully. I was so engrossed in creation mode that I didn't notice that my anxiety had gone, and my mood had lifted into a joyful, contented vibe.

The Magician's Toolkit® was born in November, and I felt like a different woman. I felt empowered, accomplished, happy, and proud to have birthed this project finally into form. Now it could serve others just as it had guided me.

Had the counselling opened a valve to the residue of unexpressed feelings? Probably.

It hadn't given me any answers, and yet it was the first part of the process that led me to empowering myself to find an alternative way, one that was right for me.

And for that, I was grateful.

PS There is a bonus a chapter available on my website which tells the full story of how *The Magician's Toolkit*® came into being. Details are at the back of the book.

The Labyrinth Speaks
of *Life as a Spiral*

Life is not linear.

It's not circular.

It's a spiral.

As we grow, we notice the same things come up and around again, only each time from a different perspective until, over time, it becomes embodied wisdom.

And at a certain point, we stop reacting and we start responding.

And then we know, we know for sure, that something wonderful has happened.

We have evolved.

We have taken a giant leap out of survival mode and into thrive mode.

And Life will reward us through greater self-love, self-kindness, and self-acceptance.

And that is pure magic.

The Soul Speaks
of *Being ENOUGH*

Decades of voices,
conditioning,
reinforcing,
projecting,
embedding,
embodying,
progressively,
solidifying.

You're too noisy.

Too boisterous.

Too shy.

Too sensitive.

Too weird.

Too different.

You're not invited.

You're too good.

Your eyes are too blue.

You're too intelligent.

Too posh.

You're not intelligent enough.

You're not accomplished enough.

Not religious enough.

You're too successful.

You earn too much money.

You're not earning enough money.

You're not public-school educated.

Not from the right background.

Not assertive enough.

Not competitive enough.

Not tough enough.

Too gentle.

You're too new here.

Too spiritual.

You've changed too much.

You're not who I fell in love with.

Not who I want you to be.

You're too outspoken.

Too much.

Too white to understand.

Too sensible.

You're too much of a risk now that you're single.

Too liberated.

Too attractive.

You're too sexy.

Too beautiful.

Too sad.

Not positive enough.

Too young.

Too old.

Not sporty enough.

Not organised enough.

You're not slim enough.

It's exhausting.

F**k it. I'm done with people-pleasing. Contorting myself to meet others' needs and expectations. Turning myself inside out and back to front, just to feel loved and welcome. Appeasing, pleasing, looking for approval, wanting SO much to be enough, to be accepted just as I am, to be ENOUGH – to FEEL SAFE.

I'm done with looking outside of myself for answers. Done.

SO f * * * i n g done.

No more.

Drawing a line in the sand here and NOW!

No more. Never again.

Take me or leave me.

Here I am.

I AM ENOUGH.

I am gloriously, magnificently enough.

Period.

I'm Worth It

Today I meet with the hip surgeon who operated on my left hip. I'm paying privately. I can't wait a whole year for an NHS appointment. I'll fund it myself. I'll find the money. I'm worth it. Enough is enough.

So, this morning, I cracked. I cracked wide open and cried. Big gulps. I've been in a lot of pain overnight, slept intermittently and I was now tired and pretty fed up.

Sitting in bed with Ian, over our morning tea and chat, I burst into tears. Pent-up tears that I've felt lurking for a few days now. My eyes have been so sore and my head hurting, I had spotted the signs of an imminent letting go and here it was. Months of frustration of not being able to progress to surgery as quickly as I needed it. Years of pain and limitation. Seeing my life shrink. Knowing that it was only going to get worse without surgery. Doing everything I possibly could to minimise the pain. Running out of ideas, options, and patience. It all came to boiling point. And it all tumbled out in a tearful stutter of words and sobs.

I let it all out.

And he listened, silently, just putting his hand on my leg, letting me know he was there, whilst I did my thing. I appreciate his understated yet full presence. Not many men have been able to hold space for me and witness me in the way that he does.

And when it felt like the tears had run out of steam, he asked me what I needed.

Journaling. That's what I needed. So, he gave me the space to write and brought me breakfast in bed.

I needed to break it all down and get it all out onto paper so that I could see the full impact of what living with osteoarthritis and chronic pain looks and feels like. Some part of me needed to see it written down. Was I looking to validate or justify myself and my tears and frustration? Maybe. Did I need to see and accept what is going on at a whole new level? Probably. Would it help? I hoped so.

I've been here before, and I don't want to put my head in the sand and deny the reality of what's going on here. I need to be brutally honest with myself. Here goes.

Pain-free days are very rare, and the state of my right hip is following the same pattern as that of my left hip. I know that this is only going to get worse. Much worse.

It's progressing much quicker than last time, probably because I can't get to the gym or have the physiotherapy or craniosacral work that I had before. The global pandemic had reduced the options available to me.

The physical pain in my hip is sharp. The pain runs from my hip, through my leg and into my toes. This referred pain is like the growing pains I had as a child when I experienced growth spurts. My right glute muscle is tight and it's causing lower back pain now too.

I can no longer walk the ten minutes to get to the beach.

I am limping all the time.

I may have to fund my own private hip replacement if the National Health Service takes the full two-year predicted time to operate. I can't wait that long. I'll be in a wheelchair.

The pain and the stiffness are affecting just about every aspect of my life.

Let's get real. Activities that are now difficult include:

walking
housework
gardening
high-street shopping
moving from a sitting to a standing position
pulling on underwear and socks

getting in and out of the bath
going upstairs (sometimes I'm on all fours when pain is spiking or I'm tired at the end of the day)
going downstairs
getting on and off a sun lounger
stepping over or around items on the floor
picking things up off the floor
walking up, down, or over a stony beach
trimming/painting toenails
getting in and out of my car.

Sometimes when the pain is high and I haven't slept well, it can take an hour to get myself up, showered, dressed and ready for work and I am exhausted before I start my day.

Everything takes so much longer.

Doing up certain shoes and sandals.
Pulling on sports socks, tights, etc.
Cycling.
Walking for more than 2 miles (it always hurts, but if I walk more than about 3 miles, I suffer for 24 hours).

I have noticed that I have started to avoid walking and this has been one of my great loves, especially on the beach.
I am limping every day.
I'm tired all the time.
I used to sleep continuously for 8-9 hours which is what I need to be operating optimally.
I now average 5-6 hours of interrupted sleep, often not able to get to sleep or waking up due to pain.
This affects my ability to concentrate and is starting to impact my mental wellbeing too.

There are so many activities that Ian and I have enjoyed together which are now out of reach or just very painful. We have weathered this storm once before. I'm sad that we must do this yet again. The situation is going to get worse before it gets better. This is creating frustration and some tension that we are having to navigate.

My life is rapidly shrinking, again.

I'm sad for what I have lost.

I'm frustrated with the hospital waiting list system.

I'm frustrated and angry that I must wait twelve months to have an appointment to get the go-ahead to have surgery, and then I could face a year-long wait. And I've waited eighteen months already. I know the signs. I know how quickly my hip is deteriorating.

I'm exhausted with the pain. It's gnawing deep inside of my hip and is always present. There is no escaping it. It's there in every waking moment and during the night too. It's affecting everything and I've had enough. Enough.

I'm running out of ways to support myself, to reduce the impact.

I'm all out of patience.

Today is not a good day.

Today may be a duvet day.

There must be something I can do; I can't be out of options.

I'm already doing so much every day just to maintain the current state of my hip:

I've lost weight.

I'm fasting intermittently as this is said to reduce inflammation in the body.

I take eight high-quality supplements each day – curcumin, MSM, collagen, high-quality multivitamins and electrolytes.

I stretch, do physio exercises, high impact interval sessions on the indoor exercise bike plus resistance weight training, all at home and daily.

I power nap when I can

I sleep with an orthopaedic cushion between my thighs for extra support.

I massage my right hip and thigh to help with circulation.

I meditate and aim to stay in the present moment with all of this so as to avoid overwhelm.

I have booked a new course of physiotherapy for the end of this month.

My self-esteem slips frequently and it's taking a lot of awareness to keep it at a level where I feel good about myself and life. I must continuously re-focus on what I can do and what is still possible otherwise I risk falling into victim mode and hopelessness. Sometimes I let myself feel this anyway rather than avoid it – but it's unhelpful to linger too long in this state. There are days when I feel helpless, hopeless, and powerless.

Thankfully, this time around, my business is thriving. That's at least one blessing. And it helps me to take my mind off the pain whilst I'm writing or working with clients. My focus is on them and not my pain.

So, what else can I do?

I'm close to being at the end of my tether. I'm losing hope but don't want to give up.

Just going to have a gentle morning before meeting with the surgeon.

*

The surgeon said YES! He will operate as soon as possible. Only downside is that I will have to pay for it, £14,000, and may have to wait up to six months. But at least six months maximum is better than two years minimum. So be it. This must happen.

27th May 2021

Unbelievable, so grateful! Can't believe my luck. Thank goodness for my intuition. I had a physiotherapy session today. I hadn't expected to but responded to a brief thought that flickered through my mind last week: 'I wonder if I am doing anything that could make my hip worse? I wonder if I'm missing a trick?' So, I booked. When I explained the situation, he couldn't understand why I had been waiting so long and handed me the name and phone number of the woman who authorises NHS funding. He said that many other people he had treated were getting surgery more quickly. When I spoke with her, she was very understanding and I'm now on an NHS waiting list too.

Let's see what happens. Hope has returned. There is an end in sight. I'm not attached to who pays for it. I want my life back.

22nd June 2021

Wow! Feeling excited and grateful. Received a phone call today inviting me to surgery in less than four weeks' time. She said they had a breakthrough, and they could fit me in earlier than expected and on the NHS list. Can't believe it. Thank goodness I followed my intuition.

Just thinking about all the steps to get to this point, the mini breakthroughs.

Not putting my head in the sand and facing this head-on.

Insisting that I have X-rays and follow-up doctors' appointments.

All the research and expense of high-quality supplements.

The powerful intention-setting that I did throughout.

Persisting in chasing results, doctors' appointments, and being relentless.

Realising that I could afford to pay for the op myself even if it took a massive chunk out of my savings or even if I had to draw down from my pension. Knowing that I was worth every penny, my health and wellbeing were worth it. My life was worth it. I could do it if I had to.

And that meant that I booked and paid for a private consultation with the surgeon much earlier than if I had waited and this ensured that I got onto his private waiting list.

Then the intuition to pay for an appointment for a private physio session and he gave me the woman's number who had the authority to authorise NHS payment, and this got me onto his NHS waiting list.

I was being led all the way by the voice within, my intuition, my Soul whispering to me. Do this. Try this. Call him. You can do this.

I am SO very grateful and happy.

Yippee! 19th July here we come.

19th July 2021

Turns out that today is Freedom Day in the UK, the day when all Covid restrictions are removed. For me it is a Freedom Day of a whole different kind. After today, the arthritic pain will be gone and within six weeks I will be walking independently with barely any pain at all.

I didn't sleep well last night. It took ages to get to sleep. My body was so excited. That feeling of bubbling excitement kept me awake for hours. Imagine that! My body knew the relief I was about to experience. My body wanted the surgery.

As I am prepped for surgery, the hospital physiotherapist arrives to run me through what to expect. She clearly hasn't read my notes, and so I politely let her know that I have already been through this once. She looks at my notes and then says,

'Poor you! That's so very unlucky to have this surgery once at your age, let alone twice.'

It was a surreal moment but one that I am so very happy about because it shows just how far I have come on this journey.

I heard her words and could almost feel the energy of them coming towards me. They didn't compute at all. It's like they reached the edge of my energy field and tumbled onto the floor like broken glass might have done. They didn't touch me, and I remember replying.

'Not at all, I feel very lucky to be having this surgery, to be having it so much earlier than was predicted and to have this paid for.'

She looked very puzzled and left the room. I never actually saw her again.

Be the Savvy Frog

One of my favourite times of the day whilst I was at junior school was the school assembly. We would all gather, sitting cross-legged on the polished wooden floor. I remember the colour and the smell of the polish and how the warmth of the sun would stream through the windows. I remember the colours and patterns on the fabric curtains that delineated the school hall from the corridor.

School assembly was a daily practice and provided a rhythm to the school day, which was very welcome to my nine-year-old self.

My very favourite part of the assembly was the story or parable. I have always loved stories. And bizarrely, of all the stories I would have listened to over the three years I was at junior school, there is just one tale that I remember.

It's the one about the boiled frog. Are you familiar with this one?

Wikipedia refers to the story of a frog being slowly boiled alive. The premise is that if a frog is put suddenly into a pan of boiling water, it will jump out immediately, but if the frog is put into a pan of tepid water, which is then brought to the boil slowly, it will not perceive the danger and a nasty end will ensue. In my time as a management consultant, this would sometimes be used as a metaphor in change management scenarios.

This memory of being back at junior school returned to me with such intensity whilst I was beginning to write this book. I was curious. It caught my attention. All manner of memories had come knocking, but why this one? And why now? I made a note of it and put it to one side, trusting that at some point, I would understand why I needed to devote a whole chapter to it.

And then I woke up one morning and understood.

I remembered times when I had been the frog that jumped quickly out of the pot and also the times when I had been the frog that stayed too long and got singed.

I had been attracted to glossy marketing courses or masterminds only to find there was no substance to them or that the values and behaviours did not match my own. And I hopped out smart.

I have avoided certain situations altogether because my intuitive antennae were screaming at me.

I have been invited to join groups only to discover that they wanted to milk me of my expertise and carry it off as their own or profit from it.

I have been part of projects that promised a lot and delivered very little.

I had begun new friendships and had quickly seen the other person's Shadow and decided that they weren't relationships that would be healthy or desirable. And I hopped to one side, dodging potential heartache.

I waited far too long to have my first hip replacement. By the time I had the surgery, I could barely walk and was 'bone on bone'.

I stayed way too long in several jobs where the culture was harmful, the job uninspiring or not as advertised.

I stayed in one of my earlier relationships much longer than was healthy because I was afraid to be alone.

In my younger days, I wasn't so connected to my feelings, and my intuition wasn't as honed as it is now, so my early warning system wasn't so good. I managed to survive situations that were unhealthy for me through distraction, disconnection, and denial. My health and my inner peace paid a high price and ultimately this would have been radiating out into my relationships at the time too.

Life Lesson: Don't be the Boiled Frog! If you're going to be a frog, be the Savvy Frog.

PS No frogs were harmed in the contemplation of this tale. x

RAGE

Here is some context to the journal entry that follows.

Towards the end of 2021, I began to feel tired, bone tired and weary. It was something that I had experienced before, so it felt familiar.

Have you ever had that feeling when you are physically and emotionally depleted? When there is no energy to be found for anything, even for the people or projects that you love? When you have to draw on reserves so deep within you that it feels like you are searching for reserves that you simply don't have?

This was the reality that I was facing. As I reflected on the previous few years, I could see why I had arrived at this point. I had been working at full tilt for two years. My business had expanded to beyond full-time throughout the pandemic. I supported many clients and led several online women's groups one after the other. I had also completed the first draft of a book. I had been in pain for much of this time, and that summer had hip replacement surgery. I had really enjoyed the variety and the pace, and it had energised me up until it suddenly didn't.

I could feel that I was being called to write and yet I had no energy for it. I could feel that something was 'off' with the women's group that I was leading and hadn't been able to pinpoint exactly what was not working. I wanted to get to the nub of it.

One evening, I ran a bath, added rose and lavender essential oils, lit a single candle, and let the water cradle and soothe me. I closed my eyes and took myself into an inner journey with the clear intention of gaining clarity on the dynamics playing out in my work. I promptly fell asleep and woke up around thirty minutes later in lukewarm water! I smiled to myself. I got what I needed even if it wasn't what I wanted. Before leaving the bath, I decided I would ask my guides for help. I asked to be given a breakthrough.

The following morning, I woke up with a very clear insight. I was no longer in alignment with running the women's group. I could feel the clarity of this awareness in my body. I could see and feel now that this had been obvious, yet it was my devotion to the individuals and the collective, and the responsibility that I had felt as leader, that blinded me from the truth. I had served my time. The contract at a higher, soul level for this leadership role had been for two years, and now it was time for me to move on.

My decision to leave, whilst understood, prompted mixed responses, and for some, triggered old wounds of abandonment. I offered to stay for several weeks to see the year out and help with the transition, and my offer was declined by the two women in supporting roles. They decided that it would be best for them to now take it forward. And I was to leave, with immediate effect. And so, I did. And I have to say that I felt relief. My energy returned almost immediately. I had an absolute knowing that it was the right thing for me to do. I knew that my leaving could trigger others. I didn't take that lightly and equally I also knew that it wasn't reason enough for me to override my calling to step out. I trusted fully that all was in Divine order. If some of us were to feel upset or triggered by the events, it would serve us, in the long run, to feel what was coming up. I knew and trusted that the wounds would serve each of us in our own personal journeys.

It meant, however, that there was only a rapid and abrupt period to say goodbye. Various admin details did not get resolved for three months. This would, in the fullness of time, trigger healing for me and, I suspect, for others too. Whilst I trusted inherently that this was part of the Design, I also felt the human intensity of the raw emotion that erupted in me, three months later.

What follows is a series of journal entries. I share this as a piece detailing the raw emotion of rage.

It is rarely spoken of let alone detailed. I wanted to give it a voice here. Feeling it fully was progress for me and sharing it here with you feels a daring and courageous act. I trust that it serves you now or in the future if Rage comes a knocking at your door.

My personal trigger came via an email several months later. I will not go into detail. My subsequent response was disproportionate to the content of the email, but such are triggers – they are not rational, and they bring to the surface far more than we could ever even know was there, hidden within us, to be felt. My guess is that this rage was not only from this lifetime but others too. I felt betrayed by women at different times throughout my life and hadn't always been able to feel it so fully. It is quite likely that it was from my ancestral line, all the women who came before me in my maternal genetic lineage. It is also possible that it was collective rage, the unconscious rage buried deep in society's psyche. In any case, I own all my feelings. It is no one's responsibility but my own and processing it in this way was hugely healing for me.

I also recognise that as a part of my soul contract, my challenge in this lifetime is to follow Spirit and my intuition without hesitation, even when I might be misunderstood, judged, or shunned. And so, it is all part of my Design. This was a precious opportunity to heal at a deep level.

Even more than that, I had allowed myself to feel the rage, the fire, for the first time in my life. Up until that point, I had either cut myself off from it or kept a lid on it. I had been scared to feel it fully. I had denied it a voice, and so it was a beautiful experience of allowing it to speak and allowing it to be felt. And this was the gift within the trigger, for which I am immensely grateful.

And within a few weeks of experiencing such raw emotion, this book began to make itself known to me. Feeling the fire had created space for a new creative project to be born.

Spring Equinox 2022

Tuesday

My heart is hurting. I can feel the anger of not being consulted, not given a voice, no choice in how I left. I was told to leave with immediate effect. No opportunity for a proper farewell, no say in how I exit. I feel pushed out. I don't feel heard or respected. I feel excluded. I feel triggered.

I ask myself: 'What's the most powerful thing I can do right now?'

The answer: FEEL it. Fully. All of it.

It feels like a fierce volcano, swirling, digging deep into the core of my body. It feels all-encompassing. Unapologetic. THIS is **RAGE**.

As I name it, my whole body begins to shiver.

Tingles all the way down my lower body, through my legs. Rage. There it is.

Rage.

Each time I acknowledge this feeling, the intensity quietens and the heat cools.

Rage.

Each time I name it and think about the circumstances, another wave of recognition moves through my body and down through my feet into the Earth.

Rage.

It has a different quality to it than anger, but I don't want to try to articulate what that difference might be because that would take me away from the feeling of it, and the feeling of it is where the empowerment lies.

Rage. Rage. Rage.

My body begins to rock and swing to and fro, and I let her do her thing.

Rage.

A stillness arrives and I sense the energy move from my heart to my throat.

I start to salivate as if to be sick, the energy of it is moving.

I yawn.

Blessed be. I acknowledge the process. It's not stuck, it's in flow.

I trust myself and I trust my process.

RAGE.

The energy now fills my entire body, and I can feel its power. I can feel **MY** power.

I engage with the energy of Rage and give it a voice through my writing.

'What would you like to say?'

'I am the voice of Rightful Rage. Of not being seen or heard. Of being swallowed down for centuries. Of being disallowed, cast out, blown out, castrated, violated, desecrated, abandoned. I am the Voice of Rage. I am not Reason. I am not Harmony. People fear me because I am so hot, so fierce, so raw, and potent. I feel chaotic. I am Life Force expressed and embodied. I am pure. I am fire. I am squashed, denied, ignored, feared, disconnected. I am avoided. I am repressed and suppressed.

I AM **RAGE**.

I will **NOT** be denied.

I am Rage.

And I lean back in my chair, and I quietly feel the Rage. I acknowledge it. I thank it for being here. I acknowledge myself for the decades, perhaps lifetimes, that it has taken for me to feel safe to feel it fully. I acknowledge my courage to share my process here on the page with you as I am processing it live. I am grateful to be able to reclaim my power in this way and to not give it away to others or external situations where I have no voice and feel powerless.

I AM more than that. I am greater than that.

I am responsible for my own response.

Let it be a powerful one. Let it be an empowered one.

And if this isn't what I was going to write about today, then so be it because **THIS** is exactly what is needed right here and right now.

Attending to **THIS**, will bring me energy to live my life more fully and more colourfully.

THIS is what Life is made of. This is Life itself. This is LIFE FORCE expressing through my body and it feels **SO** good.

It feels good to be alive and to feel this so fully, so freely, with total permission.

To have it coursing through my body.

I FEEL ALIVE!

This is fire energy.

I feel safe in my Rage. I feel safe with this feeling of power and empowerment.

I have come HOME to myself. I have come Home to love.

I will not allow others and external events to diminish how I feel about myself.

I do not have to explain or justify myself.

I do not have to dampen the fire and wait until the flames have died down before I express myself.

I AM ALIVE. And it feels GOOD.

And now I AMPLIFY this feeling through my entire body, top to toe, relishing the feeling, relishing the strength I can feel I am drawing from it.

I am grateful for this experience and my response because it has brought me Home once again to myself, my power, and my core integrity.

I AM HOME.

No longer will I give my power away, no longer will I look to others and to outside authorities for the answer to my own questions, no longer will I allow external situations to influence how I feel.

I will NOT abandon myself. I will NOT ignore my feelings. I will NOT betray myself.

I AM HOME.

And it feels so GOOOOOOD!

Wednesday Morning

It's early morning, and I check in with myself about how I am feeling, physically, emotionally, mentally, spiritually. I draw a card from my oracle deck, *The Magician's Toolkit®*. The card called The Mirror drops out of the deck and onto my lap.

Do you have a relationship creating concern or discomfort? Consider whether you share the beliefs and behaviours that are contributing to the dynamic. Chances are the other person involved may be holding up a mirror reflecting an aspect of yourself that you may have been unaware of – your blind spot. When something that was once unconscious becomes conscious, we can choose to transform or to integrate. This is alchemy in action. As within, so without. Will you rise to the challenge?

How apt. Spot on.

I want resolution with this situation.

As I tune into the sensations in my body, I see an image of the two women involved in this situation standing on the beach, feet spread out. They are dressed in khaki combat gear, and they hold rifles across their chest. They are united and they are not letting me pass.

I instinctively flip to look at me. I see that I am mirroring them. We mirror each other. We are in a stand-off. And the Shadow of all three of us is playing out. I realise that we are all stuck in the polarity of goodie/baddie, right/wrong, them/us, betrayer/betrayed.

Oh dear. I pause and take time to acknowledge my role in this dynamic.

And I also realise that a part of me wants to have the last word.

This part wants to be heard, seen, acknowledged, and given an opportunity to say what she is thinking and feeling, and this has been denied. She has been excluded and this is what has been hurting, and this explains why I feel so angry. Even when I wrote to them, I have not been acknowledged.

And I wonder …

Can we reach a neutral space?

Can we sit together and have a conscious conversation?

Is this friendship retrievable?

Do I want to retrieve it?

Although I feel sad, my answer is NO.

I've suggested all of this, and my suggestions have all been ignored.

It's time to move on.

And I take myself off for a walk on the beach.

Wednesday Afternoon

Oh wow! I feel SO incredibly alive and happy and excited about my life right now, and especially about this book, my book. I feel SO grateful for this situation to have popped up this week.

I pull a card from my oracle deck.

And I go to the guidebook and read the description.

The Wisdom of No Escape: *There is something so exquisitely unique about the situation you are in right now. What do you think or feel it might be? The unique circumstances have been orchestrated so that you can experience something new about yourself, others, or your response to Life. There may be something that you would like to be different or would like to escape from. And herein lies the wisdom of no escape. The situation you are in right now will only change when you have grasped its wisdom and surrendered to it. Once your learning has been integrated, the situation will dissipate and disappear, or it will remain but will no longer call your attention as your response to it will have changed.*

And I smile. Yes, I am right in the middle of this right now.

Thursday

I woke up early with this situation running around my head once more. Darn, I thought I had reached a conclusion, but clearly not. I can feel injustice and hurt. I began to think about how I might respond, just so that I could draw a line in the sand and move on. And yet I also know that I'm not yet clear enough in my own feelings. If I respond now, I would be responding from my wound, and I know that is rarely wise.

So, I journey within.

I lie on my back, close my eyes, and guide my awareness deep into my body. I prepare to travel into the shamanic space I call 'the Middle World'.

I invite a guide to join me. The character who calls herself the 'White Witch' appears as well as a little girl holding a teddy bear. We are all in white dresses, holding hands as we make our way through the gate into the Middle World.

The little girl has a steely look on her face and begins to stamp her feet fiercely on the ground. The rhythm of the stamping reminds me of the ticking rhythm of a grandmother clock. This continues for some time. The White Witch and I bear witness to her. She won't speak. When we invite her to speak, she shakes her head from side to side.

And now she very slowly begins to get taller. She is growing up.

Now she is a teenager. Still, she stamps. Still, she is silent.

The teenager grows a little more and becomes a young woman.

The young woman stops stamping and she begins to loudly chant, **'NO'**.

And her NO is to the same beat as her foot stamping and there is a crowd gathering.

As I scan the faces in the crowd, my head swings from left to right and back again, like a pendulum swinging, tick tock, tick tock. I recognise some of these faces from my own life. Some I don't know or perhaps haven't yet met.

As I listen to the young woman's 'NO', I can feel the whole of my lower body strengthening and tightening. My jaw clenches and relaxes in the same rhythm as her 'NO'.

NO. NO. NO. NO. NO. NO. NO.

Sacred NO.

I can feel instinctively that others will now hear and respect this young woman's 'NO' and, more significantly, FEEL the power of her 'NO'. My 'No'. She is me. My sacred No.

Her Sacred NO.

Her clear signal.

Her clear boundary.

NO.

I will not be treated like this again.

NO. This is not OK.

NO. I am worth more than this.

NO. I can speak for myself.

NO. I can decide for myself.

NO. I will be heard.

NO. My feelings will be felt.

NO. My voice counts.

NO. I will not betray myself.

NO. NO. NO. NO. NO.

And then I realise that the Young Woman and I had merged into one being.

We are One.

And I am flushed with a gentle feeling of peace.

As I leave the Middle World with the White Witch, the teddy bear I am holding turns into a little girl and she hugs me tightly, smiles and kisses me on the cheek as she begins to sing her own sweet song.

I can still feel the Sacred NO in my lower body. It is less intense and yet it is still there.

I bring myself back into everyday waking reality and reflect on what just happened. I feel so much more at peace within myself. I stretch and I smile.

My partner brings me tea and I snuggle up, feeling happy, feeling safe and looking forward to a walk on the beach before I start my day of writing.

I am Home and it feels good.

Friday

Wow, what a week. It's been a long time since I've had such a range of intense emotions running around my body. I am tired now. It's taken a lot out of me.

This morning, there is so much joy and peace coursing through my body. I am so grateful that the situation this week has been so empowering, and I feel strengthened by it all. I am grateful to the women involved for being the catalysts and to Life for bringing it to me. It was the perfect storm.

Thank you x

The Soul Speaks
of *Grace*

May there be grace in your beginnings and in your endings.
May grace be your companion in your brightest and darkest of times.
May she light your way and guide you back Home.

May she illuminate your path and give you strength when you feel weary.
May she be the voice, the nudge, the instinct to help you find your way, even when you feel lost.

May grace be with you, above you, below you and all around you.

May she wrap you in her arms and whisper,

'I love you. It's going to be OK.
Really, it is. I've got you.
You can let go now.'

I Didn't Recognise Myself

I didn't recognise myself.
I had changed beyond measure.
My values, priorities, beliefs, all lay in fractured pieces on the floor
at my feet.

My inner critical voice, once loud, now silent,
The deep, chasmic pain in my heart, flown like a bird.

My *knowing* was emerging.

Blossoming from under the rubble,
And through the barricades,
Was a sweet, gentle innocence.

A delicate flower was opening.

The Soul Speaks
of *Being Naked*

Be Someone.

Do Something.

This is the chant that echoes to us from the outside world.

Who are you if you are not Someone?

Who are you if you are not known?

Who are you if you are not loved by someone?

Who are you if you do not have someone to love?

Who are you if you have released all the conditioning that binds you?

And the demons that drive you?

Who are you when you no longer define yourself by a role?

When you own nothing?

Who are you when you have let go of striving, controlling, pushing?

When you are finally naked.

Who are You?

Who do You become?

What else is possible?

This Thing Called Life

Journal Entry, 18th May 2022

I don't know how to do this.

I don't know how to do this thing called Life.

I see so many others doing their Thing and they seem so at ease, they seem to have it sussed.

They seem to know what to do, when to do it, when and how to do it and who they are doing it for.

Me? I feel like a little kid some days, trying to figure it all out.

Adulting can be such hard work.

Lost in the jungle of ideas and dreams in my head and with no bridge to fully, truly reach out and offer them to the big, wide, world.

'Make a difference,' they say.

'Grow it big. Expand. Be consistent. Be bold. Be wild. Be unbound.'

But the truth is that I don't feel like that woman.

Not this morning, anyhow.

Today I feel hesitant. I am a gentle Soul trying her best to stay true to herself even when, and perhaps especially when, the emotional weather of the world washes through me.

What was once clear has become murky.

What once held promise now molten like wax, on the floor.

Not all potential has been realised.

And the weight of that sometimes presses heavily on my heart.

It feels a sad, stark reality

And the hand of the clock is turning, the ticking is relentless.

Tick, time is passing.

Tock, it's now or never.

Tick, what will you do with the time remaining?

Tock, how much more loss will you be able to sustain?

Tick, how much more love can your heart hold?

Tock, how much more of yourself can you give?

And when will you fully, finally, open the floodgates and let love, let Life fully in, Moriah?

If not now, when?

If not you, who?

If not any of us, then what becomes of our world?

Who will care for her?

Let the floodgates be OPEN.

Let the healing flow.

Lower the drawbridge and send out the tendrils of hope and of love to those who might find them.

May you find release in that.

May you find your joy.

May you allow the peace to come and go like the wind and be OK with that.

May you come to trust that your emotions are like the seasons and the weather and that nothing is truly ever forever.

Everything is for NOW.

For me, for you, for all of us and for the Earth. X

The Soul Speaks
of *Perfection*

Your Presence here is E N O U G H.

Just pause for a moment and allow yourself time to drink this in.

You are Enough.

Always have been.

Always will be.

You are Enough.

There will never be another You.

Your brilliance is assured.

You are unique.

You are perfect just as you are.

Life will always bring you new opportunities for growth – that's why we chose to come here to Earth's Great Playground

And in each moment of each day, You Are Enough.

Always changing

Ever evolving

A continuous dance of Master and Student

Now Student, now Master

Now Master, now Student

Yet always enough

Your Presence here is healing to others

Your Presence here contributes to the Whole.

As you learn and grow, your frequency rises

And our collective frequency rises too

As You rise, we all rise

As We rise, you Rise

A perfectly synchronous dance of becoming and un-becoming

You Are Enough.

Goddess Rising

The Goddess has re-awoken.

She is alive and rising through the Earth and through our Consciousness.

She is alert to truth and non-truths alike.

She is the hand of love and detached compassion.

She is here in full, joyous, celebration of all that is Feminine.

The Yin has returned.

I AM Woman

Here is a stream-of-consciousness writing that came to me fully formed as you read it here on these pages. I have recorded an audio set to shamanic drumming music, and this can be found on my website. I invite you to speak this out loud to receive the full transmission and power contained within and to download the audio from my website if it calls you.

Who am I?
I AM Woman.
Fierce. Tame. Loving. Kind.
I am all things
and No-thing,
and Everything in between.
I AM Woman

I am all Woman.
I am nurturing, creative, wise,
compassion, kind, visionary,
devoted.
I am love beyond measure and all that is.
I AM Woman.

I am Woman.
Fiercely protective of the vulnerable and all that is Feminine.
I protect through support and nurture so that others grow by unfolding into who they are so that they come Home, for in the homecoming is true safety and joy.
I protect through combat only when there is danger for mine is the way of love and kindness.
I am Woman.

I AM Woman.
half animal – half moon,
wild and free.
Soft of hue,
dancing to my own tune
& free to be me.

I AM Woman.
I AM Woman.
dancing free,
soaring high,
skimming the sea
& plummeting
into the depths.
I AM Woman.

I AM Woman.
Velvety rich,
chocolate dark,
milk white
& all shades in between.
I AM all WOMAN.

I AM WOMAN.
Silken to the touch
velvet smooth
the evening breeze upon your skin.
I am WOMAN.

I dance & twist & answer
to the wind.
I AM WOMAN.

Power and purpose blazing high.
Soul soaring into
the midnight sky.

I AM WOMAN.
All seeing.
All-feeling.
All-knowing.
I am Woman.

Woman.
I AM WOMAN.
Whole. Complete. Radiant.

A Beauty to behold
& a story to unfold.
Woman.
I AM WOMAN.

WOMB-MAN.
I AM WOMAN.
Divinely grounded.
Exquisitely connected.
Fully Human.
& Goddess All in One.
I AM WOMAN.

I AM WOMAN.
Creative Force.
Destructive Nature.
Fiercely Protective
& Total Love.
All One.
I AM WOMAN.

Woman.
I AM Woman.
I dance to my own rhythm,
Sing my Soul's Song.
I am Home.
Woman. I AM WOMAN.

I AM Woman.
I rise & fall,
I crash and burn,
I rise again.
I AM WOMAN.

The Labyrinth Speaks
of *Love Leading to Truth*

The light of my love leads me to truth.
The truth of my love illuminates my light.
My truth binds me to my love.
It is the way of truth and love and light to find our way Home to our one true love.
It is the path of love that illuminates the path Home to Source.
It is Source that leads us Home to our true essence.

It is our true essence that calls to our heart and soul.
It is our heart and Soul that leads us Home to Spirit.

And Spirit re-unites the sacred Feminine and Masculine, the one true love affair.
For only when we have come home to our Soul,
can we be re-united with our one true love.

And then we are bound together,
 as one love, one light, one heart and one Soul.

Home is the embodiment, the *knowing* of union.
When we are truly Home, we know ourselves as Divine.

PS Try reading this out loud.
The words bypass our linear, logical brain and help us open more to love.
How does it *feel*?

The Tale of the Labyrinth, The Void & Rennes le Chateau

Part Five

Journal Entry, 6th May 2022

Today, I'm feeling unsettled. I have been aware of the anniversary of the Labyrinth retreat to France, and I'm aware that I haven't felt like doing anything to mark the occasion. I decided to take myself into an inner shamanic journey this morning to see if I could gain an insight into why I was feeling unsettled.

I brought myself into a meditative state, called in a guide and travelled through the door between worlds and landed in the middle world, the space between the conscious and the unconscious awareness. Immediately I saw the distinctive pattern of the seven-turn Labyrinth filling the whole landscape. Today the pathway was illuminated and bright white set against a backdrop of inky black. As I walked the pathways, I was aware that my mind was busy trying to figure out where I was in relation to the pathways and chakra points of the Labyrinth. If I could figure it out, it would give me valuable information and clarity. My mind was trying to gauge which way I was going to turn next. Each time this happened, I noticed that the bright white light that formed the pathway began to dim, and I couldn't see ahead. I stopped walking and just stood still for a while, waiting for the light to brighten and for an internal signal to begin walking once more.

Once at the centre, I paused and took time to rest. It felt very peaceful here at this point. My head was clear. My heart was open and feeling expansive. It felt good. I felt content. I was fully in the moment without any thought to the past or the future or even what was happening in that moment. I felt remarkably *empty*. Walking out was easier than the journey into the Labyrinth. I flowed around the pathways without getting confused or lost, pacing myself as I took each step.

When I emerged, the guide was waiting to welcome me. She

revealed to me that my Feminine essence had been in the Labyrinth for all this time and now she had completed her time in it and had returned. It was time to celebrate.

And part of this magic is the timing. It is the anniversary of when I walked the Labyrinth in the dark. My initiation into the Void, fifteen years ago in the French Pyrenees. Today I walked the white pathway of Light, and the process was now complete. Fifteen years of diving and delving into the deepest, darkest parts of myself. Fifteen years of loss and the crumbling away of the persona, ego, and life that I knew and held most dear. Piece by piece, all my identities, masks, Shadows, belongings, and even my hips crumbled and fell away or were cut away. In so many ways, I had been led by my Soul. I had been led blindfolded, not being able to see ahead. I had not seen or guessed what might happen next. I'm guessing that if I had seen what was coming that I might have seriously thought twice. I followed my intuition and my Soul's lead every step of the way.

To come Home to myself. To let go of my innate need to belong to someone or something or somewhere, I had to learn that my belonging was to be found elsewhere.

'Your Life will never be the same again.'

This is what the message that fateful day as I boarded the plane to Carcassonne had, in part, alluded to.

Finally, fully, out of the Void.

Returning into the Light and holding the balance between the two.

I heard the message:

'The Light and the Dark now dance as One.'

In truth, it was twenty-one years ago that I first received the calling to research and immerse myself into the sacred Feminine mysteries and energy.

And now all the major and minor transformations, the many turns of the Labyrinth, all now converging, culminating at this time.

Fully.

Finally.

Coming Home to balance and harmony within myself.

The Tale of the Labyrinth, The Void & Rennes le Chateau

Part Six

Journal Entry, 7th May 2022

During the night, I felt such a feeling of expansive love washing through me again. I had a new level of understanding that this is not a personal love, it is a transpersonal love. It doesn't arrive because of a person, an event, or an outside stimulus but is available and breezes through as part of a range of emotions. Whilst I was emotionally 'walled off' for all those years, I could give love and I could feel loved by certain people, but I was walled off from experiencing the emotional *weather*. Feeling love or feeling loved was conditional on another person or on a set of external circumstances. I can see now how much pressure I put on other people, especially those I loved, and on situations being *perfect*. This was a precarious way to be living and sometimes led to disappointment. It was also unfair for those I loved and who loved me. No one and no-thing can live up to that kind of expectation. Now I see it so clearly. Now I can appreciate that the emotions I feel are simply blowing through and enjoy them as surprise visitors. I can welcome them one by one and not attach to a certain state of feeling or being. It also means that I don't put such high expectations on myself, fellow humans, or Life itself.

I can let go now.

And that feels so good.

Soul Belonging

I walk along the beach most mornings, and today I decided to walk around the spit of my local beach. I felt a desire to be amongst the sand dunes and listen to the nesting birds.

The sun was warm against my face, the clouds were high and there were clumps of seaweed along the edge where the sea meets the shore. It was a truly beautiful spring morning.

And as I walked, I became aware of words beginning to drop into my head.

They were insistent, like a bird pecking against a window pane.

'Listen, pay attention to us.'

And as I heeded their advice and listened to the words, I began to get goosebumps and shivers running head to toe.

I found a sheltered spot and sat down so that I could receive the words more fully.

I closed my eyes so that I could feel the sensations that were swirling around and through my body.

As soon as my eyelids closed, I could see a wide, cinematic image and felt myself moving quickly and steadily through a white-grey, tunnel-like form. It was like looking down through a funnel with centrifugal force. It looked and felt powerful yet gentle.

And then I was in the narrow part of the funnel. The white cloud-like formations were still present, but now it felt more intense. It looked and felt like I was a plane coming into land moving down through the layers of cloud and mist.

I intuitively made the link with a birth canal and how a baby makes its way out into the world. And yet this didn't visually seem quite right. There was a feeling of being squeezed and yet I could see so much light. Was this really what it was like to emerge through and out of the birth canal?

And then another possibility began to dawn in my mind.

This could be the Soul's birth canal into human form.

If this was the case, I was the one experiencing it here and now, both visually and viscerally.

So, this was *my* journey into form.

I felt and saw the movement from a higher vibrational space of pure, bright white light down through the birth tunnel into form, through the vibrational layers, each layer becoming thicker and denser than the last.

I saw myself move wholly and fully into the density, immersing myself until I could no longer see anything but thick, dense fog. And I felt lost and confused. I had lost my sense of direction. I could no longer get my bearings. There was nothing to give me any clues about where I was. And I saw how my connection to Soul was lost because I could no longer see it or feel it. I felt lost. And the longer this went on, I felt more alone. And I forgot. I forgot so fully that I could feel something wasn't quite right, that something was missing and yet I had no idea what it was.

In this vision, I could see my head above the clouds, looking directly at me. And I still felt the connection to her even though she couldn't feel her connection to me.

She looked so lost and yet I felt whole. I was not concerned for her. I felt expansive and good. She was now feeling anything but expansive and good.

All my life I have been wanting and waiting to belong.

I have often felt unwelcome or that I don't belong.

I have joined groups, moved into relationships, switched careers, all in a search for belonging.

A sense that something is missing.

A search for the missing thing.

A longing.

A perennial search.

'There must be more to Life than this?' kind of feeling.

And now, after six decades of feeling incomplete, I now realise that I do belong.

I belong to my Soul.

I belong to my Soul's Design for this lifetime.

I belong to my Design.

That's my belonging.

It's to my Soul.

It's with *my* Soul.

I am Soul. Just as You are Soul.

I cannot belong to You just as You cannot belong to me.

And now, today, I can *feel* this belonging. It feels tangible and real, in my body.
It's no longer a thought or a belief in my head.
Nor is it a wish or a feeling in my heart.
It is solid, and I can feel it in my lower belly.
I've arrived. Finally. Fully. At last.
I'm here.
I've landed.
And it feels so good.

Life isn't about anything else.
It's about *being* here now, experiencing ALL of this glorious life.

It's about living and breathing our Soul's Design.
Every day.
Each moment of every single day.
We are here on this Earth.

Living and breathing it.
To have an experience of being human.
This is what the Soul is here to do.
To have an experience of what it is to be human.
To feel.
To truly *feel* everything.
Everything.

This is the purpose of life.
To feel the *wonder* of life.
To feel emotions coursing through us.
To *feel* alive.
To feel *alive*.

Why else were we given all our senses?
To see, hear, feel, touch, taste.
To sense vibration in our body.
It's all Life.

And so, the only thing that has been missing – is Me.
My willingness and ability to feel all the feelings and to relish them
and how they feel inside and through my body.
To feel my life force energy coursing through me.
To feel fully alive.

THIS is what has been missing.
And now I'm Home.
Home to my Soul.
My Soul is home within me. We are Home.
Nothing is missing.
We are One.
In body.
Whole.
Complete.
Alive.
Here.
And now.
Always.
All ways.
Home.

The Labyrinth Speaks
of *Love Leading to Source*

The light of my love leads me to Source.
The Source of my love leads me to light.
The light of my truth leads me, Home.
And my Home is love.

My love leads me Home and my Source brings me light.
My light brings me Home and my Home brings me light.

In an ever-flowing dance of light and interconnectedness,
I am love, I am light, I am Source, and this is Home.
Home is in the heart,
And Home is in the Soul.

Wherever I am, as long as I remember that I am connected to Source,
Then I feel Home.

What Price Freedom?

This is the question that frequently popped up during my inner journeys. I didn't always have a clear understanding of what it meant; however, I felt the energy of it. I keenly felt the desire, from time to time, to be free, way down deep inside of me. Like a call coming up from within a well, freedom or rather the desire to be free, rippled through me like an echo reverberating around an empty room.

But free from what?

I couldn't always articulate what I wanted to be free *from* exactly or what I wanted to be free to do. It was more a sense of restlessness or unease in the current moment. Sometimes it was obvious and other times it was simply a faint unrest, not feeling quite *settled* within myself. I had wanted to be free of being at home and living with my parents and heeded the call to go to university and independent living. This is one many of us have felt. It is a natural evolution. This wasn't that kind of freedom, though.

I kept asking the question, though. 'What do I want to be free to do?'

The unsettled feeling would pop up and catch me unawares infrequently, seemingly at random moments of my life. It was always when I least expected it. It would catch me equally in those times when I had been feeling happy, settled, fulfilled as it would during the times that I had felt challenged, unsupported, or sad.

Freedom has always been a personal value of mine. If I couldn't access it externally, I would turn inwards and satiate it internally through my imagination, writing and reading. As a parent, I would get to the stage at several points during the year where I would crave space, freedom to roam, with no timetable, responsibility, or expectations. In those times, my husband or sometimes our parents would step in and give support. Sometimes for a few hours, sometimes for a weekend. This was often enough, just a few hours or a weekend away, and I felt refreshed and ready to go again. On those weekends, I would often drive the three hours to Glastonbury and spend hours in the crystal shops and the tea rooms, soaking up the chilled vibe. I would walk up to the Tor and sit in the Chalice Well Gardens for hours, absorbing the stillness and the silence.

It was only in my early fifties that I began to realise what that question really meant.

'What price freedom, Moriah?'

It coincided with another question that regularly appeared in these journeys.

'Where are we going?'

'Home.' Home was always my most instinctive response. I wasn't entirely sure where Home was or what it meant in the context of the journey and yet it was always the first word that dropped onto my head. Home to myself, home to Soul is what I imagined it to mean and again, I didn't know quite what that felt like, not yet.

It wasn't freedom from any external oppression or restriction or that I craved.

It was freedom from my Inner Critic, the limiting beliefs, and the conditioning.

Freedom from the unhealed emotional wounds.

Freedom from the unresolved ancestral trauma passing down through my genetic and spiritual lineages.

Freedom from other people's expectations, societal rules, and peer pressure.

Freedom from how I believed my life *should* look.

Freedom from how I thought my life should *feel*.

Freedom from the drama, the unmet needs, and the resulting emotional turbulence.

Freedom from the constant searching outside of myself for the answers to the questions I had.

Freedom from believing that I or my life needed to be anything other than it was in that moment.

And freedom from believing and feeling that I wasn't good enough.

It was exhausting.

I can feel that now, even as I look back.

I have so much love and compassion for the Younger Me, the woman who was genuinely doing her very best with the resources she had.

I adore Her for always wanting to do right by her family, friends, and clients, for putting others' needs first because she *cared* so deeply.

I want to send Her the longest, most loving, tender hug, for the times that she felt lost, abandoned, and lonely.

I want to tell the Younger Me that it's going to be OK. It will all work out, in the end. It may not be how she expected and yet it will be more than OK, eventually. She will be OK. Everyone will be OK. All is well. All will be well.

I want to reassure Her that there *is* a plan, and that it is unfolding *through* her and not *to* her.

I want Her to know that she is the Creator, the ultimate Designer of the plan, not the recipient, and not the victim or the helpless pawn.

The Design is of her design.

It's all perfect.

It's all here to help her grow into the woman that, at a soul level, she wants to become, she just doesn't know it yet.

I would like to show her a vision of the future, feeling happy and free. How she will be walking on her beach, writing, creating, feeling accepted, feeling loved and welcome in a relationship, supporting her clients in liberating themselves.

I would like Her to step into my body now to *feel* the difference between then and now, to give her hope that she is making a difference. Each pattern, each limiting belief, each trauma she clears and resolves. Each positive choice she makes. Each 'Yes' or 'No', each adjustment to her alignment with her purpose. Each time she listens to and acts on her intuition, all leading her closer to her goal.

And what is the result?

It is an inner peace.

It is an absence as much as a presence.

An absence of all the internal and external noise that I used to live with.

A presence of deep inner peace, of stillness within.

Being able to respond rather than react.

Freedom to choose the work that feels good, the work that I am intuitively drawn to and which serves others.

Freedom to choose where, when, and how I work.

Freedom from rules, regulations, and external expectations and conditioning.

Yes, the 'not good enough' voice emerges sometimes, even after all this time and inner work. These days it appears more as a whisper, a distant echo. I recognise it when it bubbles up or slaps me in the face. I give it space and give myself time to feel it. It doesn't last long now. It comes and goes quickly and shows up rarely.

I am deeply grateful to the Younger Me who was so devoted to her inner work. The Younger Me who diligently, daily, deliberately cleared the inner emotional and mental debris. Pattern by pattern. Belief by belief. Expectation by expectation. The Younger Me who trusted that this would bring the relief, the freedom that I value so much today.

The Younger Me who had the courage to break down the protective walls and armoury to allow herself to feel – to fully *feel*. Everything.

The Younger Me who followed her curiosity, her intuition, her spiritual signature, no matter where it led her.

She may have temporarily lost hope, faith, and trust, and yet she never gave up. She picked herself up, time and time again, dusted herself off and began again. She grew resourceful, resilient, and wise.

To Her, that Woman, I LOVE YOU x

You are a Super Star, a Superhero, in my eyes.

And in my big, bountiful, liberated Heart,

I am grateful.

I celebrate You. Your courage, your discipline, your devotion, your perseverance.

Thank you x

The Labyrinth Speaks
of *Life as a Spiral Dance*

What follows is a poem which arrived in the early hours of a full moon over two decades ago. It seems so right that it finds a home here.

The Spiral Dance

Come into the Spiral, she said so softly,
come into the ring and see.
Come and see your future, your past, your mystery.

Come see the mysteries of all time.
All space, all of me.

Gaze into the mists and see the images gently swirl.
Come feel, come taste, come see.

For I am me and you are you
and that is all there is to know.
We are united in our search and we are united in our home.
We come together to laugh and to heal.
We come together to play, yet we know one another from long ago
and we dance along the way.
For the dance is all, the dance is it, the dance is all there is to know.
It's the dance of life, the dance of time, the dance of love and all.

So, step into the dance and be present,
step into the dance and rejoice.
For this is all that you have searched for.
It is all that you came to learn.
It is all you came to remember.
It is all you came to hear.
So go in love and peace and joy

and relinquish all your fear.

Let go of that which binds you,
let go of that which hurts.
Move into the notes of wisdom
and dance with the fullness of life.

Let nature be your guide.
Let nature be your inspiration.
Let the seasons gently guide you,
let the tides and the moon steer your ebb and flow.

Step into the Spiral, my love.
Step into the flow.
Step into the rhythm of all life, step forwards and glow.
Glow with your own wisdom, your source, your power.
Glow with your inner heart and mind.
Step forwards and know that you are loved and blessed,
now, and for all time.

For yours is the wisdom, the power, and the glory.
Yours is the magic of the sea.
Yours is the wonder of a snowflake.
Yours is the wonder of all there is to see.

Step forth my loved one, step forth and simply be.
Revel in your being.
Revel in your flow.
Revel in the miracle of knowing you know all there is to know.

Enter into the spiral dance,
enter and you will see
all the mysteries of life and death, of love and fear, of All.

The choice is very simple – you only have to be
present to your humanity, present to your pain.
Release the old, bring in the new
and enter the spiral dance again.

The spiral dance is magic, the spiral dance is fun.
The spiral dance will teach you all you ever need to know
on how to unravel, how to unpick, how to unfurl all that holds you
back.
It transforms your very being.
It gets you back on track.
It takes you to Heaven
and brings you back down to Earth.

It gives you the rhyme, the reason and the wherefore and applauds
your every step.
It helps you find the answers and to know what to expect.
It will help you find your essence, your own unique self.

So, step forth, Dear One,
and dance and love and play
and may you be loved and blessed and find grace throughout your
day.

May your day be laced with kindness; may you glow with love and
joy.
May you find the clues you search for.
May your spirit flare once more.
May your angels dance alongside you.
May you feel the peace you have been waiting for.

For the peace is within you, it's within your every cell.
Come join the spiral dance and peace will prevail.

So now is the time to dance, dance, dance
now is the time to feel joy.
Create the dance you long for, create the dance of your dreams.
Step forth, step forth and dance now,
the Spiral Dance begins.

Inside Out

The Labyrinth is a key to a lock.
An opening, a doorway, of letting go and becoming.
Of becoming and unbecoming.
Releasing and embracing.

I belonged to myself so very clearly when I was young and gradually lost connection to myself and my innate nature and gifts as I disconnected from both and began to learn that I was only safe when I conformed, fitted in, and belonged to others' customs, institutions, their systems, and their rules. 'Til I conformed.

The more I conformed, the more I got lost. Looking outside of myself for answers, coordinates, for love and validation became my default setting. I sought ways to belong in relationships, places, roles, jobs, academia, by conforming to norms, societal expectations and ownership of homes, belongings, and achievements. I looked externally to academic achievements, to my birth family, my friends, my jobs, my workplace and colleagues, my husband, my belongings, and to my physical home for my identity and a feeling of belonging. I rarely felt as though I had done enough, accomplished enough, or met other people's expectations. Something always seemed to be missing. I never quite fitted in, lived up to others' expectations or got the validation I was seeking. Somehow, no matter how hard I tried it was never enough. I rarely felt 'enough'. I looked to everything and everyone outside of myself for a reflection of who I was because inside of me I had only a tenuous connection and sense of who I was.

I didn't know who I was without any of this. I did as a child but not now. To fit in and function in the world, I had believed that I had to let go of my own true nature and connection to myself, my body and to my sensory gifts.

Nothing is static.
Everything is in a state of dynamic flow.

And yet my sense of safety was in a series of institutions, traditions, beliefs, and ideals that promised stability and 'forever'. None of which recognised, valued, or rewarded the Feminine aspects of me – the intuitive, imaginative, nurturing, creative, mutable, emergent nature of my true being. I gave away my power and invested my time and energy where it was largely undervalued and unappreciated.

Looking back, I can see how precarious it is to rely on others, the form we are clinging to and its ecology, and environment. As we evolve, we naturally need to move onto the next stage so that we are in the optimum environment and ecology for our growth so that we do not stagnate. Our growth and evolution not only serve us but those whom we care for and serve too.

The difficulty is that our basic human instinct is to keep ourselves safe. As humans, many of us have done this by consciously or unconsciously seeking out and clinging to others or institutions to provide that safety. And all so that we don't activate and feel our core wounds. We become institutionalised. The thought or reality of not being safe is too terrifying to contemplate. Who do we become when we lose our identity, our home, our finances, our parents, our significant other, jobs and health? Who do we become when everything has fallen away? Where do we turn for our sense of safety and belonging?

The more I remembered to look within for my answers, to trust my intuition, to love myself, to value the gifts I have, to love the gentle power and to feel safe with my fire energy, the more my body relaxed, and I found a new way to relate to myself and to life. The less I belonged to the places and the people I had dropped anchor with, the more I had to rely on my own inner sat nav to navigate life. In following my spiritual signature, I was called to leave jobs, locations, relationships, circles of women, and friendships because I could no longer thrive there. I let go of my belongings because they no longer felt like 'me'.

The Labyrinth is a lock, and we hold the key. We ARE the key. We have the exact combination to unlock the magic within us. Looking within to our intuition and feelings help us to navigate our outer reality – not the other way around, as we are taught as infants.

Prayer – Show Me

Show me how I can serve.
Bring me those whom I can serve, who need what I have to offer.

Create through me.
Use me as a living vessel for the sacred magic of the Universe to speak, to create, to move, to inspire, to transform, to live.

I allow myself to be empty, emptied.
Fill me, oh great mystery.
Fill me with thine sacred purpose so that I might feel the joy of service.

Let me be an instrument of your Divine will.
Let me feel full, fuller, fullest.

Help me to be OK when I feel empty, emptier, emptiest.
Help me to trust in the sacred ebb and flow of Life as it expresses itself through me.

Let me be thine voice, thy sacred instrument, a vessel for your expression and presence here on Earth.

Give me wings that I might fly.
A tongue that I might express.

And help me to have the courage to allow all of this to be OK.
To be OK in the void of not knowing, not feeling, not doing.

In the space of no-thing, help me to feel OK.
Of this, I pray.

Sacred One,
Let *this* be OK.
x

Letter – The Next Decade

Dear Moriah,

And what of your next decade?

What do you wish for yourself?

Truly. Wildly. Honestly?

This requires radical honesty and deep diving into your big, beautiful heart.

For so long, you gave your power away, no more.

You gave it away by looking for external validation.

You gave it away in the name of love and by hoping for love in return.

You gave it away through overwhelm, through believing that you couldn't make it alone.

For the decisions you felt you couldn't make and because you believed other people knew better.

You gave it away because you believed others were more qualified, more confident, bolder or brighter.

You gave it away for fear of failing, not belonging and for fear of rejection.

You gave it away because you wanted to be seen, heard, loved, validated, popular, included.

You gave it away to belong.

You gave it away to prove yourself. You gave it away to keep yourself safe.

Over and over and over again.

You gave your power away because you felt yourself unworthy.

And because you didn't feel safe in your own skin, in your own power, in feeling your true heart's desire.

No more.

You've liberated yourself fully from all of this and anything that does remain is a mere echo of what used to be.

You are now free to choose.

What is your heart longing for?

What is your Soul calling you towards?

What would you love to create?

How would you most enjoy serving?

How would you love to live?

And how do you want to love and be loved in return?

All this and more are yours.

Beloved, Dear One, NOW is YOUR time.

It's your choice.

You've earned this blessing.

We await your call.

You only need to ask.

We are listening.

Life is listening.

It's time.

What would you like?

Give us a menu.

Make a list.

Create your vision

And release them into the great yonder.

It's time.

It's Your TIME.

The time is NOW.

Love from your bright, light, future self x

PS I am so proud of you and I'm willing you over the finishing line! We've got this!

The Labyrinth Speaks
of *Being You-nique*

You are an original, a masterpiece.

Be happy being different.

Break the mould,

Create a new one.

Celebrate what makes you YOU.

Look for the things that make you stand out from the crowd and LOVE them.

Focus not on what you are not nor on what you are not yet.

Instead, focus on all the mini and major things that make up YOU.

Shine.

You are here to be a bright jewel in the sky.

Let your Design move through you.

Let starlight light your way

And may the Earth root you and keep you nourished for all your days here.

You are You-nique.

So, be YOU, who else could you possibly be?

You are not alone; you have never been alone.

It was just an illusion that felt so real.

You are made of stardust and connected to the cosmos.

How could you possibly be alone?

The Red Thread

As I came close to writing the final chapter, I had begun to wonder how best to bring the book to a close. During this time, a phrase began to drop into my head – 'The Red Thread'. At first, I acknowledged it but didn't think too much about it. When it became more persistent, I began to take notice. It felt familiar, and yet I wasn't entirely sure what it meant. Its simplicity and tone felt like a message from the Labyrinth. As I began to tune into the words, a whole stream of information arrived and synchronicities began to unfold.

Online research revealed that The Red Thread features in many cultures across the world.

In Chinese legend, a red thread of fate is tied by the gods around the ankles of those that are to meet one another in a certain situation or to help each other in a certain way.

In Hindu religions, the Rakhi is a sacred red thread that a sister ties on her brothers' wrists, for their safekeeping and wellbeing during the festival of Raksha Bandhan. In return, the brother gives his sister a gift, often of money. In modern times, it is given or worn on the wrist as a symbol of protection.

The Japanese legend of the Red Thread says that everyone's little finger is tied to an invisible red string. They believe that this will lead them to another person with whom they are destined to meet and have a significant experience.

In Swedish, the phrase 'red thread' is used to describe something that follows a theme.

The expression seems to be widely accepted as coming from Greek mythology. Although there are different interpretations, the most common is that King Theseus is said to have found his way out of the Minotaur's Labyrinth by following a red thread, helped by Ariadne.

As I pondered and felt into what The Red Thread means to me

and what it means to this book, a whole trail of synchronicities, memories, and insights began to take shape and form.

It was 22nd July, the day that is traditionally associated with the feast day of Mary Magdalene. I felt intuitively that The Red Thread linked with her, her bloodline, and the experiences of the women's Red Tent tradition too. In ancient times, women who were menstruating would gather in a tent, away from domestic duties, so that they could rest and be with other females in their community. In recent times, The Red Tent has been associated with the rise in popularity of women's circles and gatherings.

Even though the words and energy of The Red Thread felt significant, I was happy to have it remain a mystery rather than try to define it.

Later that day, I set off for a quick walk before dinner. As I reached the beach, I stopped in my tracks. There was a single red ribbon tied to one of my favourite benches. It wasn't there in the morning. I took it as a sign that I was on the right track, to pay attention and to stay open to insights as they appeared.

As I dropped off to sleep that night, I was prompted to look at the photos of the last Labyrinth Day that I created six years earlier. I smiled as I made the connection. There is a story here that I would like to share with you.

I ran the Labyrinth event for seven women at a beautiful healing centre around the time of the autumn equinox. The day was designed to give them an experience of the magic of walking a Labyrinth for the purpose of transformation. I knew that I would have to create the pathways of the Labyrinth myself, and I had done this many times before using rope or very thick string. It needed to be heavy enough that it lay flat against the wooden, polished floor and pliable enough that it could be moulded into the curves of the pathways. The component parts for the Labyrinth that I'd used previously were in Dorset with a friend and it was going to be impractical to collect them. I decided to begin again with fresh components.

As I was busy with clients, I asked my partner if he would measure and cut all the pieces needed into the right lengths. He looked carefully at the seven-turn Labyrinth design and saw something I never had before.

He pointed out that the classical seven-turn Labyrinth has two continuous pathways and thus no need to measure and cut endless pieces of rope. Now he mentioned it, it made sense to me that this would be so. I wondered if the two pathways represented male and female energies. Which of course, they might. Visually, they looked to me like two serpent or dragon paths too. Now that I'm finishing the manuscript, I'm wondering also if they represent spirit and matter. The human experience and the soul, combining as one. And of course, they could represent all manner of dualities, coming into balance or unity. I am happy for it to remain a mystery.

When it came to buying the 'thread' to make the Labyrinth, I automatically thought to buy natural coloured rope. We set off to a local chandlery. They didn't have the right rope in a natural colour that was the perfect combination of weight and flexibility to create the pathways.

They did have the perfect combination, however – yes, you've guessed it – in red!

And so, the Red Labyrinth was born.

This story was still on my mind the following morning. I set off on one of my favourite walks around the sand spit that forms one of our local beaches. I never know whether I will walk clockwise or anti-clockwise until I get there and intuit it.

That morning, I sensed to turn right and walk anti-clockwise. I walked barefoot on the sand and instinctively turned off the beach and through the sand dunes until I reached the very first step of the boardwalk. And here I paused and stood still for a moment. For weeks now I had begun to feel that this was a portal to another dimension. It felt very special. It felt a sacred pathway. I put my right foot onto the boardwalk and began to walk mindfully along and up towards the harbour side of the spit.

When I reached the peak, I ran down the sand dunes onto the beach and headed towards the water's edge. It was such a beautiful summer's day that I stopped for a few minutes to paddle and to listen to the gently lapping waves.

I continued onwards around the spit and began to walk the final third of the rotation.

And then, I stopped in my tracks. I noticed a single feather. I remembered my experience at the beginning of my book writing journey, of being guided to 'follow the feathers'. I wonder if you remember that story.

I listened to my inner voice. It directed me to walk back the way I had come. The feather pointed that way too. And so, for the first time that I can remember, I retraced my steps rather than complete the circuit.

I began to wonder which break in the dunes would lead me back to the boardwalk. I couldn't see it up ahead. I climbed up one pathway and realised I'd come too far. So, I doubled back on myself and found the right one. I recognised the rabbit hole that I had noticed on my outward journey. As I got to the peak of the dunes, I saw that I was on the right track. I realised that the moment that I had thought to turn up and onto the boardwalk was the point at which I would have been walking right by the appropriate pathway to get me there.

I smiled.

I had walked a Labyrinth of sorts.

In the classical seven-turn Labyrinth that I work with, the path loops back on itself. It feels like you are moving backwards and yet you are in fact progressing forwards.

I loved how the messages and metaphors kept coming the more I listened to my intuition and followed the signs. I hoped that I could do it all justice in pulling all the threads of my book together. I knew at this point that I would write an additional chapter devoted to The Red Thread.

As I drove home, I saw an image of the black and white branding of my oracle deck, *The Magician's Toolkit*®. When I got to my desk, I reached for the deck asking for an insight. A card dropped out. It was The Labyrinth. I laughed out loud.

The Labyrinth card reminds us:

The twists and turns of the Labyrinth are akin to the ups and downs of life. This card has appeared in your selection to reassure you that the journey you are on has a higher purpose. There is a unique pathway through the current situation which is yours alone to experience. A new beginning is assured. The ancient consciousness of the Labyrinth is guiding you, Home. Relax. All is well.

As I reflect on the past 24 hours, it seems to me that there are many Red Threads that weave their way through us and our lives.

The one that connects us to our Design and guides us along our Soul's pathway.

The one that runs through our genetic, ancestral bloodline linking us to all the souls who have walked the Earth before us and from whom we originate. Within each mother is the seed of the next generation and the next.

The one that links us to all the people with whom we have made sacred agreements in this lifetime.

The one that links us with our soul mates, those with whom we incarnate, time after time.

I like the idea that there are so many possible meanings and manifestations of The Red Thread. I feel sure that it will keep revealing its' mysteries, as will the Labyrinth too.

In the writing of this book, it has felt that the Labyrinth, my Soul, and the essence of the book have all been woven together as one. I feel more integrated, more whole as a result. It has often felt like the book has called me back to my laptop; I have felt a tugging around the area of my navel, where my umbilical cord once was. So, perhaps The Red Thread is an umbilical cord of sorts too, linking us to our Soul, to Life, to all of creation and to our creative projects.

'There is a pathway through the pain' was a constant message through the times when I felt especially challenged. This may have been a reference to The Red Thread too.

The thought of a Red Thread guiding each of us to each other and home to ourselves gives me great comfort and hope. There was an invisible thread guiding me Home; my intuition and my feelings helped me to come home to myself and my body and to be able to fully feel love for myself, others, and life itself. My Design, my Soul's Contract were chosen and agreed prior to my birth, encoded into my birth name.

As I write this concluding chapter, I am smiling to myself as I remember that the cover sleeve for the first incarnation of this book, *Love Your Karma*, was to be red and white. Now I know that in the writing of *Labyrinth*, I have come to love and appreciate my karma even more. Through the remembrance of my stories and the telling of them here, I now feel more grounded and whole. I have integrated more fully the experiences of my life and in doing so, I feel at peace.

I hold dear a belief that when enough of humanity has come home to themselves, we can all come home to each other.

And wouldn't that be wonderful!

Afterword

Like Dorothy in *The Wizard of Oz*, I had walked the pathways looking for the solutions in the big, wide world, only to find that they were in me all along.

I don't miss the drama, conflict, complexity, or the intensity.

I don't miss my belongings.

I was longing for depth, meaning, soulfulness, and connection. I looked for it in others, and I ultimately found it within myself. But only when I had let go of everything. Piece by piece. One by one. It all fell away.

I was yearning for love, but I was looking for it in all the wrong places.

I let go of needing to know the whys, the hows and the whens.

I let go of needing to control.

I surrendered to Life.

I learned to allow Life to move *through* me.

I allowed myself to feel the emotional weather of Life.

I let go of needing to know what would happen next, how people might react, what people might think. I learned to trust myself and Life once more.

What I didn't know until I had experienced it was that I was moving towards a deep inner well of peace. I imagined that it was love I was seeking. Perhaps the two qualities are so closely entwined that they are inseparable. I will leave you to ponder this one.

As I look back over my life, I can see how I am the sum of all the stories within this book. Each story is a single marker in time for how my life unfolded. I can see clearly how the path was always there for me then, just as it is now. One experience, one relationship, one course, one loss, one joy, one day, one moment, one choice at a time – all leading me home to the seat of my own belonging. Home. Each of them a knot on my own Red Thread of Life, bringing me home to my own Soul connection.

It was always meant to be this way. My Soul knew it. I came to know and understand it and yet I didn't always *like* it. My Soul held the blueprint for my life and for my Soul's evolution through time, and so it also knew what I had to grow through to become the woman I chose to be prior to incarnation. My Soul holds the Design for my incarnation and the Soul's Contract that I agreed. It held the bigger picture and all the detail. It knew what was best for me, even when I couldn't or wouldn't see it for myself. It knew all my previous incarnations and it knew all of what might yet be to come. Through all the trials and tribulations, I learned to trust my Soul. I knew that it spoke to me through visions, dreams, intuition, synchronicities, feelings, and relationships. I have now come to know and experience myself as whole with my Soul. I no longer feel so separate. For the most part, I do feel the union, and I am humbled and grateful for the journey that I agreed to embark on and for the earthly woman who endured and ultimately thrived through it, even when she couldn't feel her Soul. My memory of 'something other' and 'something bigger' stirred, and I began my search. It triggered my search for something that I couldn't even find words for back then but now know as home, belonging, love and peace.

Even the seemingly small choices led to big change.

I see how there was a benevolent force guiding me even when I felt alone, helpless and had lost hope.

The postcard messages arrived to give me a reminder that I was not alone, and yet I still felt the alone-ness. I designed it this way. I needed to feel alone-ness. I needed to be with it. Befriend it. Immerse myself into it until I could feel the truth of it.

Knowing my Soul's Contract, doing my inner work, following through on my intuition, following the ten Guiding Principles that my Soul gave me and giving myself space and time to rest, dream, create, and contemplate all helped through the most challenging of times.

Mostly, I learned to be willing to show up just as I am.

To feel it all.

To trust that there is a higher order at play even when I couldn't see or feel it.

And I learned to trust and to be gentle with myself, no matter what.

Small, baby steps some days.

Braver, bolder, giant leaps other days.

Taking care of myself and loving myself radically were key to my wellbeing.

I basically had to un-learn everything that the world had taught me.

'Everything in the Labyrinth is coherent.'

I can see now ...

It facilitates the marriage of opposites, the integration of opposites ...

Within, without.

Above, below,

Feminine with Masculine.

Yin with Yang.

The opposites that I experienced and that were encoded within my birth name, all experienced, felt and ultimately integrated ...

Disempowerment to empowerment

Disconnection to connection

Hope and hopelessness.

Ultimately, it facilitates Union.

I have come to think that contentment and simplicity are underrated.

I feel more at peace with myself, life, and others than I ever have.

Ian and I have created a stripped back, simple life and we give ourselves and each other space and permission to grow. We are happy content with our lot.

In my humble opinion, peace, simplicity, and contentment are underrated.

I trust myself and the unfolding of life so much more than I did in the past. The process of writing this book has mirrored themes in my life's journey and that of the Labyrinth, and I have learned to trust myself, Life, and my journey so much more.

In my heart, I still hold a vision and the feeling of what it would be like to live in a spacious beach front house. This image dropped into my inner mind several years ago. I can clearly see the ground floor, the furniture, the layout, the colours, and textures. I can see my loved ones sitting at a long, trestle table, all laughing, chatting, and eating together. This vision makes my heart very happy. I trust that if this is part of my Design, it will come to pass.

When the topic of my book came up at a recent family gathering, my dear uncle commented, 'Didn't you start with the end in mind?' And I laughed. I have followed The Red Thread of the book's Design, its essence, and its consciousness every step of the way. In truth, now that I am in the closing stages of writing, I now feel that the voices of the book, the Labyrinth, my Soul, and I have all been in a merry dance, one with the other. A co-creation. And I love this. I haven't felt 'in control' of what the book might look or feel like, and I have thoroughly enjoyed experiencing how it has unfolded. It has felt magical. At times infuriating. But always magical. It has been a true labour of love.

And now I sense that it is time to let go. I can sense in my body that it is complete. There are so many more insights and ideas that I would like to include, and yet I can feel in my body that it is done.

Complete. Enough.

And it remains for me to say a very big thank you, dear reader, for coming on this journey with me.

Thank you for witnessing my journey and for being a part of it.

I hope that you have enjoyed reading this book and that it has worked its magic on you as it has on me.

And thank you for entrusting my book to be a part of your own journey, your Labyrinth, a small knot on your own Red Thread of Life.

If I were to leave you with a message, it would be this.

Home is within you.
You are unique.
You have full permission to do life your way.
You have full permission to be fully You, all ways and always.

The 'stuff' of this world is a distraction from what really matters most.
There is a plan for you, and it will unfold, one step at a time.
There is a pathway through the pain.
The obstacles *are* the path.
The mess *is* the way.
Each obstacle is a portal full of potential for transformation.
There is no destination but to be Home within yourself.
To *feel* is to be fully alive.

Your Soul knows the way.
Trust it to guide you.
It may lead you into some dark spaces, but it will also lead you out again.
In between, it will bring angels disguised as humans and opportunities to heal.
And it will always bring you home. Always Home. x

And as this book closes, another opens.

If you'd like to experience more of my work, please turn the pages to find out how.

My Prayer for YOU.

May your heart be free, boundless, limitless.

May your body be lithe, healthy, strong.

May your spirit express itself through you.

And may you feel the pleasure, the joy, and the ecstasy of Life

expressing itself through you in full, unbridled technicolour.

This is my wish for You.

May it be so.

With heartfelt love,

Moriah x

Contemplation Prompts

Would you like to take your experience of reading Labyrinth deeper? Here are some questions you might like to consider.

Which aspects of the book have resonated with you most? Why?

What emotions has the book evoked in you?

What are the key messages that you have taken from the book?

What might you do differently or set in motion as a result of reading Labyrinth?

What do you believe the 'Red Thread' to be?

How has it shown up in your life thus far?

What have been the key turning points in your life?

How might you have handled things differently if you had been in my shoes?

The classical labyrinth has seven turns in and seven turns on its outward path. If you were to consider your life in seven-year cycles, from birth to current time, what do you notice?

And does this differ when you consider your life in decades lived, from birth onwards?

And finally, I do hope that you have enjoyed your experience of journeying with me.

Would you like to stay connected?

On page 352, I have listed all the ways you can connect with me and my work.

I'd love to hear from you.

M x

Acknowledgements

My parents, for your steadfast love and constancy. Dad, thank you for nurturing my love of gardening. Mum, thank you for fostering my love of books and for trusting, always, that I would find my way.

Will and Josh, for your love, encouragement, and wisdom. You have been two of my greatest teachers. Thank you for choosing me to be your mum.

Ian, for truly seeing me. For nourishing me with food at the end of a long day of writing, for all the times that you were talking to me, and I didn't quite hear you because my head was full of stories and for the evenings and weekends, I spent at my laptop rather than with you.

Nicola, for being such a powerful space holder and for your invaluable support. Em for your gentle nudges and organisational wizardry. Jesse and Lynda, for your editing expertise and design magic. Lorraine for your early copyrighting support, and to the women in the Unbound Writing Mastermind for your wisdom and unbridled enthusiasm.

Stacey, for your expertise, honesty, and humour and for walking beside me during my book writing journey. That we have become friends through the process is the icing on the cake.

Early readers and reviewers of *Labyrinth*, thank you for your time, care, and feedback. Tara, Melissie, Lorraine, Marcia O', Kerry, Jackie, Catrina, Ash, Debra, Marcia N, Victoria, Sima, Ruby, Arya, Stacey, and Flo.

The 150+ members of the private online *Labyrinth* community for helping to hold space, for cheerleading and for your engagement and feedback.

To my wider family, friends and clients who have supported and nudged me to write.

To everyone, past, present, and future who has been part of my story. Thank you.

And finally, to the book itself for leading me, one story at a time, through the writing journey and to my Soul for this extraordinary adventure that is Life.

Let's Stay Connected

Thank you so much for choosing Labyrinth: My Journey to Belonging

Let's stay connected.

Here are all the ways to connect with me and keep up to date with me and my work,

Browse my website: www.amahope.net

Here you can see many of the ways I can support you in your own journey to belonging. I don't post everything on my website – too many facets and hats to display – and there is often no "one size fits all solution" - so if you're feeling a pull or a nudge to connect – please do email or book a discovery call and we can have a chat.

I send an occasional newsletter and you can also receive a weekly blog too.

My shop:

I AM Woman – my spoken voice set to music
The Magician's Toolkit
Flow Cards
Soul Contract Readings
Other audio tracks are also available.

Because I'm soul-led, there are often new items to see.

And there is a short E-book with a full A4 size 7 turn labyrinth for you to trace.

Connect via email: moriah@amahope.net

Connect with me on social media:

Moriah Ama Hope – I have a personal and a business page.

@moriahamahope and @themagicianstoolkit

I look forward to hearing from you.

About the Author

Moriah is a highly experienced Coach, writer, and empathic guide.

She helps women to navigate and make sense of life and find and fulfil their unique purpose.

She is the creator of many of her own healing systems and coaching tools, including How Cards and The Magician's Toolkit.

After many hectic years, Moriah has chosen to lead an unapologetically simple life on the south coast of England, where she divides her energies between her business, time with loved ones and restorative connection with nature.

Photo: Julia Toms Photography

Printed in Great Britain
by Amazon

16660328R00201